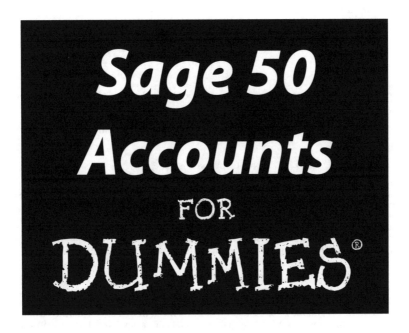

Sage 50 Accounts

FOR DUMMIES®

by Jane Kelly, ACMA

WILEY

A John Wiley and Sons, Ltd, Publication

Sage 50 Accounts For Dummies®
Published by
John Wiley & Sons, Ltd
The Atrium
Southern Gate
Chichester
West Sussex
PO19 8SQ
England

E-mail (for orders and customer service enquires): cs-books@wiley.co.uk

Visit our Home Page on www.wiley.com

For general information on our other products and services, please contact our Customer Care Department within the U.S. at 800-762-2974, outside the U.S. at 317-572-3993, or fax 317-572-4002.

For technical support, please visit www.wiley.com/techsupport.

Wiley also publishes its books in a variety of electronic formats. Some content that appears in print may not be available in electronic books.

British Library Cataloguing in Publication Data: A catalogue record for this book is available from the British Library

ISBN: 978-0-470-71558-1

Printed and bound in Great Britain by Bell & Bain Ltd, Glasgow

10 9 8 7 6 5 4

WILEY

About the Author

Jane Kelly trained as a Chartered Management Accountant whilst working in industry. Her roles ranged from Company Accountant in a small advertising business to Financial Controller for a national house-builder. For the last few years Jane has specialised in Sage software, both as a user and as a Director of a training company. She has taught a wide variety of small business owners and employees the benefits of using Sage. Jane has written and delivered a range of Sage training courses, conducted on both a one-to-one basis and in group training sessions.

This is Jane's first *For Dummies* book, but won't be the last – she is currently helping to adapt some US editions to bring into the UK market.

Dedication

I would like to dedicate this book to my daughter, Megan. I hope that she will be proud of her mum and maybe even write a book of her own one day – even if it is about Disney princesses and fairies!

Acknowledgements

I hope that this book will help the many small businesses out there who are struggling with their accounting systems. I want people to understand that if a system is properly set up it should be very easy to use, and the business will gain maximum benefit from it. In the past, I've only been able to reach small local audiences, but this book gives me the opportunity to reach the masses.

I want to thank everyone at Wiley, who have been incredibly kind and supportive through my first experience of becoming an author. I would like to extend special thanks to Samantha Spickernell who gave me the opportunity to work with Wiley and also to Steve Edwards and his development team who made the book what it is today.

I would also like to thank the support team at Sage UK Limited, who provided me with the necessary answers to awkward questions throughout this project.

Finally, I would like to thank my husband, Malcolm, and daughter, Megan, who have put up for long periods with an 'absentee wife and mother'.

Publisher's Acknowledgements

We're proud of this book; please send us your comments through our Dummies online registration form located at www.dummies.com/register/.

Some of the people who helped bring this book to market include the following:

Acquisitions, Editorial, and Media Development

Project Editor: Steve Edwards

Development Editor: Kathleen Dobie

Content Editor: Jo Theedom

Commissioning Editor: Samantha Spickernell

Publishing Assistant: Jennifer Prytherch

Copy Editor: Anne O'Rorke

Proofreader: Kelly Cattermole

Technical Editor: Rachel Heard

Executive Editor: Samantha Spickernell

Executive Project Editor: Daniel Mersey

Cover Photos: ©Martin Poole/GettyImages

Cartoons: Ed McLachlan

Composition Services

Project Coordinator: Lynsey Stanford

Layout and Graphics: Ana Carrillo, Christin Swinford

Proofreaders: Caitie Kelly

Indexer: Claudia Bourbeau

Special Help

Brand Reviewer: Rev Mengle, Zoë Wykes

Contents at a Glance

Table of Contents

Introduction

· ·

Sage is a well-known accounting system used in more than three quarters of a million small- and medium-sized businesses in the UK. The range of business software continually evolves, and Sage's developers pride themselves on listening to their customers for feedback on how to improve the software. This results in regular revisions and updates that add new features to Sage each time.

This book offers you a chance to understand how Sage 50 Accounts can help you run your business effectively.

About This Book

The aim of this book is for you to get the most from Sage. I use lots of screenshots to help you navigate your way around the system and offer tips to help you customise the programs and reports contained in Sage in language you can understand, even if you're not an accountant.

I show you how to navigate your way around Sage, and wherever possible, I show you the easiest or quickest way to do something, because you can often do the same thing in more than one way. I understand that you want a quick start, so I show you the easiest methods of doing things. You can always add details later, when time permits.

This book presents information in a modular fashion so that you get all the information to accomplish a task in one place. I don't ask you to remember things from different parts of the book; if another chapter has information relevant to the discussion at hand, I tell you where to find it, so you don't have to read the chapters in order. You can read the chapters or sections that interest you when it suits you.

Conventions Used in This Book

This book includes a lot of instructions on how to proceed with various tasks in Sage. Wherever possible, I use numbered lists to indicate the order in which to do things.

- *Italics* are used to highlight new terms and for emphasis.
- **Boldfaced** text indicates the action step in a numbered list or text that you type into Sage.
- `Monofont` is used for web addresses and on-screen messages.
- Names of windows, screens and menu choices are capitalised.
- This little arrow – ⇨ – indicates the path you click through in a series of menu options.

Because examples can help you see how a concept works in real life, I created Jingles, a fictitious party-planning company, and I use its owner Jeanette to demonstrate some of Sage's reports and functions.

Foolish Assumptions

Whilst writing *Sage 50 Accounts For Dummies,* I made some key assumptions about who you are and why you picked up this book. I assume that you fall into one of the following categories:

- You're a member of staff in a small business who's been asked to take over the bookkeeping function and will be using Sage.
- You're an existing bookkeeper who has never used Sage before or who needs to refresh your knowledge.
- You're a small-business owner who wants to understand how Sage can help in your business.

What You're Not to Read

Throughout *Sage 50 Accounts For Dummies,* I include a number of examples on how to apply particular processes within your business. If you're simply reading this book to gain an overview of Sage, you can skip these examples without detracting from your understanding of what Sage can do for you and your business.

Any text marked with a *TechnicalStuff* icon contains information you may be interested in, but that you don't need to know to understand the discussion of the topic; the same goes for the information in the grey panels called sidebars.

How This Book Is Organised

Sage 50 Accounts For Dummies is divided into six parts and includes an appendix. The appendix provides a handy glossary of important terms used in this book that you may not be familiar with.

Part I: Setting Up and Installing Sage 50 Accounts

In Part I, I discuss Sage's product range so that you can decide which version of Sage best suits your business. I take you through the installation process step by step and show you how to navigate around Sage. You see how to set up your Chart of Accounts, records and opening balances so that you can start entering information onto Sage.

Part II: Looking into Day-to-Day Functions

These chapters look at the day-to-day running of Sage. I show you how to process sales and purchase invoices and deal with your bank accounts. I also discuss how to find transactions, how to make corrections and the importance of backing up and restoring data.

Part III: Functions for Plus and Professional Users

Part III is primarily concerned with Sage 50 Accounts Plus and Accounts Professional versions. These two products contain more functions than the standard Sage program, and some of these functions are more advanced. I look at the life cycles of both sales and purchase order processing and the paperwork involved with both. I also look at running a stock system within Sage.

If you're interested in setting up projects and their associated costs, Chapter 13 is dedicated to this. And finally, for those of you who trade with foreign partners, Chapter 14 tells you how to deal with foreign currency.

Part IV: Running Monthly, Quarterly and Annual Routines

In Part IV, I look at the regular routines that you need to carry out during the year. Some of these routines are statutory obligations, such as VAT returns, but others are good housekeeping routines. Without reconciling your bank accounts, for example, you can't be certain that you've entered all your bank transactions.

I also look at the regular journals that you enter if you're planning on preparing monthly management information.

Part V: Using Reports

Part V is concerned with producing meaningful management information from Sage after you perform all the daily and monthly routines. I show you how to run a Profit and Loss report and a Balance Sheet and discuss which other reports you may like to include in a management accounts pack for the managers and owners of the business to read.

I explore alternative methods of extracting information from Sage and using spreadsheets to provide additional reports to analyse the business information. I also touch briefly upon the Report Designer function of Sage.

In addition, I cover the electronic banking function and the Accountant Link function, both of which you can use to improve the speed of processing and in some cases reduce the costs of running and managing your business.

Part VI: The Part of Tens

The Part of Tens contains handy mini chapters on some useful aspects of Sage. This part lists ten (or eleven) nifty things to do with function keys and tells you about the ten (or so) best wizards that Sage has to offer.

Icons Used in This Book

Every *For Dummies* book uses icons to highlight especially important, interesting or useful information. The icons used in this book are:

Look at this icon for practical information that you can use straightaway to help you use Sage in the most effective way.

This icon indicates any items you need to remember after reading the book – and sometimes throughout it.

The paragraphs next to this icon contain information that is, er, slightly technical in nature. You don't *need* to know the information here to get by, but it helps.

This bombshell alerts you to potential problems you may create for yourself without realising it. Don't ignore this icon!

This icon indicates that a function is available only to users of Sage 50 Accounts Plus and Sage 50 Accounts Professional.

Some functions are included only if you run the Professional version of Sage, and – guess what? – this icon indicates those functions.

Where to Go from Here

You're now ready to enter the world of Sage. If you're a complete beginner, starting at the beginning and gradually working through is probably best. If you're an existing user, but a little rusty in certain areas, you can pick the chapters that are most relevant to you, probably in Parts IV and V. This book is designed for you to dip in and out of. I hope that you find it a useful tool for developing and managing your business.

Part I
Setting Up and Installing Sage 50 Accounts

'Mr Scrimshaw, our acccountant, was schooled in the old manual way but I'm sure you two will enjoy working together on a new computerised system.'

In this part . . .

I introduce the product range and help you decide which product is going to be the most useful to you. I tell you how to install the software and what information you need beforehand. I take you step by step through setting up your records and Chart of Accounts and show you how to navigate around the system.

Finally, you discover how to enter and check your opening balances. You're then ready to rock and roll!

Chapter 1

Introducing Sage 50 Accounts

*I*n this chapter, I introduce you to the Sage 50 Accounts software range. I show you how easily you can install the software and give you a guided tour, so that you can get up and running quickly – essential for busy people!

Sage works on the principle that the less time you spend doing your accounts, the more time you can spend on your business, so makes each process is as simple as possible.

I also discuss SageCover, an optional technical support package, which is an addition worth considering. If you experience software problems, SageCover can help. For small businesses, it's like having an IT department at the end of a phone.

Looking at the Varieties of Sage

Sage's developers understand that every business is different and that each business has different needs. As a result, they've developed a range of accounting software designed to grow with your business, whatever it is. The three levels of Sage 50 Accounts software start with basic features and finish with a product that contains all the bells and whistles you can possibly want! These versions of Sage are:

- ✔ **Sage 50 Accounts:** The entry-level program. Sage 50 Accounts provides all the features you require to successfully manage your accounts. You can professionally handle your customers and suppliers, manage your bank reconciliations and VAT returns, and provide simple reports, including monthly and year-end requirements. This basic version is suitable for small businesses with a simple structure; those that need basic stock systems, and don't need systems project costing, foreign currency or sales/purchase order processing.

- ✔ **Sage 50 Accounts Plus:** Contains all the features of the entry model and also allows you to manage project costs versus budgets, control costs of manufactured and assembled products, and has an improved stock control system that you can use to produce bill of materials and allocate stock.

- ✔ **Sage 50 Accounts Professional:** Includes all the features of Accounts Plus and adds sales and purchase order processing, foreign trading, bank account revaluation and Intrastat support. Accounts Professional can also handle up to ten users and manage multiple companies. This product is suited to both small- and medium-sized businesses and offers customers a product flexible enough to suit a multitude of different businesses, including those who trade in both the UK and abroad.

Sage is best installed on a Windows operating system. XP is recommended, but Sage also works on Windows Vista, the latest Windows operating system. Installation on Apple operating systems isn't recommended (that's not to say that Sage doesn't work on Macs, it just hasn't been tested to the same extent).

Deciding on SageCover

You can purchase SageCover at the same time you buy the software. SageCover provides you with technical support in case you have any problems using Sage. It may seem an additional cost burden to begin with, but it's well worth the money if you have a software problem.

Most people who use accounting packages know something about accounting, but don't necessarily know much about computer software. When the screen pops up with an error message that you simply don't understand a quick phone call to your SageCover telephone support soon solves the problem.

You can choose between two different types of cover:

- ✔ SageCover: Provides telephone support during normal office hours, as well as email support and online questions and answers support. You also get a copy of Solutions, the Sage magazine.

- ✔ SageCover Extra: Includes all the benefits of SageCover, plus software upgrades, so you always have access to the latest version, and you can request three customised reports (for Sage 50 Accounts users).

Having someone on the end of a phone to talk you through a problem is a real bonus. Sometimes the Help button just doesn't answer your question. The technical support team can help you solve the most awkward problems that would otherwise have you throwing your laptop out of the window in pure frustration!

Installing the Software

In this section, I take you step by step through the installation process, showing you the screens as they appear on your screen. I also tell you about any differences for Vista users and Windows XP users.

I take you through the whole process and ensure that you load up the software correctly. I also let you know about any problems that may crop up while loading, so that you can deal with them effectively.

Anyway, onwards and upwards!

Getting what you need before you get started

Your Sage software package contains a CD, an installation and upgrade guide, and more importantly, a serial number and activation key. Without these last two pieces of information, you can't successfully load the software. But don't worry, if you purchased a genuine copy of Sage software, you have the necessary activation information.

You also need some details about your company:

- ✔ **When your company's financial year begins:** If you're not sure of the date, consult your accountant.

- ✔ **Whether and what type of VAT scheme you use:** Again, your accountant can tell you whether you operate the VAT cash accounting scheme or the standard VAT scheme. If you have a VAT registration number, keep it handy.

Moving to the installation itself

The following steps assume that you're loading Sage for the first time for a single company and single user. For those of you loading multiple-user programs, check the instructions provided with your software.

1. **Insert your CD into the disk drive.**

   If your CD doesn't immediately start, you may need to click Run.

2. **Follow the options on your screen to run the CD.**

   A Sage 50 Accounts welcome screen appears.

3. Choose the option to Install Sage 50 Accounts.

For Vista users, the User Account Control window appears, asking you for permission to continue installing Sage – it's a new security component. Click Continue to proceed to the software licence agreement.

XP users are taken to the software licence agreement.

You need to accept the software licence before you can continue. Be warned, the licence seems to go on forever, if you choose to read it! (Have a quick look through the software licence agreement though, just to see what you're signing up for!)

4. Select the installation type and destination folder and follow the prompts.

You have a choice between a Standard install and a Custom install, as shown in Figure 1-1. The choice you make is important.

Figure 1-1: Choosing Standard or Custom install.

Standard install is recommended for most users; it copies the files to C:\ Sage\Accounts.

Choose Custom install only if you want to control the destination of the programs being installed. For example, if you want to keep different versions of Sage separately on your computer.

If you want to use Custom install and choose a different destination folder, follow these steps:

i. Click the Custom install option.

The destination folder at the bottom of the screen automatically defaults to C:\Sage\Accounts, but with the help of the Browse button, which the arrow in Figure 1-2 points to, you can change the destination folder.

ii. **Click Browse.**

This button allows you to change the path and set the destination folder to your preferred destination.

iii. **Click OK.**

Figure 1-2:
Browsing to
customise
your desti-
nation.

Check with Sage (the company, not the program!) if you aren't sure whether to use the Custom install or not.

5. **Click Next to continue with the Accounts Set-up wizard.**

The screen shown in Figure 1-3 appears.

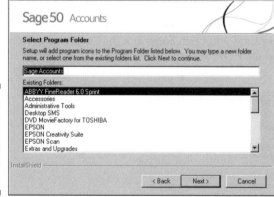

Figure 1-3:
Accepting
the Sage
Accounts
program
folder.

6. **Click Next to accept the program folder name Sage Accounts, unless you wish to designate a different folder if you're using Custom install. For example, Sage Accounts 2009.**

7. **Check that you're happy with the location of the destination folder and program folder and click Next.**

The destination folder is the one you chose in Step 4 and the program folder is the one you accepted in Step 6. If you're not happy with the destinations, click your Back button and change the destinations, as shown in Step 4.

The system then whirrs into action and starts the installation process. It takes several minutes, so you probably have time to make a quick cup of tea!

8. **Click Finish when Sage prompts you that the installation is complete.**

If you're a Windows Vista/XP user, the Select the Type of Data You Want to Use window appears. To exit this window, click the cross in the top right corner.

If you run Windows 2000 or Windows server, you're prompted to restart your PC. Click Yes to restart and then click Finish.

That's it! You have successfully installed your Sage software. You should see a Sage 50 Accounts icon on your desktop – now you're ready to rock and roll!

Be sure to remove the CD and keep it in a safe place!

Having a practice before you start

Of course, you're champing at the bit and want to get going with Sage, so double-click the new Sage icon on your desktop to get started. As this is the first time you're opening Sage 50 Accounts, you're asked to select the type of data that you want to use. Figure 1-4 shows the screen that poses this question.

If you're likely to be annoyed by seeing the Select the Type of Data You Want to Use window every time you open Sage, tick the Don't Show These Options On Start Up box and click OK to stop the window from opening each time.

Figure 1-4:
Choosing
your data
options from
the Select
the Type of
Data You
Want to Use
screen.

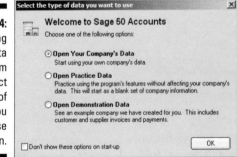

Choose an option according to your interest:

- ✔ **Open Practice Data:** Choose this option if you don't feel brave enough to start straight away with live data. You can practise using the program features without affecting your company's data. The practice company doesn't have any actual data to start with, but you can enter dummy data, for example, new records and dummy invoices, to see how the transactions are posted to the different parts of the system. In case you get stuck, tutorials help you get familiar with Sage.

- ✔ **Open Demonstration Data:** This option has some dummy company information already entered. You can use this data to navigate around the system and see how transactions are presented.

If you select one of the options above and click OK, the Sage Logon window appears, as shown in Figure 1-5. Type **manager** (not case sensitive), leave the password blank and click OK. Sage opens, using whichever data type you chose. Then click Start Practising.

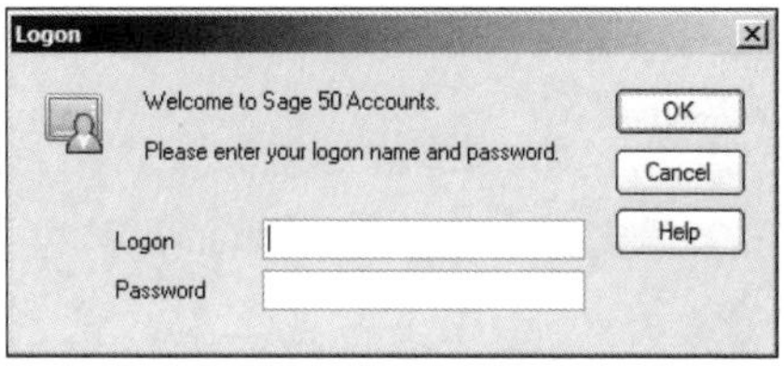

Figure 1-5:
The Sage
Logon
window.

In future, if you need to use the practice company or demo data, you can select File and then Open from the main toolbar.

If you want to jump straight in without using any of the practice data, continue to the next section.

Setting Up with the Active Set-Up Wizard

When you click the Sage icon on your desktop, the Select the Type of Data You Want to Use window appears (refer to Figure 1-4). If you decide you don't fancy using either of the practice options, you can click Set up your Company Data to open the Active Set-up wizard. You are then given three options, as shown in Figure 1-6:

✔ **Set up a new company:** If you're new to Sage, choose this first option.

You're guided through the automatic steps of the Active Set-up wizard. See the following numbered steps to guide you through this process.

✔ **Use a company already set up in another installation:** If you already use Sage and are upgrading, choose this option, which lets you copy accounts data from your previous Sage installation.

✔ **Restore data from a backup file:** Choose this option if you're restoring data from an earlier version – no earlier than Version 9 – perhaps from your accountant, so that you can use the data in your new Sage installation.

Choose whichever option is best for you and follow the screen prompts.

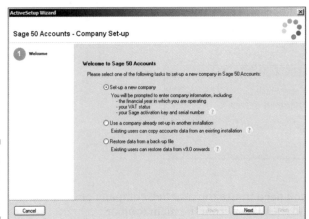

Figure 1-6:
Putting the
Set-up wiz-
ard to work.

The following steps take you through the process of setting up Sage for the first time.

1. **Click Set Up a New Company, click Next and enter your company's details.**

   You're prompted to enter your company information, such as name, address and contact details, as shown in Figure 1-7.

   Speed up the set-up by putting in just the company name. You can complete the other information later from the main toolbar by clicking Settings and selecting Company Preferences.

2. **Click Next. A screen appears that prompts you to Select Business Type, as shown in Figure 1-8.**

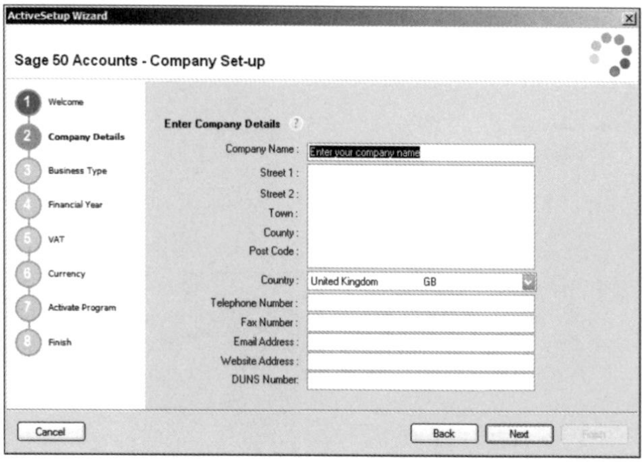

Figure 1-7:
Asking
for the
company
contact info.

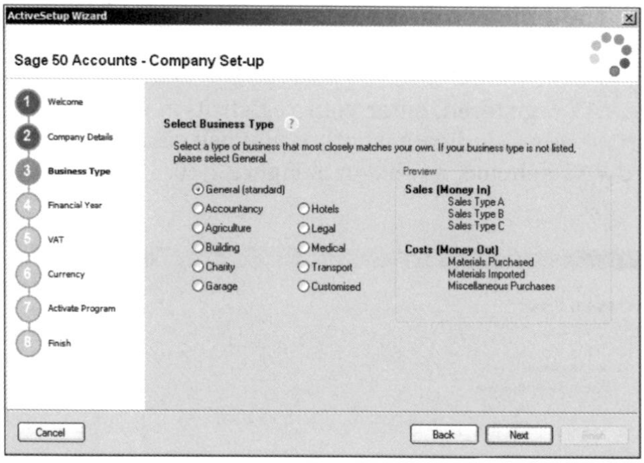

Figure 1-8:
Going with
the General
chart,
unless
you're more
specific.

3. **Accept the default setting – General (standard Chart of Accounts) – unless your company matches one of the listed categories.**

   If you don't want to select any of the categories shown, you can click Customised and create your own business type. You can then use your existing nominal codes if you're transferring accounts from a different system.

4. **Click Next and select your financial year.**

   The fictional Jingles company I invented ends its financial year on 31 March 2009, so the financial start date is April 2008, as shown in Figure 1-9.

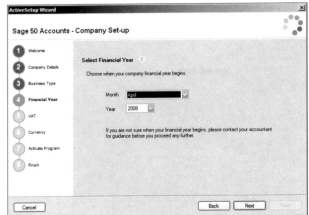

Figure 1-9:
Beginning
the financial
year.

5. Click Next and fill in your VAT details.

If you're not VAT registered, click No and go to Step 6.

If you're VAT registered, enter your registration number and tick the appropriate box to indicate whether you use cash accounting or the standard VAT scheme, as shown in Figure 1-10.

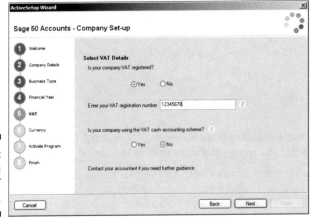

Figure 1-10:
Registering
your VAT
status.

Don't enter any transactions until you're certain of which VAT scheme you operate. Failure to use the correct scheme means that your VAT is calculated incorrectly. Sorting out the wrong VAT scheme can be extremely messy!

6. Click Next and choose the type of currency you use, as shown in Figure 1-11.

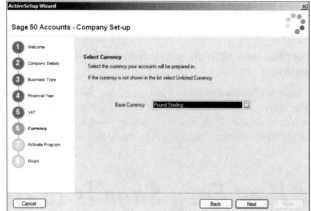

Figure 1-11:
Telling Sage
what cur-
rency to
use to pre-
pare your
accounts.

7. **Click Next and enter your Serial Number and Activation Key, as requested.**

   Look for the codes in the packet sent to you with the Sage software. They're on a set of white sticky labels or on the green delivery sheet that accompanies the software.

   The final screen summarises the data you entered on your Active Set-up wizard.

   If you need to make any changes to your data, you can click Back and revise any information.

8. **Select Finish when you're satisfied that the information is correct.**

   You're now finished!

Registering Your Software

After you install Sage, you may get a message telling you that you're using an unregistered version of the program. Don't panic! You have 60 days before you are required to formally register. You need to contact Sage (UK), Ltd, directly to obtain a new activation key; your serial number remains the same.

You can register in one of two ways:

✔ **By telephone:** Follow these steps:

   i **Open Sage 50 Accounts. From the Tools menu, click Activation and then Upgrade Program.** The Product Registration window appears.

ii **Phone the Sage Customer Care Helpline at 0845-1116666.** A customer service adviser then registers your software and provides you with another activation key.

iii **Enter the new activation key in the New Key box and click Continue.**

✔ **Via the Sage website:** Instead of telephoning Sage, follow Step 1 in the telephone instructions, but click the Web Register box in the Product Registration window. This link to the Sage website takes you directly to the Software Registration Centre; you simply follow the online instructions.

Finding Out How Easy Sage Is to Use

Sage is a user-friendly system, using words and phrases that people easily understand rather than accounting jargon. Sage also has a lot of graphics to make the pages look more appealing and easier to navigate. For example, an icon appears next to the Bank module that looks like the entrance to a grand building – like the Bank of England, perhaps?

Burying the accounting jargon

Sage uses terms that users understand and steers clear of accounting jargon. So, instead of using *debtors* and *creditors*, Sage uses *customers* and *suppliers*; rather than *nominal ledger*, it uses *company*.

Accounting terminology isn't altogether done away with, for example, you still have to print Aged Debtors reports and Aged Creditors reports, but the front end of the program uses very simple language.

Introducing process maps

Sage introduced process maps a while back. These maps look like flow charts, as shown in Figure 1-12, and they illustrate specific customer and supplier processes in a pictorial format.

Figure 1-12 shows the various stages of the customer paper trail in the Customer Process map, from the original quotation through to chasing the debt and receiving the money from the customer. You can click any one of these boxes, and Sage takes you directly to the screen necessary to process that action. For example, if you click Receive Payment, you're taken to the Customer Receipt screen, so that you can process the payment received.

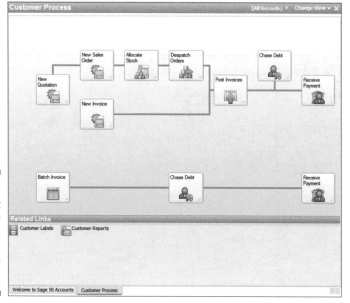

Figure 1-12:
Looking at
the inner
workings
of the
customer
process.

Looking at the screen layout

When you open Sage, the first screen you come across is the Sage Welcome screen, as shown in Figure 1-13. It provides useful links to the websites and various Help pages, including a page that shows you what's new in Sage 50 Accounts.

If you look closely at the bottom of the screen, you find two tabs. The first is for the Welcome to Sage 50 Accounts screen, and the second is called Customer Process – the arrow points to it in Figure 1-13. Refer back to Figure 1-12 to view the Customer Process map.

In the Customer Process screen, the words Change View appear in the top right corner. Clicking Change View produces a dropdown menu that gives you two more options to change the appearance of the screen:

✔ **Customers:** This view, shown in Figure 1-14, is the traditional Sage screen. The main body of the screen appears blank when you're starting out with Sage, but it eventually fills up with your customer names, balances and contact details.

Across the top of the screen, below the Customer heading, the icons that form part of the customer pages appear – Activity, Invoice and Credit, to name just a few.

Figure 1-13: Welcoming you to Sage.

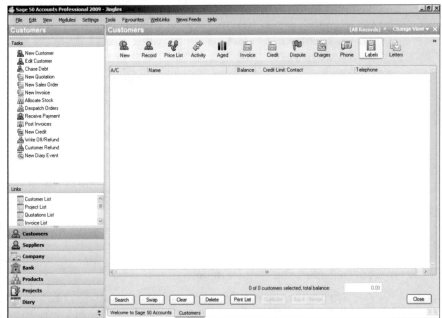

Figure 1-14: Viewing the traditional Customers screen.

✔ **Customer Dashboard**: The dashboard offers a graphic representation of the customer information. It shows the Customer Cash Overview, Aged Debt, Promised Payments and Today's Diary Events. This presentation appeals to top management, who want quick access to the key information in the accounts.

Before you input any data, the Customer Dashboard screen looks extremely boring. However, even just the Sage demonstration data illustrates the dramatic impact of presenting data this way, as shown in Figure 1-15.

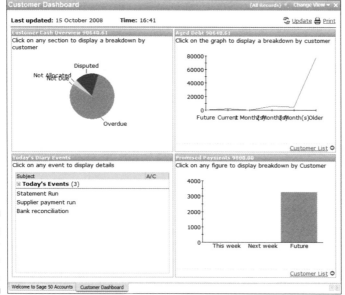

Figure 1-15: Going for the graphical view.

On the Welcome screen is a Just Practice option. Click Just Practice to get step-by-step instructions on how to access the demonstration data or the practice company, to help you grasp the functionality of Sage.

Navigating Around Sage

At the very top of the Sage Welcome screen is the name of your version of Sage – Sage 50 Accounts Professional 2009, for example – followed by the company name you entered when you set up Sage. (Refer to the 'Setting Up with the Active Set-Up Wizard' section, which walks you through getting Sage up and running.)

From the Welcome screen, use the browser toolbar that runs horizontally across the top to navigate through the program. For example, if you misspelled your company name in your excitement at setting up, or missed off *Ltd*, you can amend the error by using the browser toolbar.

Exploring the browser toolbar

The browser toolbar is the traditional way of navigating around the system. Sage introduced the navigation bar that runs down the left side of the screen more recently. Refer to Figure 1-16 to see both the browser toolbar and navigation bar. The navigation bar includes the Task pane, Links list and Module buttons (see the 'Navigating the Task pane, Links list and Module buttons' section later in this chapter for more detail).

By clicking the different browser toolbar options, you gain access to submenus and different parts of the system. The next sections talk about each option on the browser toolbar in turn.

File

Nothing counter-intuitive here; clicking File gives you options for creating, accessing, saving and sharing data. The submenu options are:

- **New Report:** Takes you into a Report wizard that enables you to design new reports.

- **New Batch Report**: Allows you to bundle a set of individual reports together and view, export, print or email them at the same time. Click F1 for Sage Help and type **batch reporting** for more details.

- **Open:** Enables you to access the demonstration data and practice data from here, open a report and open previously archived data, including the VAT archive.

- **Close:** Closes the dropdown menu.

- **Backup**: Allows you to back up your data. You can also back up your data when you exit the program.

   Back up your data each time you use Sage, or at least at the end of each day. Back up more often during the day if you're processing significant amounts of data.

   Sage automatically gives the backup a filename, which is usually SageBack DD-MM-YY.001. (Sage backup files always have the file extension .001.) If you do more than one backup on the same day, differentiate the file name, otherwise Sage uses the same date and the same file name and simply overwrites the previous backup.

✔ **Maintenance:** Enables you, amongst other things, to correct data, delete records, check data or even, as a very last resort, rebuild the data. I talk about maintenance in more detail in Chapter 9.

✔ **Restore:** Allows you to retrieve data from a previous backup, if necessary. You may need to do this if you have problems with the current data – perhaps the data had become corrupted and you want to return the data to a known point in time when the data was free of problems.

✔ **Import:** Allows you to import records, such as customer records, stock records and project records, from other sources, like Microsoft Excel, as long as they're in a pre-determined CSV (comma separated values) format. This option is very useful when you're setting up Sage and have other information or records that you wish to import. You can speed up the data-entry process if you import information instead of keying in each individual record. I cover importing and CSV formatting in more detail in Chapter 19.

✔ **Office Integration:** Using this option, you can export data to Microsoft Excel, Word or Outlook (if you have a compatible version of Microsoft Outlook).

✔ **Send:** Enables you to send a message by using your default e-mail program.

✔ **Exit:** Lets you exit the program altogether. You can also exit the program by clicking the black cross in the right top corner of the screen.

Edit

You can use Edit to cut, copy, paste, insert or delete rows, duplicate cells, or memorise or recall data.

View

The *status bar* is the narrow strip across the bottom of your screen, showing the name of your Sage product, today's date, the start of the financial year and the current transaction number. You can switch it on and off. You can also view the user list, which shows who is currently logged onto Sage.

Modules

The *modules* are essentially the different components that form the whole of the Sage accounting system. The modules include the usual accounting ledgers, such as Customers, Suppliers, Bank, Nominal Ledger and reporting functions, but they also include (depending on which version of Sage you purchased) additional components, such as Projects, Sales Order Processing and Purchase Order Processing. You can also access the Invoicing function, wizards and the new diary that has been recently added to Sage.

Access modules by clicking Modules on the browser toolbar and selecting the module of your choice, or by clicking the much larger buttons on the navigation bar at the bottom left side of the screen. I prefer the buttons at the bottom – they're easier to use and more visible.

Settings

The settings include the Configuration Editor and Company Preferences, which hold some of the basic information about your company and the way Sage was set up upon installation. Settings also include many of the default screens for the ledgers, which save you time when setting up records at a later date. If you need to change the system date or check the financial year, you can do it within settings. You also have access to the security settings for accessing the software and can set up passwords to protect your accounts data. The settings include:

- ✔ **Configuration Editor:** Holds the basic information you enter when you complete the Active Set-up wizard. Have a look at the numerous tabs within this option and familiarise yourself with them. Examples of things you can do include: editing your customer and supplier trading terms; amending your VAT codes; and managing your project cost types and cost codes.

- ✔ **Company Preferences:** Allows you to enter extra information if you didn't add it all when using the Active Set-up wizard. You may want to update your address information. Company Preferences provides many more tabs to look at, too many to comment on here, so have a flick through at your leisure.

- ✔ **Customer/Supplier/Bank/Product/Invoice and Order Defaults:** Gives you the opportunity to amend parts of the default data you set up on installation.

- ✔ **Financial Year:** Identifies the start of the company's financial year, as input during the Active Set-up wizard. This date is fixed when you start to enter data.

- ✔ **Change Program Date:** Allows you to change dates when running a month-end or a year-end report. The date is normally set to the current day's date, but there may be times, such as period ends, when you wish to change the date, albeit only temporarily.

- ✔ **Currencies:** Enables you to edit your currency requirements if you're using multiple currencies.

- ✔ **Countries:** Lists all the countries in the world in the Countries table, together with country codes, and identifies those countries that are currently members of the EU. The Sage 50 Accounts Professional package uses Countries information to comply with Intrastat reporting requirements. (Chapter 17 talks more about Intrastat.)

   You can amend the Countries table as and when countries enter or leave the EU.

✔ **Control Accounts:** Gives you an at-a-glance list of all the control accounts within Sage. A *control account* is a summary of all entries contained within a specific ledger. For example, the Sales Ledger control account includes all transactions for all sales ledger accounts and the balance on the control account tallies with the sum of the sales ledger accounts. Control accounts are used as a check on the numerical accuracy of the ledger accounts and form part of the double-entry system that Sage performs when you enter transactions.

If you're going to change the control accounts, do so before you enter any transactions, otherwise leave them alone.

You can reconcile a control account. Just click Help and follow the instructions for reconciling debtors or creditors.

✔ **Change password:** Allows you to change your password periodically as part of your data protection and security routine.

✔ **Internet Resources:** Provides you with an Internet Resources list that you can use to set your courier and credit bureau information, if you have them. You can launch your website browser from within Sage and go to your credit bureau to check the status of a customer or go to a courier's website to track the progress of a parcel.

Tools

The tools option is a hotchpotch of items. You can run the Global Changes wizard, carry out contra entries, run period ends, open up Report Designer and convert reports, to name but a few. The options are outlined below:

✔ **Global Changes:** Allows you to globally change customer or supplier credit limits, turnover values, nominal budgets, product sales or purchase prices, reorder details and discount table values.

✔ **Contra Entries:** Enables you to match sales invoices against purchase invoices, which often happens at the point of sale as the supplier usually raises an invoice of the same value to offset against your sales invoice. No money officially changes hands, just the provision of goods and services.

✔ **Activation:** Allows you to upgrade your program, enable third-party integration or Construction Industry Scheme. *Third-party integration* enables you to use add-on software, developed by a third party, which is tailored to your specific industry. Sage has a separate module for the Construction Industry Scheme (CIS) and the recording of payments to subcontractors. Activate this scheme by clicking Tools and then Activation for businesses that fall under the scheme.

You can use the Upgrade Program option to register after your initial 60-day Sage trial period runs out.

✔ **Period End:** Enables you to run the month-end, allowing you to post accruals, prepayments and depreciation. This option also clears the current-month turnover figures. You can run your year-end, which sets your Profit and Loss nominal accounts to zero for the new financial year.

You can choose *consolidation,* which can consolidate multi-company accounts. You also have the opportunity to clear stock and clear your audit trail. (See Chapter 16 for further information on clearing stock and audit trails.)

✔ **Transaction Email:** Gives you the ability to exchange invoices and orders with your customers and suppliers via Microsoft Outlook. You can import any orders or invoices that you receive via email directly into your Sage accounts.

✔ **Report Designer:** Allows you to edit or create new reports, customised for your business.

✔ **Convert Reports:** Gives you the opportunity to convert reports from earlier versions of Sage. Often, Sage does this automatically when you update your program, but this gives you an additional opportunity to update any bespoke reports that do not form part of the automatic update.

✔ **Batch Reporting:** Opens up a Report Browser; refer to the Help file supplied with Report Designer to find out how you can best utilise this option.

✔ **Event Log:** Shows a history of system events. If you contact the Sage helpline with a system problem, the event log may come in handy.

✔ **Options:** Gives you options to change the settings and appearance of Sage. For example, you can change the default view of the Customers and Suppliers screens from the process map to customer or supplier lists.

Favourites

You can store your favourite reports under this heading. To find out how to set up favourite reports, use the Help menu supplied with Report Designer (which can be accessed via Tools on the browser toolbar – Chapter 18 goes into more detail about the Report Designer).

Weblinks

Weblinks gives you a number of links to useful websites, such as Sage shop and HM Revenue and Customs, provided that you're hooked up to the Internet.

News Feeds

The Sage RSS News Feeds option keeps you informed about updates on the Sage system. It can update you on the content of blog entries, news headlines or podcasts.

Help

Help is the last entry on the browser toolbar, but probably one of the most useful. If you want to understand more about the system and want to know how to do something, click the Help option. The Contents and Index option allows you to type in key words that may help with answering your question.

Internet Options

An internet option screen opens, which has four tabs:

- ✔ **Software Update:** Allows you to decide when to check and download the latest software updates. Several automatic options exist, along with a manual option.

- ✔ **Sage Accounts:** Gives you access to Sagecover services over the internet.

- ✔ **Network Setting:** Defaults to 'Use my browser settings' and should not be altered without the guidance of your network administrator.

- ✔ **Data Settings:** Provides remote access to business information held in your Sage software, so that everyone in your business can work together.

Navigating the Task pane, Links list and Module buttons

An alternative method of navigation, and probably the easiest, is to use the navigation bar, which is down the left side of the screen. It includes a Task pane and Links list, as well as buttons at the bottom of the bar for opening up your modules.

As you may have gathered by now, Sage offers a variety of ways to navigate to the same point. For example, if you want to open a new customer record, you can click New Customer in the Task pane or use the browser toolbar and click Modules, Customers and then the New icon (assuming you've changed the view to Customers and haven't left it on the process map – refer to the 'Looking at the screen layout' section earlier in this chapter).

As you get used to using Sage, you'll see that the first navigation bar to open is the Customers bar. Figure 1-16 shows the navigation bar in the Customer module, where you can see these features:

- ✔ **Task pane:** The topmost menu is the Task pane, which is different for each module.

- ✔ **Links list:** The Links list offers different links for each module within Sage. The Customer Links list take you to customer-orientated pages, such as Customer Invoices, Orders or simply a list of customers.

✔ **Module buttons:** These buttons sit at the bottom left side of the screen and enable you to switch between modules. They are wide buttons that start with a little icon and then a description. The first button is Customers, the next is Suppliers, then Company, Bank, Products, Projects and Diary.

Just below the Diary button is a tiny chevron with a small arrow directly beneath it. Clicking the chevron gives you the option of showing fewer buttons or adding or removing buttons. You can play about with the buttons and decide which display you prefer. (The Diary button is a new feature recently added to Sage. It assists with credit control and is discussed in Chapter 6 in more detail.)

Clicking the various tasks, links or Module buttons automatically moves you to the relevant part of the system.

I prefer the Module buttons, finding it easier to navigate with them as they're more visible and easier to click than the Task pane or Links list.

Browser toolbar   Modules toolbar

Figure 1-16:
Identifying
the
Navigation
bar, the
Task pane,
the Links
list, the
Module
buttons,
and the two
toolbars
as viewed
from the
Customers
module.

Module buttons

Navigation bar

Using Wizards

A number of wizards wield their technological magic through Sage. You can access these helpful creatures, whose job is to help you through a wide variety of set-ups and tasks, by clicking Modules on the browser toolbar and then Wizards.

A wizard's work is to make your work easy; all you have to do is follow the prompts and enter the information the wizard requests.

Wizards can help you both in setting up Sage and in day-to-day processing. Wizards assist you in setting up new records for customers, suppliers, nominal accounts, bank accounts, products and projects. But you can also use them to do the otherwise tricky double-entry bookkeeping, for items such as opening and closing stock, fuel-scale charges and VAT transfers. You can also use a wizard to set up the Foreign Trader features.

In addition, whenever you click the New icon on the Modules toolbar, you go straight into the Record Set-up wizard. For example, if you click the Customer module and click the New icon. See Chapter 22 for more details about wizards.

Chapter 2

Creating Your Chart of Accounts and Assigning Nominal Codes

In This Chapter

▶ Getting familiar with some accounting concepts

▶ Charting your accounts

▶ Adding nominal codes in your Chart of Accounts

▶ Changing your Chart of Accounts

*I*n this chapter, I get down to the nitty-gritty of the accounting system – the Chart of Accounts (COA), which is made up of nominal codes. Think of the Chart of Accounts as the engine of the accounting system. From the information in your COA, you produce your Profit and Loss report, your Balance Sheet, your budget report and prior-year reports. Set it up properly, and the Chart of Accounts grows with your business, but set it up wrongly and you'll have problems forever more!

Luckily, Sage gives you a lot of help and does the hard work for you, but you still need to understand why Sage is structured in the way that it is and how you can customise it to suit your business.

Understanding as Much as You Need to about Accounting

To use Sage, it helps if you have an appreciation of accounts and understand what you're trying to achieve. But you certainly don't need to understand all the rules of double-entry bookkeeping. The next sections give you the basics of accounting principles so that you can use Sage more comfortably.

Dabbling in double-entry bookkeeping

Accounting systems and accounting programs such as Sage use the principle of *double-entry bookkeeping*, so called because each transaction is recorded twice. For every debit entry, you record a corresponding credit entry. Doing the two entries helps balance the books.

For example, if you make a cash sale for £100, your sales account receives a £100 credit and your cash account gets a £100 debit.

Some knowledge of double-entry rules helps. That way, you can interpret information a little more easily. The following is a short summary of the rules of double-entry bookkeeping:

- **Asset and expense accounts:** Debit the account for an increase in value; credit it for a decrease in value.
- **Liability and income and sales accounts:** Debit the account for a decrease in value; credit it for an increase.

Fortunately, you don't need to book yourself into a bookkeeping evening class, as Sage does the double-entry for you . . . phew! (If you're intrigued by the double-entry system though, please pick up a copy of *Bookkeeping For Dummies* by Paul Barrow and Lisa Epstein, published by Wiley, which explains double-entry and more.)

Having said that, understanding the double-entry method does help, particularly if you intend to do your own nominal journals. This knowledge also comes in handy if you intend to produce monthly management accounts. Sometimes, you need to post nominal journals to correct mistakes, and understanding the principles of double-entry bookkeeping lets you confidently process journals. Don't panic though – Sage has many wizards, which can post things like depreciation, accruals and prepayments for you. So some familiarity with the double-entry method is important, but thorough knowledge isn't essential. If you struggle with journals, leave them to your accountant or at least seek advice if you aren't sure.

Naming your nominals

In accounting and in Sage, you bump into the term *nominal* quite a bit. And for good reason, as several key concepts use the word:

- **Nominal account:** Every item of income, expense, asset and liability is posted to a Nominal Ledger account. The Nominal Ledger accounts categorise all your transactions. The individual nominal accounts are grouped into ranges and can be viewed in your Chart of Accounts.

✔ **Nominal code:** A four-digit number given to each account that appears in the nominal ledger. For example, 7502 is the nominal code for telephone expenses, which is an account in the nominal ledger.

Sage categorises each nominal code into nine different ranges, and these categories form the basis of your Chart of Accounts.

✔ **Nominal ledger:** The nominal ledger is an accumulation of all the nominal accounts – it's the main body of the accounting system. Each nominal account shows all the transactions posted to that specific code, so it follows that the nominal ledger represents all the transactions of the business in one place. Deep joy, I hear you say!

Sage tries to complicate things by referring to the nominal ledger as Company.

✔ **Nominal record:** An individual record for each nominal code. So, to create a new nominal code, open up a new nominal record and give it the new nominal code as its reference. See Chapter 3 for more details about nominal records.

Sage categorises the nominal codes in a specific way, so don't change them without careful consideration. Using common sense and planning at the early stages of implementing Sage can pay huge dividends in the future. You need to correctly categorise your nominal codes in order to create meaningful reports.

Preparing reports

One of the reasons you're investing in Sage is probably so that you can run reports to see how your business is doing. And your money is well spent, for Sage has many reports you can run at the click of a button. The important thing to remember is that reports are only as good as the information contained within them. The old saying, 'Rubbish in, rubbish out' is never truer.

The two key financial reports every business and every accounting system use are:

✔ **Balance Sheet:** This report shows a snapshot of the business. It identifies assets and liabilities and shows how the business is funded via the capital accounts.

✔ **Profit and Loss report:** This report shows the revenue and costs associated with the business for a given period and identifies (as the name suggests!) whether the business is making a profit or loss.

The Profit and Loss and Balance Sheet reports are created from the information in the Chart of Accounts, so it's important to get the COA right!

I discuss the Profit and Loss report and Balance Sheet more fully in Chapter 18, where I also cover producing monthly accounts and the types of reports you're likely to need.

Looking at the Structure of Your Chart of Accounts (COA)

The Chart of Accounts is a list of nominal codes, divided up into the nine categories below:

- ✔ Fixed Assets
- ✔ Current Assets
- ✔ Current Liabilities
- ✔ Long-term Liabilities
- ✔ Capital and Reserves
- ✔ Sales
- ✔ Purchases
- ✔ Direct Expenses
- ✔ Overhead

The first five categories form the Balance Sheet; the remaining categories create your Profit and Loss report. So the COA is a pretty important part of the system!

A look at the nominal list on the Nominal Ledger screen shows that the list runs in numerical order, with the Balance Sheet codes first. If you click the COA icon within the nominal ledger, the Profit and Loss codes show up, followed by the Balance Sheet codes.

Checking out the default COA

Being a caring, sharing software developer, Sage provides a default Chart of Accounts for you to use, with a ready-made list of nominal codes. (You select the type of COA you want using the Active Set-up wizard, which I go through in Chapter 1.) Your COA is determined by the type of business you operate. For most businesses, the default Chart of Accounts based on the general business type is the most appropriate, and it's the one I use here.

Whilst Sage can spot if a new nominal code is outside the range of the usual Chart of Accounts, it can't really help with the structure of the coding system that you chose to use, so plan ahead to avoid costly mistakes.

You can choose from other Chart of Accounts, including accountancy, building, garage, legal, transportation, charity, agriculture, hotelier and medical. Use the F1 Help key and type **standard Chart of Accounts** to see these other layouts and their nominal code lists. For example, the hotelier Chart of Accounts includes 'Food stock for use in Kitchens' and 'Function organisation costs'.

Even if you choose a COA other than the general business type, this section contains information you can use.

You can also customise the default Chart of Accounts to suit your business. (I tell you how in the 'Editing Your Chart of Accounts' section a little later in this chapter.)

The COA is in the Company module. To display it, click Modules on the main (browser) toolbar and then select Company, or you can simply click the Company button from the navigation bar down the left side of the screen. (Make sure that you click Show More Buttons at the bottom of the navigation bar so that all the buttons are visible).

The navigation bar is in full view all the time you're using Sage.

The opening screen for the Company module is shown in Figure 2-1. On the navigation bar, Sage uses the word Company as a title for the Nominal Ledger module, and you access the COA from there.

Check out the name of the opening screen of the Company module – Nominal Ledger, the name Sage uses within the Company module. Sage has slipped seamlessly into accounting mode – are you visualising the grey suits? The Nominal Ledger screen shows a series of icons, one of which is COA (Chart of Accounts). You can also create and amend nominal codes from this screen, and create journals, accruals and prepayments, as well as run a series of Nominal Ledger reports.

For a better look at the Chart of Accounts screen, follow these steps:

1. Click the COA icon on the Nominal Ledger toolbar.

The COA icon is second from the end of the icons across the top of the screen. The Chart of Accounts window opens, which gives you a list of all the Chart of Accounts you created. At first, only the Default Layout of Accounts shows, but any subsequent Charts of Accounts you create also show here.

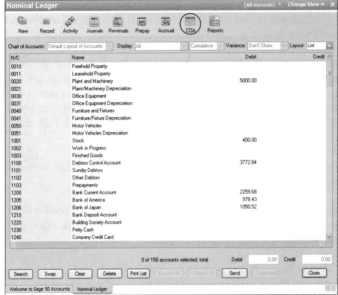

Figure 2-1:
Going
through the
nominal
ledger to get
to the Chart
of Accounts.

2. **Highlight the Chart of Accounts you want to view and click the Edit button at the bottom of the next screen.**

   Initially, the COA you want is the Default Layout of Accounts.

   The Edit Chart of Accounts window for the Default Layout of Accounts screen opens, as shown in Figure 2-2. This screen shows the category types on the left side and a description of the nominal code ranges contained within each category on the right side.

   As you click each category type, the nominal codes shown in the Category Account window change to match the category type. Have a go and see for yourself.

In the Category Account window, all you see is nominal code ranges. For example, in Figure 2-2, Sales is highlighted in the Description column of the category type, so the Category Account columns show the High and Low ranges of nominal codes within each Sales category. I explain the nominal code ranges in the next two sections.

If you're not sure which nominal codes fall into the range described, you can print a complete list of nominal codes. Alternatively, you can click the number in the Low or High column and use the dropdown arrow next to the field to see which account the nominal code is referring to. You can then scroll down the list of accounts that appear and view the range of codes.

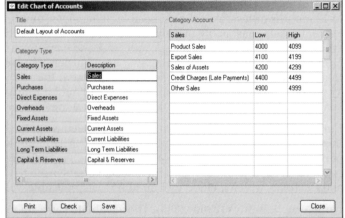

Figure 2-2:
Looking
at the Edit
Chart of
Accounts
window.

To print a hard copy of the nominal list, use the following steps. The list usually consists of two or three pages, but the length depends on the number of codes you create. The more codes, the longer the list!

1. **From the navigation bar, click the Company button.**

2. **Click the Print List button at the bottom of the screen.**

   A command is sent to your printer to run off a hard copy of the existing codes.

The list of nominal codes may look rather daunting at first, but I talk you through the basics in the next sections.

Identifying Balance Sheet codes

The *Balance Sheet* is a snapshot of the business at a fixed point in time. It identifies the company's assets and liabilities and shows how the business has been funded via the capital accounts. To achieve this snapshot, the Balance Sheet looks at the assets the business holds and its liabilities, so it draws on the numbers in a range of nominal codes:

✔ **Fixed assets (0010–0051):** A *fixed asset* is an item likely to be held in the business for a long period of time – more than 12 months. The range of fixed-asset codes is used for transactions relating to freehold and leasehold property, and other items the company plans to hold for a while. You can add other capital items, such as computer equipment, to this list.

✔ **Current assets (1001–1250):** A *current asset* is an item that has a lifespan of 12 months or less. You should be able to *liquidate* (turn into cash) current assets reasonably quickly. Common current assets include stock, debts owed to the business, and bank and cash items. Current assets are normally ordered in the least liquid order first, meaning items that take the longest to convert into cash appear at the top of the list. Therefore you expect to see cash, which is so liquid it runs through some people's hands like water, at the bottom of the current assets list.

✔ **Current liabilities (2100–2230):** *Current liabilities* are amounts the business owes normally outstanding for less than 12 months. At the top of the list is the Creditors control account, which is basically the total owed to all suppliers. But it also includes amounts owed to HM Revenue and Customs, which include VAT and PAYE, if applicable.

✔ **Long-term liabilities (2300–2330):** These liabilities are amounts owed by the business for a period of more than 12 months. They include long-term loans, hire-purchase agreements and mortgages.

✔ **Capital (3000–3200):** Capital accounts show how the business is funded. These codes include those for share issues, reserves and the current Profit and Loss balance.

Reserves is another word for earnings retained within the business – they're officially called *retained earnings.* Annual profits swell this account and any distributions of dividends to owners of the business reduce the balance.

In order for the Balance Sheet to balance, the Capital account includes the current-year profit, as shown in the Profit and Loss report.

Table 2-1 shows the range of nominal codes that form the Balance Sheet.

Table 2-1	Balance Sheet Nominal Codes	
Category	*Low*	*High*
Fixed Assets		
Property	0010	0019
Plant & Machinery	0020	0029
Office Equipment	0030	0039
Furniture & Fixtures	0040	0049
Motor Vehicles	0050	0059
Current Assets		
Stock	1000	1099
Debtors	1100	1199

Category	Low	High
Current Assets		
Bank Account	1200	1209
Deposits & Cash	1210	1239
Credit Card (Debtors)	1250	1250
VAT Liability	2200	2209
Current Liabilities		
Creditors: Short Term	2100	2199
Taxation	2210	2219
Wages	2220	2299
Credit Card (Creditors)	1240	1240
Bank Account	1200	1209
VAT Liability	2200	2209
Long-term Liabilities		
Creditors: Long Term	2300	2399
Capital & Reserves		
Share Capital	3000	3099
Reserves	3100	3299

Looking at profit and loss codes

In the default set of nominal codes, all codes from 4000 onwards are Profit and Loss codes, which, appropriately enough, include the numbers that show how much money the business brings in and how much it spends. The Profit and Loss codes include the following:

- ✔ **Sales (4000–4999):** Sales codes apply to goods or services that your business offers; they indicate how you earn your money. The 4000–4999 range also includes income other than sales, for example, royalty commissions.

   The default descriptions against the sales codes are nonsense. Sales Type A, B, C, D and so on are not meaningful to anyone; they're just a starting point. You need to change the sales types to make them applicable for your business. If you own a card shop, for example, instead of Sales type A, you may have nominal code (N/C) 4000 for birthday cards, sales type B may become N/C 4005 for get-well cards, and so on. I look at editing nominal codes in Chapter 3.

- ✓ **Purchases (5000–5299):** These codes identify material purchases and purchasing costs such as carriage, packaging and transport insurance. *Material purchases* is a very general term for the purchase of the raw materials used to make the products the business sells. For example, flour is a material purchase for a bakery.

- ✓ **Direct Expenses (6000–6999):** A *direct expense* is a cost directly associated with the product being manufactured or created by the business. Labour costs, including sub-contractors, come under these codes, which also include expenses such as sales commissions, samples and public relations costs that can be associated directly with the products.

- ✓ **Overheads (7000–9999):** By far the largest range of codes is *overheads*, which covers all other expenses not directly associated with making and providing the products or service. Table 2-2 shows the smaller sections into which overheads can be broken.

Table 2-2 lists the nominal codes that form the Profit and Loss report.

Table 2-2	Profit and Loss Nominal Codes	
Category	*Low*	*High*
Sales Revenue		
Product Sales	4000	4099
Export Sales	4100	4199
Sales of Assets	4200	4299
Credit Charges	4400	4499
Other Sales	4900	4999
Purchases		
Purchases	5000	5099
Purchase Charges	5100	5199
Stock	5200	5299
Direct Expenses		
Labour	6000	6099
Commissions	6100	6199
Sales Promotion	6200	6299
Miscellaneous Expenses	6900	6999
Overheads		
Gross Wages	7000	7099
Rent & Rates	7100	7199
Heat, Light & Power	7200	7299

Category	Low	High
Overheads		
Motor Expenses	7300	7399
Travelling & Entertainment	7400	7499
Printing & Stationery	7500	7599
Professional Fees	7600	7699
Equipment Hire & Rental	7700	7799
Maintenance	7800	7899
Bank Charges & Interest	7900	7999
Depreciation	8000	8099
Bad Debts	8100	8199
General Expenses	8200	8299
Suspense & Mispostings	9998	9999

Use Suspense and Mispostings nominal accounts when you can't find a suitable nominal code to put something to. They serve as holding pens – somewhere to post an item whilst you're trying to find a better code to post it to. At the end of each month, you need to review the Suspense and the Mispostings accounts and put the items in their correct locations. Unfortunately, the suspense account in particular can become a dumping ground. Avoid the use of these accounts as far as possible and only use when absolutely necessary.

Leaving gaps and mirroring codes

Notice that the ranges of codes in the preceding sections leave plenty of gaps between the categories. For example, Sales codes start at 4000 and the next range of Purchase codes doesn't begin until 5000. You can fill the large gap between 4000 and 4999 with Sales codes, which gives you a great deal of flexibility for a growing business.

I suggest leaving gaps of ten between each code to allow for growth, but it's entirely up to you to decide the best fit for your business. You may decide that gaps of 50 are quite sufficient.

You may consider mirroring corresponding Sales and Purchase codes, so that the last two digits are the same for the sale and purchase of each item, as in Table 2-3, which shows some of Jingles' nominal codes. (Jingles is the fictional card shop and party-planning company I created to serve as an example throughout this book.)

Table 2-3		Mirroring Nominal Codes	
Nominal Code	**Description**	**Nominal Code**	**Description**
4000	Sale of greetings cards	5000	Purchase of greetings cards
4010	Sale of party balloons	5010	Purchase of party balloons
4020	Sale of party gifts	5020	Purchase of party gifts

Accommodating floating nominals

A *floating nominal* is a code that can be placed as a Current Asset or Current Liability, depending on whether the balance is a debit or a credit. For example, if your bank account is in the black, it's a Current Asset, but if the account is overdrawn, it should show as a Current Liability. Another example is the VAT Liability account, as you can sometimes get a refund from the Inland Revenue.

The Sage program automatically places the code to the correct side of the Balance Sheet, but only if you've identified those specific codes that can be treated as an asset or as a liability in the Floating Nominal Accounts section on the Edit Chart of Accounts screen. Sage normally designates accounts as floating nominal codes, so you don't have to do anything.

Editing Your Chart of Accounts

One of the first things to consider when setting up Sage is how well the Chart of Accounts suits your business. Have a look at the categories and nominal codes to make sure that they contain suitable descriptions for your products or services. For example, the Product Sales category doesn't suit a business that primarily provides a service. You may want to change a few categories, or you may decide to make wholesale changes, in which case it may be simpler to create an entirely new Chart of Accounts. The next sections tell you how to change and create COAs.

If you place a nominal code in the wrong category, it can cause inaccuracies in the reports you produce; miscodings are every accountant's nightmare! When creating new codes, be sure that you know whether the code should be a Balance Sheet or a Profit and Loss item. You can usually rely on your common sense, but if you're unsure, give your accountant a quick call. Accountants don't mind answering a quick question like this, but they do mind if you mix up Balance Sheet and Profit and Loss codes, and they then have the task of unpicking your mistakes!

Amending your Chart of Accounts

You can edit the default Chart of Accounts to suit your business.

In Figure 2-2 (in the earlier 'Checking out the default COA' section), the category types are on the left side of the screen, starting with Profit and Loss items and followed by Balance Sheet items. If you move your cursor down the list of sales types, the Sales account headings on the right side of the screen change to reflect the heading names and nominal codes contained within the highlighted category types. To view the nominal code ranges in more detail, click the nominal code and then use the dropdown arrow to identify the name of the nominal code.

Don't change the category types on the left side of the COA screen: they are fundamental accounting descriptions, and the layout of both the Profit and Loss report and Balance Sheet should conform with recognised financial reporting standards.

However, you can change the category accounts on the right side of the Edit Chart of Accounts page. The headings aim to describe the group of nominal codes linked under the heading.

One of the first things to change is the Product Sales headings. These headings are very general descriptions and won't suit all business. For example, if you're a baker using Sage, you may want to change the sales types to bread sales, cake sales and so on.

The headings in the Chart of Accounts show up in your Profit and Loss report and Balance Sheet, so you need to give careful consideration to which headings you want to see on your financial reports. If you don't want an extensive list of different types of sales categories on your Profit and Loss account, consider grouping together several nominal codes under more general headings.

After you decide on the level of detail that you want to show on your reports, you're now ready to amend your Chart of Accounts by following these steps:

1. **From the navigation bar, click Company and then click COA.**

2. **Make sure that you highlight Default Layout of Accounts and then click Edit.**

3. **Make any changes to headings within the category account.**

   Changes available are:

   - **Rename a heading:** Simply click the title and overtype with the new name.

     So Jeanette, the owner of Jingles, would change Product Sales to Shop Sales.

TIP

When you rename a heading, make sure that all the nominal codes included within the renamed heading relate to the new heading.

- **Insert a new heading:** Click the line below where you want to insert a line and press the F7 function key. A message comes up to say that inserting a line moves all categories down by one. Click Yes and don't panic when the codes above disappear from view! They're still there, they've just moved up. Scroll up the category accounts to see where your line has been inserted. Type the name of the new heading and then enter the range of nominal codes to which it relates.

Figure 2-3 shows the newly created Party Fees heading for Jingles. At the moment, the new heading has only one relevant nominal code (4150 Party Organising), so this code is both the Low and High range. If Jeanette wants to add more nominal codes at a later date, she can include them in the High range. So if the new code was 4170, the range of nominal codes for Party Fees would be 4150–4170.

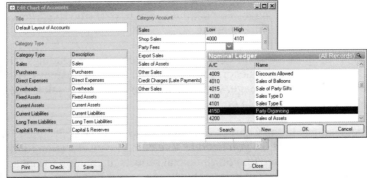

Figure 2-3: Inserting a new heading in the Chart of Accounts.

- **Delete a heading:** You can use F8 to delete a heading line, but you must ensure that you're not likely to want to use those nominal codes.

4. **Click Save when you're happy with the changes you've made.**

   You need to go through your Chart of Accounts for errors, so check out the 'Checking your Chart of Accounts' section later in this chapter.

Creating a new Chart of Accounts

If the existing Chart of Accounts doesn't suit your business at all, you may find that creating your own COA is less work than adapting the one Sage provides. You may decide to use your existing nominal codes from your old accounting system, so you can customise the Chart of Accounts with your existing codes.

Alternatively, you might find that your business has particular geographical locations or segments that you wish to report on. You can create a new Chart of Accounts for each segment or location, but make it specific for your business. For example, you may have an office in London and one in Edinburgh. With the creation of suitable nominal codes, you can produce a Profit and Loss report to the gross profit line for each office. So you group together all the Sales codes associated with the London office and deduct from them all London office Purchases and Direct Costs. This results in a London office gross profit. You can do the same exercise for the Edinburgh office with a separate COA, and then you can compare the two, to see which office was the most profitable.

It requires an extremely complex set of nominal codes to be able to analyse any further than gross profit. (Please speak to your friendly accountant, who can assist with complicated nominal code structures.)

When adding a new Chart of Accounts with the purpose of producing a Profit and Loss report to gross profit level, be aware that you can only select the nominal codes specific to that geographical location or segment of the business. As a result, the word *partial* appears after the COA name because you haven't selected all of the nominal codes. In addition to the Gross Profit reports, you must always have a fully complete Chart of Accounts for the whole business, which must be checked for errors prior to running reports. See the 'Checking your Chart of Accounts' section later in this chapter. Don't try to check a Chart of Accounts that has *partial* in the title as Sage always brings up a list of codes that are missing; always check your complete Chart of Accounts for accuracy.

To add a Chart of Accounts, follow these steps:

1. **From the navigation bar, select the Company module and click COA.**

2. **Click Add from the COA window.**

   The New Chart of Accounts window appears.

3. **Enter the name of your new Chart of Accounts and click Add.**

4. **Select each category type by clicking the Description field and entering a description in the Category Account on the right side of the screen.**

5. **Use the Category Account pane on the right side of the screen to enter new headings and assign a range of codes for each heading.**

Figure 2-4 shows a new COA called Jingles Card Shop. The Jingles business consists of two definite parts. One is the card shop, which sells cards, balloons and so on, and the other is party-planning. To see the gross profit made on each part of the business, I created a separate Chart of Accounts for each segment. I selected only the nominal codes specific to the card shop and ignored any party-planning codes. Because I didn't include all the nominal codes in this COA, Sage includes the word *partial* in the title.

However, to get accurate reports for the whole of the business, I need to use the default COA, as this COA includes all nominal codes.

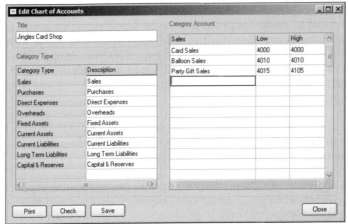

Figure 2-4:
A new Chart of Accounts created for the Jingles Card Shop.

After you add a new Chart of Accounts, you can run your Profit and Loss report to see what information pulls through. Pay attention to the descriptions that you use in your Chart of Accounts, as they transfer through to your Profit and Loss and Balance Sheet reports. At this point, you can see the gross profit for each part of the business and determine what is making money or not, as the case may be.

When editing your Chart of Accounts, you can use the F7 function key to insert a line and the F8 key to delete a line.

Also, if you want just one code within the range, then the code is the same in both the High and Low columns.

Deleting a Chart of Accounts

You may find that while you've been playing around designing new Charts of Accounts, you created too many variations and want to delete some of them.

Follow these steps:

1. **Click Company and then Chart of Accounts.**

   The Chart of Accounts window opens.

2. **Highlight the Chart of Accounts that you want to delete and click Delete.**

3. **Click Yes to confirm that you want to delete it.**

   If you decide that you don't want to delete, click No and return to the main Chart of Accounts window.

Checking Your Chart of Accounts

After you make any changes to your Chart of Accounts, you need to ensure that your COA doesn't contain any errors. If an error is present, the Profit and Loss or Balance Sheet reports may be incorrect, and a warning message flashes up every time you run these reports.

To check your Chart of Accounts, follow these steps:

1. **Go to the Company module and click COA.**
2. **Click Edit.**
3. **Click Check.**

If no problems are present, Sage tells you that no errors were found in the Chart of Accounts, and you can breathe a sigh of relief. However, if a little window entitled Chart of Accounts Errors appears, be prepared to take corrective action.

Previewing errors

The Chart of Accounts Errors window gives you four output options for displaying the error report:

✔ **Printer:** Sends the report directly to your printer.

✔ **Preview:** Lets you look at the errors on the screen before deciding to print or exit.

✔ **File:** Saves the report to a new location.

✔ **Email:** Offers the facility to email the document to another person.

Usually, the best method is to preview the report first, to make sure that it's providing you with the information you expected, and then you can print a hard copy if you like what you see.

Make sure that the option you want has a filled-in circle next to it and then click the Run button at the bottom of the pop-up screen. Figure 2-5 is a sample Error report, showing that a nominal code is not represented in the Chart. The missing code must be included within the nominal code ranges to stop the Error report coming up.

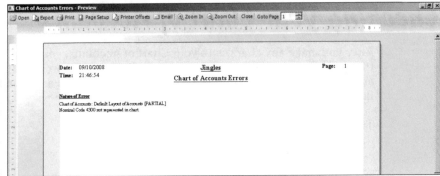

Figure 2-5:
An error
shows up in
a COA Error
report.

Looking at some common errors

Whenever you add new nominal codes, the chance exists that they may not fit within the nominal code structure currently in place. This common oversight leads to errors within the COA.

Check the steps in the 'Amending your COA' section earlier in this chapter for advice on how to fix the errors I list here.

Other common errors include:

- ✔ **Overlapping ranges:** The same nominal code occurs in two different ranges and is therefore counted twice.

  For example, Jeanette, the owner of the Jingles Card Shop, assigned the Sales of Cards category nominal codes from 4000 to 4199, and then assigned the Sale of Balloons category codes from 4100 to 4299. The Error report pointed out that the categories overlap between 4100 and 4199. Jeanette needs to amend the ranges so that they don't overlap.

- ✔ **Enclosing one range within another range:** Assigning a range of codes that's within another range is a big no-no.

  For example, Jeanette assigned the Sale of Balloons category a range from 4100 to 4299, and then assigned the Sale of Party Gifts codes from 4200 to 4250, which is within the Sale of Balloons range. She needs to fix it so that she knows whether she's selling mostly balloons or party favours.

- ✔ **Using a floating code in one category but not in its complementary category:** You may require a floating code so that an item such as the Bank account can be both a Current Asset or a Current Liability, depending on whether the account is overdrawn or not. If you set up a floating code in Current Assets but not in Current Liabilities or vice versa, you get an error message.

Chapter 3

Setting up Records

· ·

In This Chapter

▶ Choosing a quick start or step by step

▶ Setting up records for customers and suppliers

▶ Registering your bank accounts

▶ Accounting for your products

▶ Depreciating your fixed assets

· ·

*A*fter you install your Sage software, you quickly realise that the hard work is only just beginning! You now have to create the records necessary to operate your accounting system, including creating records for your customers and suppliers and your existing bank accounts. Depending on your business, you may also need to set up stock and project records. This chapter tells you how.

Choosing How to Create Your Records

Setting up records may seem a daunting task, but Sage provides at least two ways of doing things: a quick way, using the Record icon within the relevant module and the step-by-step way, which involves using the wizards. If you like the belt and braces approach, choose the wizards, as they help you complete each section of the record thoroughly. However, if you're a bit of a speed freak and want to get on with things as quickly as possible, and don't mind leaving a few less important data fields blank (you can always update them later), choose the quick start option outlined in the next section. I always use this method, as time is always of the essence.

Getting a quick start using the Record icon

If you're looking for a quick start, the first thing you need to do is locate the Record icon. To set up records for nominal accounts, bank accounts, products and projects, click the relevant Module button from the navigation bar, and you're presented with the associated icons for each module, including the Record icon. You can also click the relevant Edit option on the Task pane for each module. A record opens for you to start entering data.

For customer and supplier records, after you click the module button from the navigation bar, you're presented with a process map, which is currently the default screen. If you prefer not to have the process maps as a default and want to see a list of customers and suppliers with icons across the top of the screen, you can switch the process maps off. (See the 'Switching off the process maps' section later in this chapter.)

If you want to keep the Process screen as your default screen, you can simply use the Task pane to open up the Customer or Supplier Record screen. To do this, click the relevant module and then Edit Customer/Supplier in the Task pane to bring up the Record screen. You can enter your details by using the following steps:

1. **From the Customer/Supplier Process screen, click Change View (in the top right corner of the screen).**

2. **Select Customers/Suppliers from the dropdown menu.**

   Look for the icons available at the top of the screen.

3. **Click Record.**

   You can start entering your customer/supplier details; I tell you how in the upcoming 'Creating Customer and Supplier records' section.

As soon as you close the Process screen, the default screen reverts to opening with the process map.

Switching off the process maps

You can choose not to display the process maps as your default screen for customers and suppliers. I personally don't like the process maps, as I prefer to use the icons shown on the Toolbar screen. Incidentally, for those of you who have used Sage before, the Toolbar screen is more like the screens used to be before all the fancy graphics. (Now I'm showing my age!)

If you want to switch off the process maps and see the Customers or Suppliers screen instead, follow these steps:

1. **From the main toolbar, click Tools.**

2. **Select Options.**

3. **Click Yes to the confirmation screen, if you have other windows open.**

4. **In the Options menu, select the View tab. Click the small dropdown arrow next to Customers Process Maps and select Customers List. Do the same for Suppliers.**

   Figure 3-1 shows the Options screen.

5. **Click OK.**

Now, as soon as you enter either the customer or the supplier ledger, the default screen shows the icons. You can click the Record icon to create as many records as you require. See the 'Creating Customer and Supplier Records' section later in this chapter.

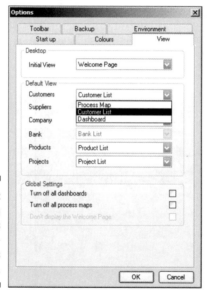

Figure 3-1: Changing the defaults from process maps to lists.

Following the wizards brick by brick

Like Dorothy and friends finding their way to the Emerald City, going brick by brick or step by step can take some time, but it most assuredly gets you where you need to be. This method is slower than using the Record icon, as it guides you through the completion of every box in each record. For example, if you're keen on keeping customers within their credit limit and offer discounts for early settlement, you may want to use the Customer wizard to guide you through setting up the intricacies of your credit control.

To awaken a wizard, click the module you want to create a new record within and then click New. The program takes you through a step-by-step wizard, which prompts you to dot every *i* and cross every *t*. The wizard is very thorough, but using it can be very time-consuming. (For more information about wizards, check out Chapter 22.)

Creating Customer and Supplier Records

Because setting up customer and supplier records is essentially the same process, I cover both of them in this section. Wizards can walk you through creating both types of records (just click New in the relevant module), but for the quick start method, read on:

Click the Record icon using one of the methods outlined in the preceding 'Getting a Quick Start using the Record Icon' section. A blank customer record appears, as shown in Figure 3-2.

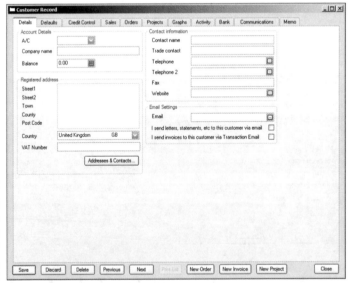

Figure 3-2: An example of a blank customer record.

Notice that several tabs appear across the top of the record:

✔ **Details:** Type the usual contact details in these fields.

WARNING!

Decide how you want to set up the account reference prior to beginning your data entry. Think carefully about this first data-entry field and the eight-digit short name you give each account. Sage recommends that you use an *alphanumeric* reference, meaning you use letters and numbers. Sage suggests this because you may have a number of clients with the same surname, for example, Smith, so you need to give them unique references, such as Smith01, Smith02 and so on. Alternatively, ignore any numbers and continue with just words. For example, Julian Smith is SmithJ, Sarah Smith becomes SmithS and so on.

After typing in the account reference, you can tab through the other fields and enter the relevant information.

If you're transferring from a different computer package, you may be able to import the customer records from your old system to Sage. See Chapter 19 for details about how to do this.

✓ **Defaults:** The basic defaults are shown in each record, and you can override the details for each individual record if desired. You can specifically tailor the defaults for your customers as well.

For example, the default nominal code is currently set at 4000, but if you have a customer for whom this code never applies, you can easily change the code to something more suitable. For example, Jingles may sell one customer only balloons, therefore it makes sense to set the default nominal code as Sale of Balloons for that customer.

✓ **Credit Control:** You can enter your credit control details here for both customers and suppliers. For example, you can set credit limits so that if a customer exceeds those limits, Sage warns you and you can take steps to get that customer account back under control again. You can note details such as credit reviews and settlement discounts to assist you in your credit control.

To avoid a nervous breakdown, tick the Terms Agreed box in the bottom left corner of the Credit Control screen. If you don't, every time you open that record, you get an audio and visual prompt saying that terms haven't been agreed with this account. You'll go crazy after a very short space of time! So if you do nothing else with this page, make sure that you tick the Terms Agreed box.

✓ **Sales (customer record):** You can view a history of all invoices, credit notes, balances, receipts and payments against this account. You can identify trends in your customer's monthly transactions.

✓ **Purchases (supplier record):** You can view a history of all invoices, credit notes, balances, payments and receipts applied to this supplier account. You can see trends developing with your transactions with this particular supplier.

✓ **Orders:** You can see the history of all sales orders applied to this account. Double-click any of the orders to enter the detail of the sales order record. You can also create a new sales invoice or a new order from this screen.

✓ **Projects:** You can view a list of all the projects associated with this customer. You can also create a new project record for this selected customer by clicking New Project Record. (See Chapter 13 for more details.)

✔ **Graphs:** Prepare to be wowed with a graphical representation of the history of the transactions month by month.

✔ **Activity:** I use this screen a lot. It shows a list of every transaction ever made on the selected account. You can see all the invoices and credit notes, payments and receipts. It also shows a balance, amounts paid or received and turnover for that account.

Each line on the Activity list represents a single invoice, credit note, receipt/payment or a payment on account. You can drill down into additional detail, where it exists, by clicking the plus sign (+) on the left side of the transaction line. You can also view the aged detail of your customer or supplier accounts, shown at the bottom of the Activity tab. Future, Current, 30 days, 60 days, 90 days and Older buttons show values according to the age of the outstanding amounts.

✔ **Bank:** You can enter bank details on each record. This option is useful if you do a lot of online banking, particularly payment of suppliers.

✔ **Communications:** You can record details of telephone conversations with both customers and suppliers. For example, if you're making a credit control call, you can make notes of promised payments and follow-up dates for call backs, which creates an event in your Sage Diary. This information also appears in the Task Manager.

If your business charges on a time basis, you can directly invoice a customer from the Communications tab for time spent on a phone call. See Chapter 6 for more details.

✔ **Memo:** You can attach electronic documents and files for all your customer and supplier records, using the Document Manager function. For more details on this, see Chapter 19.

You can also make notes about your customers and suppliers, including details of phone calls.

Setting customer and supplier defaults

Whenever you create a customer or supplier record, you enter details such as the credit limit, discounts and terms of payment. If all the same terms apply to all your customers or suppliers, you can set up this information once only, and it then applies to all customer or supplier records that you create. This option can save you time, particularly at the start when you're creating lots of records. If terms are different for a few individual customers or suppliers or if the terms change for some reason, you can override the defaults in each individual customer or supplier record at any time. If all your customers and suppliers are different, then don't set up defaults.

The following steps apply to setting up the Customer defaults, but you can use the same process for Supplier defaults:

1. **Click settings from the main tool bar, then customer or supplier defaults.**

   The customer defaults screen opens on the Record tab. Here you can enter the currency if Foreign Trader is enabled (otherwise it is greyed out). You can also edit the VAT code, nominal code and any discounts as applicable.

2. **Click the Ageing tab if you want to switch from Period Ageing to Calendar Monthly Ageing.**

   Period ageing sets periods of less than 30, 60 and 90 days, and 120 days or more. So if an invoice is dated 15 January 2009, it falls into the current period between 15 January to 13 February (within 30 days) and the 30-days plus period between 14 February and 14 March, and so on.

   Calendar monthly ageing means that all the month's transactions are classed as outstanding on the first day of the month. For example, if the invoice is dated 15 January 2009, the invoice falls into the current period if an aged report is run between 1 January and 31 January. If the aged report is run between 1 February and 29 February, the invoice falls into Period 1, and so on.

3. **Click the discount tab if you apply different discount percentages, depending on the value of the invoices.**

   This option applies to Customer defaults only.

Deleting customer and supplier records

You can delete a record only if there are no transactions on the account and the account balance is zero. If neither condition is met and you try to delete an account, Sage lets you know in no uncertain terms that you can't do it! But if you can, and if you must, find out how here.

You may want to delete a record if you set up duplicate accounts in error. For example, you set up a new account before checking to see if one was in existence already.

If there are no transactions on the second account, you can delete it following the steps here. If you have unwittingly added transactions to the duplicate account, you can change them by using the File Maintenance option, which I tell you how to use in Chapter 9. The second account then needs to be renamed with the words *Do Not Use!!!* in the title.

To delete a record, follow these steps:

1. **Open the customer or supplier ledger as appropriate and select the account you want to delete.**

2. **Click Delete, and when the confirmation message appears, click Yes.**

Creating Your Nominal Records

Nominal records are the main body of an accounting system. They are categorised into a Chart of Accounts structure, which I explain in Chapter 2.

Exploring your nominal records

To explore your nominal records, click Company to open up the Nominal Ledger screen. You can change the way the information is presented on the Nominal Ledger screen by using the dropdown arrow next to the Layout field. Figure 3-3 shows the Analyser layout.

Figure 3-3: Looking at the nominal ledger through the Analyser layout.

The main body of the screen shows the categories of the nominal codes. To see which codes lie within the categories, click the plus sign (+) next to each category. Doing so drills down to the next level and shows the subcategories. You can click the plus sign next to a subcategory to see the actual codes that form part of that subcategory.

Alternatively, you can view all the nominal codes at a glance. To do this, follow these steps:

1. **Click the Layout dropdown menu at the top right corner of the screen.**

2. **Select List.**

The screen changes its appearance and shows a list of all your nominal codes along with a description/name. After you have transactions entered, you also see Debit and Credit columns with figures in, next to each nominal code.

3. Scroll up and down this page to see the numerous codes.

They start at 0010 and finish at 9999! You may think this is an awful lot of numbers, but the numbering system has gaps. I've never felt inclined to count them all, but suffice it to say, Sage has a lot!

You can choose the Graph layout, which shows a pie chart layout of the nine categories of accounts within the nominal ledger. This option is colourful, but not particularly useful. My preferred option is the List layout, which shows the nominal codes in their clearest format.

Renaming existing nominal records

You may want to rename some of your nominal records. For example, Sage helpfully gives you several Sales Type codes from _A_ through _E_ – meaningless descriptions that you need to change to suit your business.

For example, Jeanette, the owner of Jingles, wants to change nominal code 4000, currently designated as Sales Type A, to Sale of Greeting Cards.

Follow these steps to rename the nominal records:

1. Click Company.

2. On the Nominal Ledger toolbar, click the Record icon.

3. Type the number of the nominal code you want to change in the N/C (nominal code) box and press Enter.

In the Jingles example, Jeanette types in 4000.

4. Place your cursor in the Name box and delete the current name. Replace it with the name of your new sales type.

For Jingles, Jeanette replaces Sales Type A with Sales of Greeting Cards.

5. Click Save and then Close.

Adding a new nominal record

When you're adding a new nominal record, you need to make sure that the nominal code you use fits into the correct part of the Chart of Accounts. Refer to Chapter 2 to see the nine different ranges of nominal codes that make up the Chart of Accounts.

If you're adding new codes into your range, you need to decide where you can slot them into your existing structure. For example, if you want to add a nominal record (which requires a new nominal code) for mobile phones, look at the Profit and Loss account, because it's an expense item. It's not a direct product cost, so place it in the Overhead section, close to the telephone costs for the business, around the 7500 range of nominal codes.

In the Jingles example, Jeanette wants to add a new Sales nominal record, Sale of Balloons, with a new nominal code, 4010.

Here's how to add a new nominal record:

1. **Click Company.**

2. **On the Nominal Ledger toolbar, click the Record icon.**

3. **In the N/C box, type the new nominal code number and then tab to the Name field.**

   The new nominal code for Jingles is 4010.

   The words new account pop up next to the nominal code because Sage doesn't recognise this nominal code; it isn't part of the default list of nominal codes.

4. **In the Name field, type the name of your new record.**

   For Jingles, Jeanette enters Sale of Balloons.

5. **Click Save and close the box.**

Figure 3-4 shows Jingles' new nominal record.

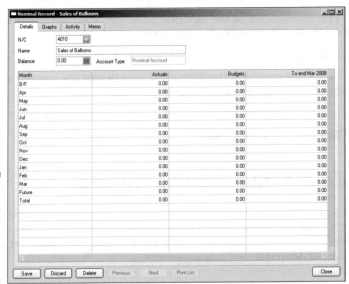

Figure 3-4: Adding Sale of Balloons to Jingles' nominal ledger.

You need to check that your Chart of Accounts is free of errors; refer to Chapter 2 for instructions on how to do this.

Looking for a nominal record

Each nominal record has its own nominal code, but not every nominal code is immediately easy to find. Not that Sage tries to make things difficult, but an awful lot of codes need slotting into categories. Some codes sit into categories better than others.

Because I know a lot of the nominal codes by heart, I know where to start looking, but as a beginner you need to have some tricks up your sleeve to find those elusive codes!

Searching for a record alphabetically

If you know the name of the record you're trying to find, but not the number (nominal code), follow these steps:

1. **Click Company and then Record.**

2. **From the N/C (nominal code) field, click the right dropdown arrow.**

   A list of all your nominal codes appears, in number order.

3. **Click the grey heading Name to reorganise the nominal codes into alphabetical order. Press the appropriate letter and locate the code you're interested in.**

   If you're looking for the nominal record for Telephone, press **T** on the keyboard, and Sage takes you to the first record beginning with the letter *T*, which just so happens to be Telephones! Looking across at the nominal code, you can see that it is 7502.

To see where a record sits in the overall range, sort the nominal records back into number order by clicking the grey N/C (nominal code) heading and scrolling down to the appropriate codes.

After you sort the records back into number order, if you want to get to a specific number range again, type the first digit of the nominal code. Sage takes you to the first code that starts with that number, so you save time.

Finding a record numerically

If you know the approximate nominal code range, 7500, for example, but you don't know the specific code to use, follow Steps 1 and 2 from the preceding section and then scroll down to the code range.

In the Jingles example, the telephone codes show no space to insert a code for mobiles. However, directly after Telephone is nominal code 7503, classified as Telex/Telegram/Fax. As Jeanette doesn't think she'd use this code, she renames it Mobile Phones.

Looking around a nominal record

Sage provides a number of different ways to view the information contained within a nominal record.

Sage also provides you with some demonstration data, and I sometimes find it helpful to explore parts of the system with dummy data already entered.

To view the demonstration data, use the following steps:

1. **From the main toolbar, click File⇨Open⇨Open Demo Data. Click Yes to the confirmation window that appears.**

2. **Type** manager **into the Logon field. There is no password, so click OK.**

3. **Click Company and then Record.**

4. **Type a code in the Nominal Code field and press Enter.**

   To follow this example, type **4000** to bring up the Sales North nominal record, which is shown in Figure 3-5.

Notice the four tabs at the top of the nominal record:

✔ **Details:** You are already in the Details screen. This screen shows you actual amounts posted to this account on a month-by-month basis and prior-year figures if they're available. You can see a column for budget figures. You can edit the Budget field and enter figures directly into each month for each nominal record as part of your budget-setting process. These figures then appear on the Budget report, which I tell you about in Chapter 18.

If you can't see the column for budget figures, you need to change your budgeting method from Advanced to Standard on the Budgeting tab in Company Preferences. For more details on advanced budgets, look at the Sage Help menu by pressing F1.

✔ **Graphs:** You can view a graphic format of the account information with lots of pretty colours!

✔ **Activity:** One of the most well-used screens! You can scroll up and down the screen to see exactly what transactions have been posted using this nominal code. Any credit notes or journals also show here.

As 4000 is a sales code, you can see exactly which invoices have been posted.

✔ **Memo:** You can make notes that relate to this account. Or, you can attach electronic documents with the Document Manager, which I talk about in Chapter 19.

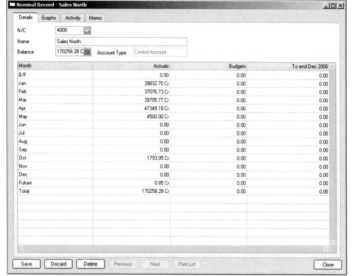

Figure 3-5: Looking at a nominal record with Sage's demonstration data.

Deleting a nominal code

You can delete nominal codes that you never use, to tidy the list. For example, if you sell just one product, you may want to delete the codes associated with Sales Types B, C, D and E. Just follow these steps:

1. **Click Company.**

2. **On the Nominal Ledger toolbar, click the Record icon.**

3. **In the N/C box, type the number of the code you want to delete and press Enter.**

4. **Click Delete. Click Yes when the confirmation box appears.**

You can only delete a nominal record if there are no transactions associated with that code.

Recording Your Bank Accounts

Sage automatically gives you seven bank accounts – including a new one for version 2010 named Cash Register. These are shown in Figure 3.6. The accounts range from an Ordinary Bank Current Account to a Credit Card Receipt account. You need to review the list of bank accounts and rename some, add new ones or delete those that don't apply to your business. The next sections tell you how to do these tasks.

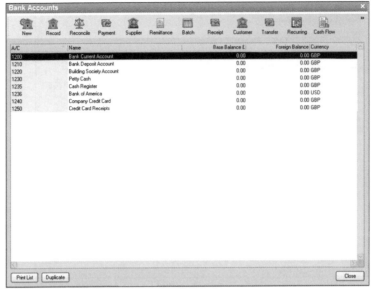

Figure 3-6:
The default
list of bank
accounts
that Sage
provides.

Renaming an existing account

You may find that the number of bank accounts that Sage gives you is sufficient, but you probably need to rename them to suit your business. For
example, you may want to specify the name of the bank or type of account,
such as number one account, number two account and so on. . . .

Don't create a new account if you can simply rename an existing one. You
then don't need to amend your Chart of Accounts for new nominal codes.

To rename an account, follow these steps:

1. **Click Bank and then Record.**

2. **Use the dropdown arrow to select the account you want to rename
   and then overtype the new name in the Nominal Name field.**

3. **Click Save.**

Creating new accounts

If you have a lot of bank accounts, you may need to create additional bank
account records to accommodate your business needs. You can choose from
three ways of creating a new account. You can:

✔ Set up a new account by using the wizard. Simply click Bank on the navigation bar and then New Account from the Task pane or the New icon from the Bank Account Module toolbar.

✔ Duplicate an existing account. From the Bank module, highlight the account you want to duplicate and click the Duplicate button at the bottom of the screen. Give the account an appropriate nominal code and name, click Save and off you go.

✔ Use a blank record and follow the steps I give here.

I demonstrate how to create a bank record with the same method used for creating customer, supplier and nominal records so far. The steps are:

1. **From the Bank module, click Record.**

   A screen appears, as shown in Figure 3-7.

   The screen shows the account reference as 1200, which is the default nominal code for the Bank Current account.

2. **Click the dropdown arrow in the Account Reference box.**

   All the existing bank accounts and their nominal codes are listed.

3. **Decide on a new nominal code reference for your new bank account and enter it in the Account Reference field.**

   Try to keep all the current accounts and deposit accounts between 1200 and 1229 and credit card accounts between 1240 and 1249. The Chart of Accounts is more presentable that way.

4. **Tab down to the Nominal Name field and give your new account a name.**

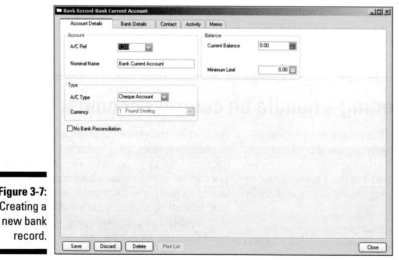

Figure 3-7:
Creating a
new bank
record.

5. **From the Account Type box, use the dropdown arrow to select cash, cheque or credit card account.**

6. **Skip the Balance box – don't enter anything.**

   Have a look at Chapter 4 for information on opening balances.

7. **If you're operating foreign currency accounts, select a currency.**

8. **Check *No bank reconciliation* if you're not intending to reconcile this bank account.**

   You'll probably only choose this option for the Petty Cash account. You need to reconcile all accounts, including credit card accounts, to a bank or credit card statement to get a good picture of how your business is doing.

9. **Click Save.**

Deleting a bank record

You may find that you want to delete a bank record. For example, Sage provides you with a Building Society account, which you may not want. Although you may decide to rename this account, you can choose to delete the account completely and tidy up your bank account list. However, you can only do this if the following conditions apply:

✔ The bank account has no transactions associated with it.

✔ The balance is zero.

✔ It is not a control account.

If the account meets these conditions, highlight the bank account concerned and click Delete. You receive an affirmation message. Click Yes to continue or No to return to your original record.

Getting a handle on control accounts

Sage uses control accounts to make double-entry postings. The Debtors and Creditors control accounts enable you to see total figures for all your debtors and creditors without having to add up all the individual invoices and credit notes.

To see a list of all the control accounts, click Company and then Control Accounts on the Links list. You don't need to alter these accounts because they're default accounts. In fact, if the Debtors, Creditors and Sales Tax or Purchase Tax control accounts have balances on them, you can't make any changes to these codes. Only journal to them if you're confident with your double-entry bookkeeping. Otherwise, leave them to your accountant!

Getting Your Product Records in Order

Planning your nominal codes is important, but planning your product records is just as important. The product records that you create eventually become your product list – a list of all your stock items. As the business grows, the number of stock items grows, so you need to design a stock-coding system that's easy to use and can easily identify products. You need to be able to identify a product type quickly and easily from a stock list or stock report.

Creating a product record

You can create a product record three ways:

- ✔ Use the wizard: click Products and then New.
- ✔ Duplicate an existing record: click the product and then Duplicate.
- ✔ Type your details directly into a blank product record, as detailed here. Follow these steps to use the blank record method:

1. **From the Products module, click Record.**

   The Details screen, shown in Figure 3-8, appears.

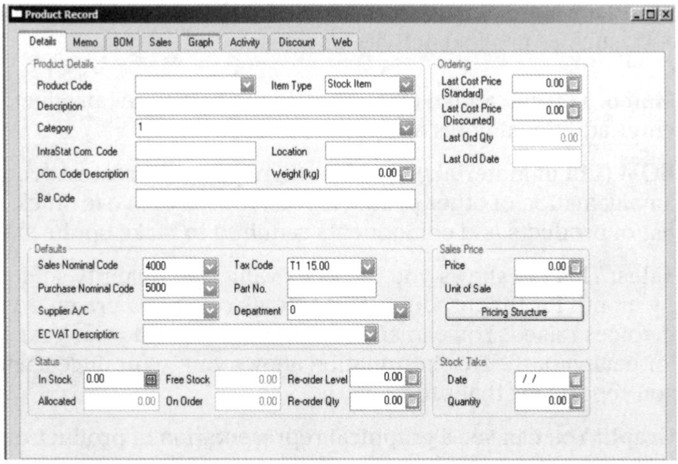

Figure 3-8: Viewing a blank product record.

2. **Enter your chosen product code, using 30 digits or fewer.**

3. **Type in a description of the product and fill in as much of the product details as you can. Note: The product field now allows you to enter the bar code for your product, alpha-numerically and up to 60 characters in length.**

In the default section, you may need to change the default sales nominal code and purchase nominal code. For example, a stock record for birthday cards requires a nominal code for birthday cards. You need to check the nominal codes and change if necessary.

When entering your product details, you can choose an Item Type:

- **Stock Item:** A regular item of stock, which has a product code and description. You can give a stock item a project code and issue it to a project.

- **Non-Stock Item:** An item that isn't a usual item of stock, perhaps purchased for use within the business instead of to sell. Non-stock items can't be posted to a project as they aren't classified as stock and can't be issued.

- **Service Item:** Usually a charge, for example, a labour charge, that can be set up as a product code. Service items can't be posted to a project as they aren't physical products in stock and can't be issued.

4. **When you've finished entering your product details, click Save.**

   Your first record is saved, and the screen goes blank again, waiting for your next record.

The other tabs that belong to the product record are outlined next. You may need to enter details in the BOM tab if you're using Bill of Materials. (See Chapter 12 for more details on this.) Other tabs can just be used as monitoring tools, such as product activity or sales.

✔ **Memo:** You can attach electronic documents to the product record or enter additional notes about the product.

✔ **BOM (Bill of Materials):** BOM is where you can create a product from an amalgamation of other products that you may have in stock. BOM is a list of products and components required to make up the main product.

✔ **Sales:** This tab shows you the sales value and quantity sold month by month for that product. The Actuals column is driven from actual invoices raised. You can enter budget values and prior-year information for each month. This information allows you to produce useful comparison reports for that product.

✔ **Graph:** You can see a graphical representation of products sold against budget and the prior year at a glance.

✔ **Activity:** Shows the individual transactions created for each product. For example, goods in, out, transferred or stock adjustments. You can also view the quantity of the item in stock, on order, allocated and available.

✔ **Discount:** Allows you to give up to five different quantity discounts per product.

✔ **Web:** You can enter information about your web shop, including images of your product.

Editing a product record

You can edit a product record at any time by double-clicking the chosen product. The Product Record screen appears. You can then make the necessary change, click Save and close the screen.

Deleting a product record

As with the other records, you can only delete a product record if the following criteria are met:

✔ The product record has no transactions on the product activity. Any history needs to be removed; see Chapter 16 for information on how to do this.

✔ The In Stock, On Order and Allocated balances are all zero.

✔ The product is not a component of a Bill of Materials.

✔ The product has no outstanding transactions, such as outstanding orders.

If all these conditions are met, you can delete the product with a couple of steps:

1. **From Products, highlight the product you want to delete.**

2. **Click Delete. An affirmation message appears. Click Yes.**

Creating a project record gives you a place to hold all the relevant information describing your project.

Setting up a project is covered in Chapter 13, but in this section, I give you an overview of the information contained within a project record.

Entering a project record

You can create a project record in one of the following ways:

- Summon the Project Record wizard in one of two ways: from the Projects module, click the New icon; or select New Project from the Task pane.

- From the Customer Record window, click New Project.

- Enter details directly into a blank project record, which I describe next.

- When you create a sales order with the product code S3, you have the option to create a project for that order.

To enter project details from a blank record, click Record from the Project module. The project record opens on the Details tab and gives you access to other relevant tabs:

- **Details tab:** Enter your project details, including start dates, completion dates and contact names and addresses here. You must have a unique project reference before you can save the project. If you need to, you can link a project directly to a customer by clicking on the A/C Ref field in the Customer Details section and selecting your customer using the dropdown arrow. If the project is internal, leave this blank (in other words, don't select a customer).

- **Analysis tab:** You can enter the price quoted for a project on this screen. All the other information falls into the look-but-don't-touch category – you can see it, but you can't change it. As you create and post invoices to raise bills to your customer for the project, the billing total is updated. You also have an analysis of the total budget and costs associated with this project.

- **Activity tab:** You can view the transactions posted against a project here – invoices, costs and product movements, for example.

- **Budgets and Structure tabs:** The Budgets tab records monies allocated to the project. The Structure tab is used to maintain a project that has several phases; both are applied to the project record after it has been created. As the project is being created, you apply all costs associated with it.

- **Memo tab:** Using the Attachments pane, you can add electronic documents or filing references to each project. You can edit the memo pad as you require. See Chapter 19 for more information on Document Manager.

After you enter the project details, click Save, and your new project appears in the Projects screen.

Setting Up Fixed Asset Records

Fixed assets are items usually held in the business for at least 12 months or more. When the business purchases a fixed asset, such as a building, a vehicle or machinery, instead of deducting the whole expense at the time of purchase, the asset is *depreciated* over the extent of its useful life. (Sorry, I'm going into accountant-speak here.) Basically, the charge to your Profit and Loss account is apportioned over a longer period of time. For example, you may apportion the cost of a car over a four-year period instead of charging the whole cost in the first year.

To keep track of your depreciated items, you need to set up a fixed asset record, so that Sage knows what items are fixed assets, and over what period and at what rate they need to be depreciated. To set up a fixed asset record, follow these steps:

1. **Click Company and then select Manage Fixed Assets from the Task pane.**

   To begin with, the main screen is blank. As you start to record your assets, the screen fills up with detail, one line per asset.

2. **Click Record. Use the Details tab to describe the asset and give it a reference.**

   Enter information as necessary on the Posting tab, as shown in Figure 3-9 and detailed here:

   • Select a Department if required.

   • Use the Balance Sheet Depreciation N/C dropdown arrow to select the appropriate code. Remember, this record requires a Balance Sheet code, so it starts with 00. For example, Plant and Machinery Depreciation is 0021.

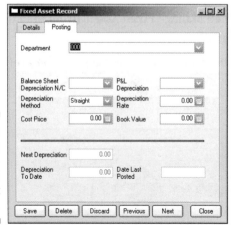

Figure 3-9: Entering information onto a fixed asset record.

- Use the Profit and Loss Depreciation dropdown arrow to select your code. Now you need a Profit and Loss code, so take care to select the correct one. For example, Plant and Machinery depreciation is 8001.

  You may feel confused by the two codes for depreciation – one in the Balance Sheet and one in the Profit and Loss account – but remember that Sage operates a double-entry bookkeeping system and needs two codes to post your transactions to. Just be careful when setting up your codes to select the correct ones.

- Select the Depreciation Method, usually straight line or reducing balance. If you're not sure, check with your accountant. After you select the method, you can't change back, except to write off the asset.

- Set the Depreciation Rate. The depreciation rate is the percentage rate that reduces the value of the asset. For example, if you're depreciating a car over four years and applying the straight line method, you apportion the value of the asset equally over four years and apply a 25 per cent depreciation charge per year.

- Enter the cost price, net of VAT of the asset.

3. **Enter the current book value of the item you're depreciating.**

   If the item is brand new, the book value is the same as cost price. If the item has already been depreciated, the book value is cost price less depreciation. If you decide to use the reducing balance method, the book value is the value used to calculate the depreciation amount. Sage automatically updates the remaining boxes.

4. **Click Save when you're happy with the information you've entered.**

Sage posts depreciation when you run the Month-End option. For more details, go to Chapter 16. If you have to delete an asset – because you sold it or it was stolen or damaged – follow these steps:

1. **Click Company and then Manage Fixed Assets (from the Links list).**

2. **Select the asset and click Delete.**

3. **Click Yes to agree to the confirmation message or No to return to the previous menu.**

Chapter 4

Recording Your Opening Balances

. . . .

In This Chapter

▶ Choosing the right time to switch to Sage

▶ Getting your opening balances

▶ Recording your opening balances

▶ Checking for accuracy

. . . .

*I*n this chapter I explain how to transfer the individual account balances from your previous accounting system, whether it is manual or computer-ised, into Sage 50 Accounts. Effectively, you're taking the values that make up what your business is worth on the day you swap from your old system and start using Sage. You need to set up your nominal records before recording balances, so check out Chapter 3 if you haven't done that yet.

Opening balances give you a true picture of your business's assets and liabilities to use as a starting point. If you don't enter your opening balances, you don't have accurate information about who owes you money, how much money you owe or how much money you have in the bank. You won't even be able to reconcile your bank balance. In short, without opening balances, the information in your Sage program isn't worth the paper it's printed on!

Entering your opening balances can be a bit tricky, so make sure that you're not going to be disturbed too much! After you've done this, you can print an opening balance sheet, which is an important tool to check that your balances have been entered correctly.

Timing Your Switch to Sage

The best time to start with a new system is at the beginning of a financial year. You roll the closing balances from the previous year-end forward so that they become your opening balances for your new year. Take advice from your accountant if you have one, as everyone's circumstances are different.

If you can't wait until the new financial year to switch to Sage and you're VAT registered, at least wait until the start of a new VAT quarter. This way, you avoid having a mixture of transactions in your old and new system, which makes reconciling your data extremely difficult.

Enter your opening balances before you start entering transactions. You can then check your accuracy by proving your opening Trial Balance matches your Closing Trial Balance from your previous system. Without the clutter of day-to-day transactions you can check much more easily!

Obtaining Your Opening Balances

Whether you're transferring from a manual bookkeeping system or a computerised one, the process is still the same. Essentially, you transfer into Sage the balance sheet information that shows the net worth of your business.

An opening *Trial Balance* is a list of all account balances carried forward from the previous year-end. Your previous accounting system is your source for your Trial Balance. As you zero-down your Profit and Loss items at the end of the financial year, any retained Profit and Loss items from the previous year now sit in your balance sheet, so an opening Trial Balance contains only balance sheet codes. An opening Trial Balance report looks quite short and shows debit and credit entries for all your balance sheet items, with grand totals at the bottom of both your Debit and Credit columns.

If you're starting to use Sage at the beginning of a new financial year, your accountant can provide you with your opening balances.

If you're transferring from a manual bookkeeping system, you need to ensure that you've balanced off all your individual accounts for the previous period. You may find it easier to print off a list of your newly created nominal accounts in Sage and create two columns, one for debit balances, and the other for credit balances. (To print a nominal list, click Company, which takes you to the Nominal Ledger screen, and then click Print List.) You can then total each column to create an opening Trial Balance.

The figures contained within a Trial Balance are simply the accumulated value of items. For example, the Debtors control account is simply the combined value of all monies owed by customers at that point in time. To establish your opening balances, you need to know the specifics of exactly which customers owe you money and what invoices are outstanding. The same applies to your suppliers: you need to see a full breakdown of who you owe money to. You obtain this information from a variety of sources. Table 4-1 shows the types of reports you need from a computerised system or a manual one.

Table 4-1   Information Sources for Entering Opening Balances

Category	Computerised System	Manual System
Customers For a standard VAT system, record the transaction including VAT. For a VAT cash accounting scheme, record both the net and VAT amount. If this figure isn't the same as your opening Debtors Balance, you need to investigate why.	An Aged Debtors report, showing a breakdown of who owed you money at the start of the year/period.	A list of customers who haven't paid at the year-end, including the amount out-standing.
Suppliers For a standard VAT scheme, include the VAT amount. For a VAT cash accounting scheme, show both the net and VAT amount. If this figure isn't the same as your opening Creditors Balance, you need to investigate why.	An Aged Creditors report, showing a breakdown of who you owed money to at the start of the year/period.	A list of suppliers who you haven't paid at the year-end, along with the monies owed.
Bank When you start reconcil-ing the first month's bank account you may see cheques from the prior year clearing through the bank account. You don't need to worry about these unpresented cheques and lodgements as they've already been taken into account in the previous year and are included in the opening balance for your bank account. Simply mark the items on your bank statement as being prior-year entries. Don't post the items through again.	A copy of the bank statements showing the balance at the year-end. A copy of the bank reconciliation showing a list of any unpresented cheques or outstanding deposits. (Your accoun-tant can help with this.)	A copy of the bank statements showing the balance at the year-end. A copy of the bank reconciliation showing a list of any unpresented cheques or outstanding deposits. (Your accountant can help with this.)
Products	A stocktake list showing the number of items in stock at the start of the year/period.	A stocktake list showing the number of items in stock at the start of the year/period.

Entering Opening Balances

The opening balances represent the financial position of your business on the day you start entering transactions into Sage. Even a new business has opening balances as the funds used to start it up need to be accounted for – the owner's money or grant funding, for example.

Work through your opening Trial Balance systematically and tick off each balance as you enter it into Sage. At the end of this process you can print an opening Trial Balance from Sage that replicates the one from your previous accounting system – in theory at least!

Entering customer and supplier balances

Despite the fact that customers owe you money and you owe money to suppliers, the process for entering opening balances for both is pretty much the same, so I talk about them together in this section.

You only need to record customer balances if you keep customer records. So if you run a shop that collects all receipts at the till and doesn't send out invoices, you don't need to keep customer records.

If you send invoices to your customers, keep records for each customer and record how much each one owes you at the start of your new accounting period with Sage.

In the supplier records you created earlier (I tell you how in Chapter 3), enter the opening balance for each supplier to whom you owe money at the start of the accounting period.

If you used wizards to create your customer and supplier records, you've already entered your opening balances because the wizard asks for them.

I use the Record icon as opposed to the wizard option when setting up records (as explained in Chapter 3), so I use the Record button to enter opening balances, as outlined in the upcoming steps.

Using your Aged Debtors report or debtor list for customers and your Aged Creditors report or creditor/supplier list for suppliers, access each individual account and enter each opening balance, recording each invoice individually.

You have the options of entering a zero balance (which is appropriate if you haven't yet dealt with a new customer or supplier), one lump sum figure or individual transactions. I recommend entering each transaction so that you can see at a glance on the Activity record exactly which invoices make up the opening balance. I strongly urge you to avoid entering a lump sum – it's not best practice and can cause you problems later on.

Depending on whether you're entering balances for customers or suppliers, you start from different places:

✔ **Customers:** From the Customer module, click Record.

✔ **Suppliers:** From the Supplier module, click Record.

Then follow this process:

1. **Select the account using the dropdown arrow and then click the OB (Opening Balance) button located to the right of the Balance box.**

   The Opening Balance Set-up window appears (see Figure 4-1).

Figure 4-1:
The Opening
Balance
Set-up
window.

Opening Balance Setup				
Ref	Date	Type		Gross
	18/06/2008	Invoice		0.00

Save   Cancel

2. **Click the Reference field and type** opening balance.

3. **Tab to the Date field and enter the original date of the invoice/credit note.**

   Entering the original invoice date ensures that the invoices are allocated to the correct period when printing Aged Debtors or Creditors reports.

4. **Tab to the Type field and select Invoice or Credit.**

5. **Enter the invoice or credit amount in the Gross field.**

   Record the gross amount including VAT for standard VAT accounting users; record the net amount and VAT separately if using the VAT cash accounting scheme.

6. **Press Enter to move down to the next line if you have more transactions to enter for that customer/supplier and repeat Steps 2 to 6.**

7. **Click Save to accept the details you entered. Click Cancel if you aren't happy with the accuracy of your entries and want to return to the main customer record without saving.**

8. **Check that your customer balance agrees with your Aged Debtors or customer list for customers, and your Aged Creditors or supplier list for suppliers.**

Recording opening bank balances

You need to record the opening balance for each bank account associated with your business.

Only post opening balances by using nominal journals (see Chapter 16 for information about nominal journals) if you're confident using double-entry bookkeeping. To avoid complications, I recommend that you use the Opening Balance button in each individual bank record in the same way as when entering customer and supplier opening balances.

You may have uncleared payments or receipts already included in your bank balance shown on the opening Trial Balance. The best way to deal with uncleared payments is to obtain a copy of your bank reconciliation statement at the year-end and identify those items shown as unpresented cheques or outstanding paid-in items. After your bank statement arrives, mark these items on your statement as being pre-year-end transactions. When you come to reconcile your bank account in Sage, you can ignore these items as they're already included in your opening balances.

Use the following steps to enter opening balances for each bank account:

1. **From the Bank module, highlight the bank account you wish to enter an opening balance for and click Record.**

2. **Click the OB button next to the Current Balance box.**

   The Opening Balance Set-up window opens. The Reference automatically defaults to O/Bal (Opening Balance), which is fine, leave it as it is.

3. **Enter the date.**

   You want to enter the prior year's end date. For example, if you're starting with Sage on 1 April 2009, the date should be 31 March 2009 to ensure that Sage posts this as an opening balance.

   The closing balance as at 31 March is the same as the opening balance as at 1 April.

4. Enter the account balance.

If the account is in the black, enter the account balance in the Receipt box. If the account is overdrawn, put the amount in the Payment box.

5. Click Save when you're happy that the opening balance figure is correct.

Recording nominal opening balances

If you use the opening Trial Balance or list of account balances as your checking document, or if you followed the order of this chapter, you've already entered the Debtors control account, the Creditors control account and the opening bank balances, so you don't want to enter them again.

When you enter the individual opening balances on to each customer record, Sage does some double-entry in the background, crediting the Sales account and debiting the Debtors control account; therefore when you come to enter the remaining nominal account balances from your Trial Balance, don't post the Debtors control account total, otherwise you are double-counting. If you do post the Debtors control account balance in error, you need to reverse the posting by using a nominal journal. Turn to Chapter 16 for information on journals.

Working in a methodical manner, enter all the remaining balances, such as fixed assets, stock, loans and so on, using the following steps:

1. From Company, click Record.

2. Enter the nominal code.

If you're using the Sage default set of nominal codes, use common sense and match the items from your opening Trial Balance to those of Sage. For example, Accruals in Sage has the nominal code 2109. Take the balance for Accruals from your opening Trial Balance and use nominal code 2109.

If you're using your own existing nominal codes, enter them here. (If you're using your own codes, you should have elected to use a cust-omised Chart of Accounts when you set up Sage – refer to Chapter 1 for company set-up information.)

3. Click the OB button next to the Balance box.

The Opening Balance Set-up window appears.

4. Keep the reference (Ref) as O/Bal (opening balance) and tab along to the Date field and enter the closing date of the prior period.

5. Tab to the Debit or Credit column and enter a debit or credit figure from the opening Trial Balance.

6. Click Save.

You must use the prior year-end date as your opening balance date so that the Trial Balance you bring forward is correct. If you inadvertently enter 1 April as your date, the figure you enter drops into the current year and not into the brought-forward category. To rectify this, enter a nominal journal to reverse the previous journal that Sage automatically posted for you. (See Chapter 16 for help.) If you want to view the automatic journal that Sage has posted, click Company from the navigation bar and then click Financials from the Links list.

Putting in opening balances for products

You only need to do this if you want to track stock items.

Make sure that you create product records for all the items of stock that you wish to put an opening balance to before you try to enter opening product balances. (Refer to Chapter 3 for information on creating records.)

Jingles, the fictional card company, is serving as the example in the following steps. Jeanette, the owner, created a record with the product code Card-HB for birthday cards. Her stocktake at the year-end showed 1,000 cards in stock.

1. **From the navigation bar, click Products. Highlight the product you want to enter an opening balance on to and click Record.**

   For Jingles, Jeanette highlights Card-HB.

2. **Click the OB button next to the In Stock button.**

3. **Keep the reference as O/Bal and enter the date as the prior year-end.**

4. **Enter a quantity and cost price for the item.**

   In the Jingles example, Jeanette enters 1,000 as the quantity and 50p as a cost price, as shown in Figure 4-2.

Figure 4-2: Registering a thousand birthday cards.

Opening Product Setup			☒
Ref	Date	Quantity	Cost Price
O/BAL	18/06/2008	1000.00	0.50
		Save	Cancel

5. **If you're happy with the details entered, click Save.**

   If you're not happy, click Cancel to return to the product record and start again from Step 2.

After you click Save, Sage posts an Adjustment In (AI) transaction to the product record, which you can see in the Activity tab. To view activity on an item, from the main screen, click the stock item you want to view and double-click the product to take you into the record. Click the Activity tab to see the adjustment posting.

 The product opening figures don't automatically update a stock value into your nominal ledger. Opening stock is one of the figures you enter as part of your nominal ledger opening balances – see the 'Recording nominal opening balances' section earlier in this chapter.

Checking Your Opening Balances

Make sure that the figures you entered are correct and agree with the opening Trial Balance you used to enter those figures. The best way to do this is to print your own opening Trial Balance from Sage and compare it to the document you've been working with. If you find discrepancies, you can go back and fix them.

Printing an opening Trial Balance

Follow these instructions to run an opening Trial Balance:

1. **From the navigation bar, click Company and then click Financials in the Links list.**
2. **From Financials, click the Trial icon at the top of the page.**
3. **Select Preview and Run in the Print Output box.**
4. **Change the date in the Criteria Values box to Brought Forward, using the dropdown arrow.**
5. **Click OK.**

   This previews the opening Trial Balance.

6. **Click the Print icon to print the Trial Balance and check your report.**

Look for the following information on the report:

- ✔ Check that the *suspense account* (the temporary account where you put problematic transactions until you determine where they properly belong) shows a zero balance.

> ✔ Check that the totals on your new Trial Balance are the same as the totals on the Trial Balance from your previous system.

If you have problems with either of these balances, see the next section.

Dealing with errors

If the suspense account doesn't have a zero balance, first check that you haven't entered the Debtors or Creditors control account twice. If you've entered something twice, turn to Chapter 16, which tells you how to reverse out the duplicated item using a nominal journal.

If you find that your total balance doesn't match the total of your opening Trial Balance, make sure that you've entered an opening balance for each nominal code and that you haven't missed anything out by mistake.

After you enter all your opening balances and your opening Trial Balance matches that of your previous system, you're now in a position to begin entering your transactions, so turn to the next chapter!

Part II
Looking into Day-to-Day Functions

'There – we've got to stop storing petty cash in a tin and use a computerised petty cash system.'

In this part . . .

I look at the day-to-day functionality of the system, taking you through issuing sales invoices, entering purchase invoices and doing banking transactions. I show you how to maintain and correct your transactions, which hopefully leads to correct information and good reporting!

Chapter 5

Processing Your Customer Paperwork

In This Chapter

▶ Entering sales invoices manually

▶ Posting credit notes

▶ Allocating customer receipts

▶ Getting rid of invoices and credit notes

*I*n this chapter I tell you how to process the sales invoices for your company. If you want to process invoices created manually or from another system, such as Word, this is the chapter for you! Alternatively, if you prefer to produce your sales invoices directly from Sage, check out Chapter 6.

Posting Batch Entry Invoices

Don't you just groan when you see a huge pile of invoices that need entering? Well, Sage can help you speed your way through them by allowing you to post batches of invoices. In other words, you can enter several invoices on the same screen and post them all at the same time as a batch onto the system. (*Post* is a way to say *enter information into an account.*)

Use this method to record sales invoices raised from a system other than Sage. For example, you can issue invoices with Microsoft Word and then enter the invoices onto Sage by using batch entry.

You can enter any number of invoices in one sitting. For example, if you have 20 invoices to process for the day, you can enter them all onto one screen and then check the total of that batch to ensure accuracy. Larger companies often process large quantities of invoices in a number of smaller batches, which makes processing a more manageable task.

You can enter one invoice per line on your Batch Entry screen, but remember that if you have an invoice where the value needs to be split into two different nominal codes, you need to use two lines for that one invoice.

When you have a batch of invoices in front of you, follow these steps:

1. **Click Customer and then click the Invoice icon.**

   The Batch Customer Invoices screen appears.

2. **Click the A/C (Account) field and use the dropdown arrow to select the correct customer account for the invoice.**

3. **Enter the invoice date.**

   Sage automatically enters the system date, which is usually the current day's date. Make sure that you change this date to the one on the invoice.

4. **Enter the invoice number in the Ref (Reference) field.**

   Every invoice needs a unique number derived from a sequential system.

5. **Add any additional references in the Ex Ref field.**

   You can choose to leave this field blank or enter order numbers or other references.

6. **Change the nominal code, if necessary, in the N/C (Nominal Code) field.**

   This field automatically defaults to 4000, unless you changed the nominal default code on the Default tab of your customer record.

7. **Click the department (Dept) applicable for your invoice.**

   You can leave this field blank if you don't have any departments set up. If, on the other hand, you want to be able to analyse information from different offices or divisions within the company, setting up departments is the way to go:

   • From the navigation bar, click Company.

   • Click Department from the Links list.

     You can then enter departments as you wish, using the New/Edit icon.

8. **If you're using projects, click the dropdown Project Ref arrow to select the appropriate project.**

   You can leave this field blank if you don't use projects.

9. **Describe what the invoice is for in the Details field.**

10. **Enter the amount net of VAT in the Net field.**

11. **Choose the tax code applicable for this invoice in the T/C (Tax Code) field.**

Some common VAT codes:

- T0: Zero-rated transactions.
- T1: Standard rate 17.5 per cent.
- T2: Exempt transactions.
- T4: Sales to VAT-registered customers in the European Community (EC).
- T5: Lower VAT rate at 5 per cent.
- T7: Zero-rated purchases from suppliers in the EC.
- T8: Standard-rated purchases from suppliers in the EC.
- T9: Transactions not involving VAT, for example journal entries.

The system updates the VAT field according to the tax code you choose.

Make sure that the VAT Sage calculates is the same as the amount on the invoice. Sometimes Sage rounds up the VAT, and you may find you have a penny difference. If that happens, overwrite the VAT amount in Sage so that the amounts match.

12. **Perform a quick check of the total value of the invoices you're about to post.**

    To do this:

    - Add up the gross value of the pile of invoices you've just entered.
    - Check this total against the total on your Batch Entry screen (in the top right corner of your Sage screen).

    If the totals are different, check each line on your Batch Entry screen against the invoices.

13. **Click Save when the totals in Step 12 are the same.**

To speed up the entry of invoices, you can use the function keys. To see how the F6, F7 and F8 keys can help you, have a quick look at Chapter 21.

Creating Credit Notes

A *credit note* is the opposite of an invoice. Instead of charging the customer, as you do with an invoice, you refund money to a customer through a credit note. Posting a credit note reverses or cancels an invoice you entered previously.

You use credit notes for a number of different reasons. Invoices may need to be cancelled because the product sent was wrong, the goods have been returned and so on.

To ensure that you raise the credit note correctly, you must identify which invoice you're trying to correct. You need to know the invoice number, the date it was raised and the nominal code it was posted to. It's important that you use the same nominal code on your credit note as you used on your invoice. This way, the double-entry bookkeeping posts the entries in the correct nominal codes, so you don't find odd balances showing in the accounts!

You can produce credit notes from the Invoicing module described in Chapter 6, but if you're not invoicing directly from Sage, you must use the batch-entry method for processing them, which is what I describe here.

To enter a credit note, follow these steps:

1. **Click Customer and then the Credit Note icon.**

   Note that the font colour changes from black to red. This feature is useful, as the Credit Note screen looks identical to the Invoice screen. You wouldn't be the first person to merrily continue entering credit notes rather than invoices!

2. **Select the account (A/C) you wish to enter the credit note against.**

3. **Change the date in the Date field if necessary.**

   Unless today's date is acceptable, remember to change this to your desired date for raising the credit note.

4. **Put the credit number in the Credit No field.**

   Use a unique sequential numbering system for your credit notes. Some people prefer to have a separate numbering system for credit notes, others just use the next available invoice number. The method you choose really doesn't matter, just as long as you're consistent.

5. **Enter any additional references in the Ex Ref field.**

   This step isn't necessary if you don't have any further references.

6. **Make sure that the nominal code (N/C) is the same as the invoice you're trying to reverse.**

7. **Select the department (Dept) the original invoice was posted to.**

8. **Select the project that the original invoice was posted to in the Project Ref field (if you are using projects).**

9. **Use the Details field to record the specifics of the credit note.**

   Put something like 'Credit note against Invoice No. 123', and if possible add a description as to why the credit is necessary – the goods were faulty, for example.

10. **Enter the Net, Tax Code and VAT.**

    If you're completely refunding the invoice, these three values are the same as on the original invoice. Otherwise you need to apportion the net amount and allow the VAT to recalculate.

11. Click Save when you're happy with the information you've entered.

Sage posts the credit note: it debits the Sales account and credits the Debtors control account.

You can check to see if the credit has been posted properly by viewing the Activity screen for the nominal code you used. (See Figure 5-1 for an example.) You can see the original invoice being posted to the sales nominal code as a credit and then the credit note showing the debit in the nominal code at a later date. If you've written a description in the Detail field linking the credit note to the invoice, it comes in useful here.

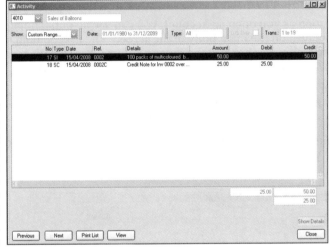

Figure 5-1:
A credit note and invoice on the Activity screen for nominal code 4010.

Registering Payments from Your Customers

Whenever you're dealing with money, whether a payment to a supplier, a cheque from a customer or any other kind of money transaction, use the Bank module. Don't forget this as you process your transactions!

The Bank module has several icons across the top. Use the Customer icon to post a customer receipt.

Don't go directly to the Receipt icon as the info under this icon helps you process things like bank interest received, grants received and so on – it doesn't record the money you receive from customers.

Matching payments to invoices

Ideally, when a customer sends you a cheque you also receive a *remittance advice slip.* This slip identifies which invoices the customer is paying with the cheque sent in. You then pay the cheque into the bank, using a *paying-in slip,* which is kept for your accounting records.

To match the cheque to the correct invoices, follow this procedure:

1. **From the Bank module, click Customer.**

2. **Select the account you wish to post the receipt against by using the dropdown arrow.**

   As soon as you open an account, you can see all outstanding items displayed on the main body of the screen. The first column shows the transaction number and the second column displays the transaction type: *SI* marks a sales invoice; *SC* indicates a sales credit.

   The top part of the Customer Receipt screen is split into three sections: the first column identifies the bank account; the second shows the customer details and the third shows the receipt details.

   Figure 5-2 shows a list of three outstanding invoices and credit notes on the Village Shop account – a Jingles Card Shop customer.

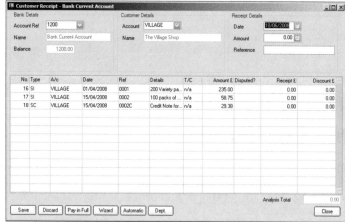

Figure 5-2:
Outstanding items on a customer's account.

3. **Enter the date that the money was received in the Receipt Details column.**

   If you're recording a cheque paid into the bank, type the date from the paying-in slip.

4. **Tab past the Amount field without entering an amount.**

5. **Type** BACS **(for Bankers' Automated Clearing Services) in the Reference field if the invoice is being paid automatically. Or, put a paying-in slip reference if paid by cheque.**

6. **Tab to the next field.**

   Sage takes you to the Receipt column of the first line of transactions.

7. **Click the Pay in Full button at the bottom of the screen.**

   The top right box (the Amount field you ignored in Step 4) now shows the amount of the invoice paid. In the Jingles example in Figure 5-3, the amount shows £235, which is the total of the first invoice.

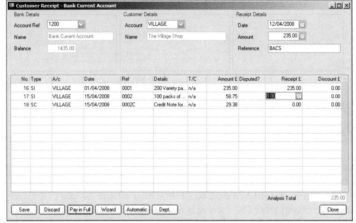

Figure 5-3: A customer receipt after clicking the Pay in Full button.

8. **Click Save at the lower left of the screen if you're happy that the receipt amount is correct.**

   If things aren't right, click Discard. A confirmation button appears: click Yes to continue discarding and your data is cleared ready to start again.

   After you click Save, the screen returns to the original Customer Receipt screen ready for your next customer receipt.

9. **Click Close to finish after you're done entering all your receipts.**

You need to enter and save each receipt individually.

If you want to see what's happened in your Customer account, click the Activity tab. Figure 5-4 shows the Activity tab for Jingles' customer, the Village Shop. The sales receipt is showing on the account. However, two unallocated items still remain on this account. In the next section, I show you how to allocate credit notes to invoices, rather than payments to invoices.

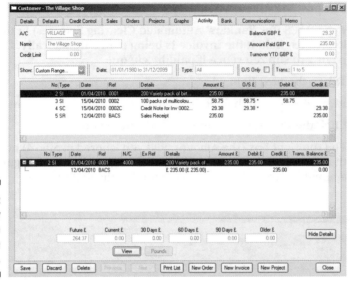

Figure 5-4:
The Activity
tab for the
Village
Shop.

Giving credit where due – allocating credit notes

As well as knowing how to allocate a payment specifically to an invoice, you also need to know how to allocate a credit note against an invoice. Because a credit note is usually raised to cancel the whole or part of an invoice, it stands to reason that the two are matched off against one another.

Allocating means matching a specific invoice to a specific payment or credit note.

Referring back to Figure 5-4, you can see that two of the entries each have an asterisk against them. The asterisk means that the item is unallocated or unmatched. The two unallocated items are sales invoice number 0002 and the credit note 00002C. You can tell that they should be allocated against each other because the description on the credit note refers to invoice 0002. However, the value of the credit note doesn't exactly equal the invoice, so you need to be careful, as you can't match the two items by using the Pay in Full button.

The steps to allocating a credit note are almost identical to allocating a customer receipt:

1. **From the Bank module, click Customer.**

2. **Select the customer account that you need to allocate the credit note to.**

3. **Put the date of the credit note in the Date field.**

   In the example, the date is 15.04.08.

4. **Tab past the Amount field and the Reference field, down to the Credit Note line. With the cursor sitting in the Receipt column on the Credit Note line, click Pay in Full.**

   Figure 5-5 shows the Village Shop account with a -£29.38 balance in the Analysis Total field in the bottom right corner. This indicates that the credit note value is ready to allocate against the invoice.

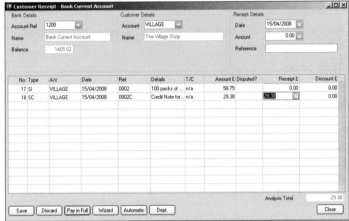

Figure 5-5:
Allocating
a credit
note to a
customer
invoice.

5. **Click the Receipt column on the line that has the invoice you wish to allocate against and manually enter the value of the credit note you're allocating.**

   The Analysis Total now reduces to zero.

6. **Click Save if you're happy that you've allocated the correct amount against the invoice.**

The Customer Activity tab for the Village Shop now shows an outstanding balance of £29.37 – the remaining part of invoice 0002. The small letter *p* against the balance indicates that it's been part paid or part allocated.

Recording payments on account

You may receive payment from a customer that you can't match to a specific invoice. For example, a customer may have inadvertently paid an invoice twice (it does happen) or have forgotten to include the remittance advice slip, so you're not sure which invoice to allocate the payment to.

You can still enter the receipt onto your customer account, but you may not be able to allocate it against a specific invoice.

To enter the receipt, follow these steps:

1. **From the Bank module, click Customer and then select the customer account.**

2. **Enter the date of the receipt in the Date field.**

3. **Enter the amount received in the Amount field.**

4. **Note in the Reference field why the payment isn't allocated against an invoice.**

   For example, if you believe that the customer has duplicated a payment enter 'duplication'.

5. **Click Save.**

6. **Click Yes after you see the message saying that there's an unallocated balance and asking if you want to post this payment on account.**

The Customer Activity screen shows a payment on account as transaction type SA. In the event of a customer overpaying, you may find that the account now has a negative balance. To rectify this, you can send the customer a cheque or leave the balance on account and wait until you start raising more invoices to net this off against.

Deleting Invoices and Credit Notes

The traditional accounting method for reversing an invoice is to create a credit note for the same amount. However, Sage has made it even easier to sort out such problems: you can simply delete the invoice. That way, you don't have to raise the credit note or allocate it to the invoice. You maintain an audit trail, as any deleted items still show and are highlighted in red, so your accountant can always see what you've been up to!

You can use the Maintenance option to cancel unwanted transactions. See Chapter 9 for details on how to delete a transaction.

Chapter 6

Invoicing Your Customers

- -

- -

*Y*ou can generate invoices directly from your Sage accounting software, which means that you can streamline your paperwork process by printing invoices quickly – even directly from sales orders if you're using Sage Accounts Professional. So you have more time to make more money for your business – or more time to take a break from making money for your business.

Sage is an integrated system, which means that when you produce a sales invoice, the system automatically updates the nominal ledger and the customer account, along with products and projects if you're using those options.

Deciding on an Invoice Type

Depending on the type of business you run, you issue mainly one of two types of invoices:

> ✔ **Product invoices:** Used for businesses that sell physical items – cards, widgets, folderols and what-have-yous. A manufacturing company issues product invoices, using product codes.

> ✔ **Service invoices:** Used for businesses that don't sell tangible products, but provide a service to their clients.

A business that sells physical products may need to generate a service invoice occasionally. For example Manufacturers of Widgets might service some of the products they manufacture, and the engineer's time is charged using a service invoice. However, a business that provides services rarely needs to send a product invoice. For example a consultant charges for the time spent providing a service, but usually doesn't need to issue product invoices.

If you need to send invoices with both service details and product items on the same invoice, you need to have Sage Accounts Professional; otherwise you have to send one invoice for service items and another for product items. For example, a car repair centre needs product invoices for the sale of parts and service invoices to show the labour costs for servicing vehicles.

Creating Invoices

You can create both product and service invoices in much the same way, so I combine the two methods in this section and simply highlight the differences between the two as I go along.

Before you start your product invoices, make sure that you've set up your product records, which I explain how to do in Chapter 3.

To begin creating your invoices, from the Customers Task pane, click New Invoice. The Product Invoice screen comes up, as shown in Figure 6-1. The next sections cover the four tabs on the Product Invoice screen.

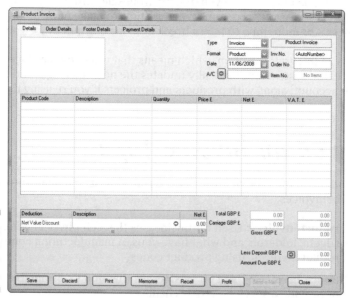

Figure 6-1: Creating a blank product invoice.

Issuing a proforma invoice

A *proforma invoice* is an invoice supplied in advance of the goods or services being provided. It is a more formal and detailed version of a quote.

You can create a proforma in the same way as a sales invoice. However, after you receive payment for a proforma, you need to convert it to an actual invoice. To do this, open up the proforma and change the Type field from Proforma to Invoice using the dropdown arrow in the top right corner of the screen. You can then update the record.

Note: A proforma invoice isn't considered a valid VAT invoice and can't be used in your VAT return.

Putting in the details

The Invoice screen opens with the Details tab, where the default invoice-type is for a product invoice, as indicated in the upper-right corner of the screen.

Starting in that corner, you can set options for your invoice, including:

- ✔ **Type:** Use the dropdown arrow if you want to change from an invoice to a credit note (or proforma if you're using Professional – refer to the preceding sidebar, 'Issuing a proforma invoice').

- ✔ **Format:** You can choose product or service invoice. (In the Professional version, you can produce invoices that include both elements. The following sidebar 'Mixing product and service invoices' tells you how to do this.)

- ✔ **Date:** This automatically defaults to today's date, so change it if necessary.

- ✔ **Account:** Select your customer account, using the dropdown arrow.

- ✔ **Invoice Number:** The `<Autonumber>` notation here unsurprisingly indicates that Sage automatically numbers your invoices. It starts with number 1 and then automatically increases by one for each subsequent invoice. If you want to start with a different number, from the navigation bar, click Customers, and then click Invoice/Order Defaults from the Links list and select the Options tab.

- ✔ **Order Number:** You can enter your own order number here or leave it blank. However, if you're using Professional and generated the invoice using Sales Order Processing, an order number automatically appears within this box.

- ✔ **Item Number**: This shows the item line of the invoice that the cursor is currently sitting on.
- ✔ **Rate:** This field appears only in Professional versions of Sage when you enable the Foreign Trader facility (Chapter 14 explains Foreign Trader).

Getting to the main attraction

The main body of the invoice has the most differences between product invoices and services invoices. As you would expect from a product invoice, you must select the product code, which in turn comes up with the product description and a Quantity field. A service invoice doesn't require these items; instead it has a Details field.

Producing product invoices

Enter the following fields when creating a product invoice:

- ✔ **Product Code:** Normally you set up product codes within product records. You can type in the relevant product code directly or use the dropdown arrow.

  You may encounter instances where a regular, everyday product code isn't suitable and you need a special product code, such as:

  - **M Message Line:** Use this to add extra lines of description or to make comments about the products.

  - **S1 Special Product Item Tax Chargeable:** Use this for product items that are standard VAT rated and don't have their own product code.

  - **S2 Special Product Item Zero Rated:** Use this code for zero-rated items that don't have their own product code.

  - **S3 Special Service Items Tax Chargeable:** Use S3 when you want to add service items to product invoices and sales orders. This uses the standard VAT code.

  If your S1–S3 codes don't appear in your dropdown list, using the navigation bar, click Customers and from the Links list, click Customer Invoice/ Order Defaults and make sure that you tick the Show Special Product Codes invoicing box.

- ✔ **Description:** The product description displays automatically from the product record, but you can overwrite it if necessary. You can also click F3 to edit the item line and add any one-off product details or comments.

✔ **Quantity**: Enter the number of items you're invoicing. Sage automatically shows a *1* if a quantity is in stock or *0* if no items are in stock. If you don't have enough stock for the quantity you enter, Sage issues a warning – it's difficult (not to mention illegal!) to charge people without delivering the product, so pay attention to the warning.

✔ **Price**: The unit price for the product record appears here, but you can change this if you need to.

Selecting service invoices

A service invoice has fewer columns in the main body than a product invoice.

After you enter the header details for your invoice (customer details, date and so on), you then need to add the details of the service provided.

✔ **Details:** You can expand the information entered in the Details field by using the F3 key. This function allows you to add additional information to the invoice detail. You can only use F3 after you've entered some information into the Details field.

✔ **Amount:** You can enter the amount using the Edit Item Line window that appeared if you used the F3 key in the Details field. Alternatively, if you didn't need to use the F3 key for additional details, add only one line of detail on the main screen and then tab across to the Amount column and enter the amount there.

Figure 6-2 shows what happens after the insertion of the detail Hire of Clown for Party into the Details field. As soon as you type in the description, press F3 and the edit box appears. Sage duplicates the words typed into both the Description and the Details field.

Mixing product and service invoices

If you're using the Professional version of Sage Accounts, you have the facility to produce invoices that include both products and service elements. To do this, start by simply raising a product invoice and then at the point you want to raise a service charge, select the S3 special product code. The Edit Item line for a service invoice opens. Follow the steps in the 'Selecting service invoices' section later in this chapter for details on how to complete this transaction.

You can process all other details, including order details and footer and payment details, in the normal manner.

You can save the invoice and print it whenever you decide. If you're not happy with the invoice contents, click Discard prior to saving to clear your entries and enable you to start again.

Even though you've saved the invoice, you can still make changes and resave it.

Figure 6-2:
Use the F3
function key
to expand
the details
of the ser-
vice invoice.

You can now apply the number of hours the clown worked and enter the unit price. You can also check that the nominal code is one that you want to use or adjust it where necessary. In this case, you may choose to change the nominal code shown in the Jingles illustration from 4000 for Sale of Cards (the default nominal code) to a more suitable code, such as Party Organising. Because Party Organising isn't an existing code, you'd then need to create a new nominal code. Refer to Chapter 3 to see how to do this.

After you're happy with the details on the main body of the invoice, the following steps are the same for both product and service invoices:

 ✔ **Net:** This is an automatic calculation, which also applies any discount attached to this customer account. Change the discount by using the F3 key if you need to.

   An additional Discount and Discount Percentage column shows if you selected this option within Invoice/Order defaults. Click the Discount tab and tick the Show Discount on Main Invoice/Order box.

 ✔ **VAT:** Sage automatically calculates this column. You can only edit it if you selected the Item VAT Amendable box on the VAT tab of Company Preferences on the main toolbar.

Then you get to the bottom of the Invoice screen, where Sage does much of the work for you:

Editing the service invoice with the F3 key

When you press F3 from the Description line of an invoice, an edit box appears where you can amend some of the detail of your invoice. The nominal code, tax code and department all appear in the posting details in this edit box. The details shown are those chosen as defaults. You can amend both the tax and nominal codes for each item line on the invoice by using the dropdown list. Alternatively, if you want to use the same nominal code and tax code for all lines of the invoice, you can click the Footer Details tab of the invoice and enter the appropriate codes in the Global section. The new codes then overwrite any code used on an individual line of the invoice.

✔ **Total:** Sage totals the invoice, showing net, VAT and any carriage charges applied.

✔ **Deposit:** This new feature has a smart link – a little grey arrow that takes you to the Payment tab of the invoice if clicked, so you can record any deposits received against the invoice.

Sage 50 Accounts also offers a Pay by Card option, but you have to register for Sage Payment Solutions to use it. To find out more about this, from the main toolbar, click Weblinks and select Sage Payment Solutions or click Help from the main toolbar and type in **Sage Payment Solutions**.

✔ **Deduction:** With this new feature, you have the ability to provide a net value discount on the Details tab of your invoice (see the next point). You can use this feature to offer seasonal discount promotions or one-off offers.

✔ **Net Value Discount:** Click the dropdown arrow in the Description box to reveal an Edit Item line. You can enter information referring to the discount and a discount value and then press Tab, and Sage automatically calculates the percentage discount. If you enter a discount percentage, the value is calculated for you.

Filling in the order details

You can use the Order Details tab to fill in details of where the goods are being delivered and who took the order. You can also add up to three lines of text. If the order can be left outside by the chicken shed, this is the place to share that information!

Getting down to the footer details

You can enter carriage terms, settlement terms and global details in the Footer Details tab:

- ✔ **Carriage terms:** You may want to assign carriage costs to the invoice. You may have postal or courier costs. You can set up specific nominal codes to charge carriage costs. If you set up departments, use the drop-down list to select the appropriate one. You can also add the consignment number and courier details and track your parcel by accessing the courier's website.

  To set up a courier on your Footer Details tab, click Help from the main toolbar. Using the Contents and Index option, type in **couriers** to see how to add a new courier.

- ✔ **Settlement Terms:** Some information may already be present in these boxes if you entered the details on the customer record. You can enter the number of days during which an early settlement discount applies, if any. You can see what discount percentage is applied, if any. It also shows you the total value of the invoice.

- ✔ **Global:** This section enables you to apply global terms to the whole of the invoice or credit note. If you chose to do this, only one line is added to the audit trail, although carriage is always shown as a separate line.

  You can apply one nominal code to the whole invoice. If you do, you can also enter details to accompany the posting to the nominal ledger. Up to 60 characters are available for additional details, which appear on your reports.

  The same global effect can be applied to your tax code and also your departments (if required).

- ✔ **Tax Analysis:** The tax analysis for each product item appears at the bottom of the Footer Details tab. The list shows a breakdown of all the VAT into the separate VAT codes (assuming the Global Tax option hasn't been used).

Credit notes are prepared in a very similar way to product and service invoices. The screens look exactly the same; however, after you type in the details of the credit note, the font becomes red.

Follow the same principles as you do to create an invoice, but make sure that you change the Type box on the Details tab to credit note. Refer back to previous sections of this chapter for assistance.

Going over payment details

In Accounts Plus and Accounts Professional only, you can record a payment directly to your sales invoice. You can enter details of deposits already received; make a payment on account if you don't want to allocate the payment to a specific invoice or you can allocate the money to a specific invoice.

If you're entering a deposit, Sage updates the details of the deposit on the Details tab of your invoice. If you click Payment Already Received, Sage displays the deposit but doesn't post a receipt transaction. You don't want to double count the deposit receipt if it has already been posted. After you're happy with the detail on your invoice, click Save to keep a copy of your invoice on the Invoice list. If you're not happy with your invoice, click Discard.

You need to remember to update your credit notes in the same way as you do invoices. If you don't, the credit notes aren't updated to the nominal ledger.

Checking your profit on a product invoice

This is a nifty little device! You can check the profit you've made on each invoice. Treat it with a little caution, as it only compares the sales price of your product against the unit cost price, but at least you've an idea of whether you're making any money!

To check your profit, follow these steps:

1. **From Customers, click Invoice List.**

2. **Double-click the invoice you want to check and then click Profit.**

   Sage calculates the profit using the information you entered in your product record. It simply displays the difference between the sales price less the cost price. If either of these fields isn't completed in the product record, the calculation doesn't work.

   You're then given a profit value in pounds sterling and the profit percentage.

3. **Click Close to return to your invoice.**

   Alternatively, you can print the information.

Communicating is Key

Communication and credit control are key to the success of any business. With this is mind, Sage has a revamped Communications tab (previously known as Contacts). Upon opening the Communications tab, you can record details of telephone calls, emails, letters or meetings and record follow-up actions. This function is particularly useful for credit controllers as they can record follow-up phone calls to customers, and Sage makes diary entries to remind them of their future tasks.

A new button on the navigation bar called Diary lets you access and view any appointments or follow-up calls made via the Communications screen.

Invoicing from a telephone call

This option enables you to charge your client whilst making a phone call. For service businesses that bill by their time, this service is essential. For example, if you're a solicitor, you may need to charge clients for the time you spend on the phone with them. (You're a fancy solicitor after all, and certain behaviour is expected!) So, before you pick up the phone, follow these steps:

1. **From Customers, choose the Record icon.**

2. **Click the Communications tab. Click New at the bottom of the screen.**

   The Customer Communications History window appears, as shown in the accompanying figure.

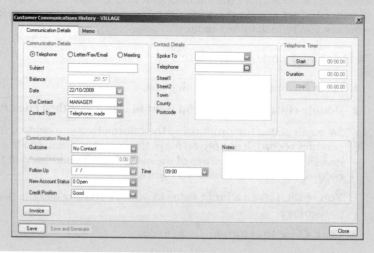

3. **Enter the topic or client in the Subject field and then dial the telephone number. When the call is answered, click Start on the Telephone Timer.**

   The system automatically starts recording the duration of the call. You can type notes in the Communication Results part of the screen. When you have finished the call, click Stop on the Telephone Timer.

4. **Click Invoice to raise an invoice for the time spent on the phone call.**

A Communication Invoice Details box appears, as shown in the following figure, which gives you the opportunity to enter the hourly rates, nominal codes, departments and VAT details. Any notes from the Communication Results field pull through to the Details To Invoice field, where you can edit them as necessary. The time of the telephone call is recorded in the Invoice Details box.

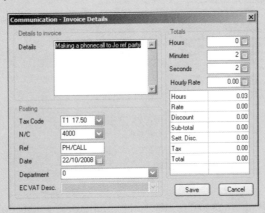

If you simply want to record details of the phone call without billing for it, skip this step.

5. **Click Save when you're happy with the details. A confirmation message appears. Click Yes to raise the invoice and then**

click Save again, and you return to the customer record.

The invoice now appears on the Invoice list. Click Customers and then Invoice List on the Task pane to view it.

Managing Your Invoice List

After you safely save an invoice, it appears on your Invoice list, and you can do all sorts of business-like things with it. The next sections tell you how.

Printing

As soon as you save your invoice, you can print it. If you still have the invoice open in front of you, simply click Print. The Invoice Printing window appears, displaying different print layouts, as shown in Figure 6-3. If you haven't got the invoice open in front of you, click Customers from the navigation bar and select Invoice List from the Links list. Highlight the invoice you want to print from the list and click the Print icon to open the Invoice Printing window.

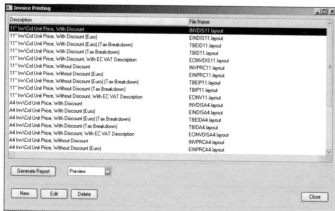

Figure 6-3:
Choose your
invoice lay-
out prior to
printing your
invoice.

The layout choices are pretty self-explanatory; you choose one based on paper size and whether the customer is offered a discount.

You can preview the invoice prior to printing to make sure that the details are correct. Click Generate Report, ensuring that the button to the right of Generate Report says Preview.

When previewed, you can print the report or email it directly to the customer. You can print the invoice without previewing it, but I always check to be sure that I'm happy with the details. You can edit or change an invoice at any point prior to sending it to the customer and updating the ledger.

Alternatively, you may choose to print your invoices at a later time. To do this, follow these steps:

1. **From Customers, click Invoice List in the Links list.**

2. **Highlight the invoice that you want to print and click the Print icon.**

   You can print off a number of invoices at the same time by highlighting all the invoices you want to print and clicking Print.

On the right side of the screen is a column headed Printed and another headed Posted, so you can easily identify which invoices have already been printed.

Updating

After you are 100 per cent happy with your invoices, you're ready to *update,* a process that posts the invoice to both the nominal ledger and the customer ledger.

You can update invoices individually or in batches. First, check and see which invoices have been updated and printed already. To find out the status of each invoice:

1. **From Customers, click Invoice List.**
2. **Look at the last two columns – the Posted and Printed columns.**

   The word Yes indicates whether an invoice has already been printed and/or posted.

To update the invoices:

1. **Highlight the invoices you want to update.**
2. **Click Update. When an affirmation box appears, click OK.**

   Notice that the main screen now has a Yes against that invoice in the Posted column.

You've now updated your invoice, and an Update Ledger report appears on your screen. You can print this if you want to, but it isn't really necessary.

Deleting

Deleting invoices and credit notes is easy, but be aware that if you've already posted the invoice to the nominal ledger, deleting the invoice or credit note doesn't reverse the posting in the ledger.

1. **From Customers, click Invoice List. Select the required invoice or credit note from the Invoice list.**
2. **Click Delete. An affirmation message appears. Click Yes to continue or No to exit.**

That's it; your invoice is deleted from the Invoice list.

Saving Time while You Ask for Money

When creating invoices, it's useful to know about some of the time-saving features that you can use.

Duplicating existing invoices

If you need to send the same invoice details to a number of different clients, this function is very useful. From the Invoice list, highlight an existing invoice and click Duplicate at the bottom of the screen. The system produces an exact replica of the original, but you can edit the details, for example, change the dates and customer. Check all the details of the invoice before saving and amend where necessary.

Repeating recurring transactions

This feature is useful if you're invoicing the same product or service on a recurring basis. After you set up your recurring transaction, you can then continue to process the invoice in the same way.

To set up a recurring sales invoice, follow these steps:

1. **From Customers, click New Invoice.**

2. **Enter your invoice details as shown in the previous 'Creating Invoices' section.**

3. **Click Memorise.**

   The Memorise box appears, and you're asked to provide the following:

   - Reference and description for your recurring item.

   - Frequency – is it every day, week or month, and when does it start and finish?

   - Last processed – for ongoing recurring transactions the date shown is the date the invoice was last processed.

   Ensure that the transaction you're creating shows Invoice or Order in the Type box. It must also have a customer account reference, contain at least one item line and if foreign currency is enabled (available in Sage Professional only), then you must set an exchange rate for that customer, otherwise the frequency details aren't made available.

4. **To save your recurring transaction and return to the invoice, click Save. To exit without saving, click Cancel.**

Every time you open Sage, you're asked if you want to post your recurring entries. Choosing Yes posts the transaction, but choosing No allows you to use your program without posting the transactions.

You can turn this reminder off by clicking Company⇨ Company⇨Preferences⇨Parameter tab and then select the No Recurring Entries at Start-up check box.

To process the transactions, follow these steps:

1. **From the Invoice list, select the Recurring icon.**

   The Memorised and Recurring Entries box appears.

2. **Click the item you want to process and click Process.**

   The Process Recurring Entries box appears, which asks you what date you want to process transactions up to. After you put your date in, Sage lists all the items included. Make sure that all the transactions you want to process have a green tick in the box next to them. If you don't want to include a transaction, make sure that the box doesn't have a tick in it.

   If you clear a tick from the Process Recurring Entries box and then click Process, the system asks `Do you wish to update the last posted date for excluded transactions?` Select No if you want to post them at a later date. If you're excluding the transaction because you don't want to put it through this month, click Yes.

3. **Click Process.**

   Sage processes the recurring items and says `Processing Complete`.

4. **Click Cancel to return to the Invoice List screen.**

Using defaults

You may have invoices or credit notes that have similar items or characteristics, and as such you can enter defaults for them. For example, you may want to assign carriage costs to your customers.

To access the defaults, within Customers, scroll down the Links list and click Invoice/Order Defaults. To adjust carriage defaults, click Footer Details.

For help with other invoice defaults, select Help from the main toolbar and then click Contents and Index and select Invoices followed by Defaults.

Chapter 7

Dealing with Paperwork from Your Suppliers

In This Chapter

▶ Getting and posting bills

▶ Entering credit notes

▶ Recording supplier payments

▶ Sending remittance advice notes

*Y*ou receive lots of invoices from your suppliers, so you need to put systems in place so that you can easily locate the invoices if required. Sometimes Sage contains enough detail to answer a query about an invoice, but on some occasions you need to pull the actual invoice out of the file.

As you process each invoice, Sage allocates it a sequential number. Use this sequential number as a reference, so you can always track down an invoice quickly and easily.

Receiving and Posting Invoices

You need a good system for capturing all the purchase invoices that come into your business, so that bills get paid, and you can continue doing business. The two steps in making sure that this gets done are receiving the invoices properly and then posting them.

Setting up your receiving system

Send all invoices to one person or department (a choice that depends on the size of the business). You don't want lots of different people receiving the invoices as more people mean more chance of invoices getting misplaced or entered incorrectly.

Enter invoices onto the accounting system as soon as possible after receiving them so that the liability is recorded in the business accounts. Depending on the size of the business, you may want to make a copy of the invoice so that you can keep one copy within the Accounts department and send the other copy to the person who requested the goods, so that they can check the details for accuracy and also get the invoice authorised for payment.

Posting invoices

The term *posting* doesn't mean posting the invoice into a letter box! In accounting terms, *posting* means processing an invoice to the nominal ledger. (Chapter 2 talks about the nominal ledger.)

You can post a number of invoices in one sitting. If you have large quantities of invoices to process, separate them into smaller batches and total the values of each batch so that you can check those same values against Sage to ensure that you haven't made any mistakes.

Users of Sage Accounts Professional have two different ways of posting invoices:

✔ If you receive an invoice as a result of raising a purchase order, you can update your order details and Sage automatically posts the invoice. See Chapter 11 for more information about purchase order processing.

✔ If you don't have an order for your invoice, you need to use the Batch Entry screen to process your invoice – a method I describe in the following steps.

Sort the invoices into date order before separating them into batches. This ensures that they get entered in chronological order, which helps when you are viewing them on screen.

To enter a batch, follow these steps:

1. **From Suppliers, click the Invoice icon.**

   This brings up the Batch Suppliers Invoice box.

2. **Select the correct supplier account for the invoice.**

   When you have several items on an invoice, enter each item from the invoice separately on the Batch screen as you may need to give each item a different nominal code. However, you can use the same supplier account, date and reference, so that Sage can group those items together.

   After you post the invoice, you can view it on the Supplier Activity screen, which is split into two parts. The top part has one line entry for each transaction (in other words all the individual lines of each invoice are grouped together), and the bottom part has the detail of each transaction. Clicking an invoice highlights it in blue, and the bottom part of the screen shows each line entry of that invoice.

3. Put the invoice date in the Date field.

Be careful as Sage automatically defaults to today's date, so you need to overtype the invoice date here. If you don't, Sage won't age the invoice correctly, and you'll have a distorted view of the transaction on the Aged Creditors reports.

4. Enter your sequential number in the Ref (Reference) field.

Your *invoice reference number* is the number order in which you file your invoices.

5. Add details in the Ex Ref field, if desired.

You can add more references here or leave this field blank.

6. Select the nominal code in the N/C field, using the dropdown arrow.

7. Click the department applicable for your invoice in the Dept field.

You can leave this field blank if you don't have any departments set up.

8. Click the dropdown Project Ref arrow to select the appropriate project, if applicable.

9. Enter the Cost code if you are using project costing.

See Chapter 13 for further details on project costing.

10. Enter information describing what the invoice is for in the Details field.

Put as much detail as you can here. I usually put the supplier's invoice number first followed by the description. You can then identify the invoice quickly using the supplier's number. If you need to contact them about an invoice, it helps to use their reference numbers, so it makes sense to record it here.

Note: You can use the Ex Ref field for this purpose, but that field doesn't show up on every report.

11. Enter the amount net of VAT in the Net field.

12. Choose the tax code applicable for this invoice in the T/C (Tax Code) field.

Depending on the tax code, Sage updates the VAT field.

Make sure that the VAT Sage calculates is the same as the amount on the invoice. Sometimes Sage rounds up the VAT, and you need to overwrite the VAT amount in Sage to match the VAT on the invoice.

13. Repeat steps 2 through 12 for each invoice in your batch.

14. **Check that the total of your batch of invoices matches the total in the right corner of the Batch Entry screen (see Figure 7-1), and if they do, click Save.**

Doing the check ensures that the data you entered is accurate. When you click Save, Sage posts the invoices to the nominal ledger, posting a debit to the Cost account and a credit the Creditors control account.

Figure 7-1:
A batch of purchase invoices entered onto Sage prior to posting.

Check out Chapter 21 to see how the function keys can help speed up the batch-entry process.

Memorising and recalling batch invoices/credit notes

You can use the Memorise and Recall functions in Sage Accounts Plus and Professional versions to save you having to re-enter the same information again and again. For example, if you regularly buy the same product from the same supplier, you can use the Memorise function to save time when ordering the product.

Another great function is the ability to memorise a batch of invoices that you are in the middle of, so that you can come back and amend them

later. You can save the batch, go away and check some details and then come back, recall the batch, make the amendments and post.

To memorise a batch of invoices from within the Batch Entry screen, click Memorise, add a filename for the batch and click Save. To recall a batch of invoices, click Recall from within the Batch Entry screen, select the appropriate file and click Open.

Getting Credit

Credit notes can be raised for a variety of reasons. The goods delivered may have been faulty or the wrong colour, for example. The supplier assumes that you have already posted the original invoice supplied with these goods and sends a credit note to reduce the amount you owe them. The credit note may completely reverse the value of the original invoice or partially credit the invoice.

Processing a credit note is done in much the same way as processing an invoice, so follow the steps in the previous section, 'Posting invoices', paying special attention to the following points:

✔ **From Suppliers, click the Credit icon instead of the Invoice icon and select the account to enter the credit note against.** The screen looks very similar to that of the Invoice screen, but the font colour is red rather than black, to help alert you to the fact that you are processing a credit note. You wouldn't be the first person to merrily continue entering credit notes, when they should be invoices!

✔ **Remember to change the date, unless today's date is acceptable.**

✔ **Enter a credit number instead of a ref number.** Use a unique sequential numbering system for your credit notes. Some people prefer to have a separate numbering system for credit notes, others just use the next available invoice number. It really doesn't matter, as long as you're consistent.

✔ **Make sure the nominal code (N/C) is the same as the invoice you're reversing.** This ensures that the correct cost code is reduced in value.

✔ **Put some notation in the Details field.** Something like 'Credit note against Invoice No 123' with a description as to why it is necessary, if possible.

✔ **If the credit note is reversing just part of an invoice, apportion the Net and VAT amounts.**

When you click Save, Sage posts the credit note, crediting the Purchase account and debiting the Creditors control account.

You can check to see if everything is posted by viewing the Activity screen for the nominal code you used. The Jingles example in Figure 7-2 shows the Activity screen for nominal code 5000. You can see transaction number 25, the purchase of get-well-soon cards (debiting code 5000) and transaction 27, the credit note (crediting the nominal record). The Activity screen shows the original invoice posted to the purchase nominal code as a debit and then the credit note showing at a later date, crediting the nominal code. This is where it is useful to have a description in the Details field linking the credit note to the invoice.

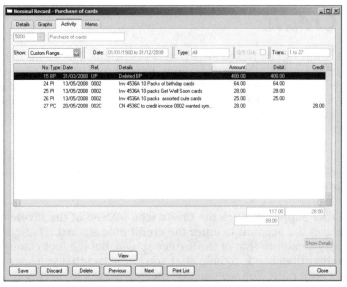

Figure 7-2:
The
nominal
code
Activity
screen
showing a
credit note
posted for
the
purchase of
cards.

Allocating a Credit Note

You allocate credit notes the same way you make payments, though you need to allocate a credit note specifically against an invoice.

You can tell if something hasn't been allocated if a transaction in the Supplier Activity screen has an asterisk against it.

To allocate a credit note, follow these steps:

1. **From Bank, click Suppliers.**

2. **Select the account you require.**

   All outstanding transactions are shown.

3. **Enter the date, usually the date of the credit note.**

4. **In the Payment column, click Pay in Full Against the Credit Note.**

   This puts a negative value in the Analysis total at the bottom right side of the screen.

5. **Move up to the invoice that you wish to allocate the credit note to, and type in the value of the credit note.**

   The Analysis total becomes zero.

6. **Click Save.**

   This posts the allocation, as shown in Figure 7-3.

Figure 7-3:
Allocating a
credit note
to a supplier
invoice.

Paying Your Suppliers

When you come to process the payments for your supplier, you need to use the Bank module.

1. **From Bank, select Suppliers.**

   A screen that looks a bit like a cheque book opens up.

2. **Check that the Bank A/C Ref field shows the correct account.**

   This field automatically defaults to account 1200, which is usually the Bank Current account. If this isn't the account you wish to use, select the appropriate account.

3. **Enter the supplier name or use the dropdown arrow to select the payee.**

   As soon as you select an account, Sage brings up a list of outstanding transactions for that account.

4. **Enter the payment date in the Date field.**

   Usually you use the date on your cheque stub or the date of the direct debit or other form of payment.

5. **Record the cheque number or method of payment in the Cheque No field.**

Type **DD** for direct debit, **BP** for bank payment or any other short description that helps you identify the transaction when you reconcile your bank account.

6. **Click the Payment column.**

You have several options here:

- **To pay in full,** click the Pay in Full button at the bottom of the screen. This puts an amount in the £ box at the top of the screen, as Figure 7-4 shows.

Note: If you're taking a discount for early payment, enter the discount amount in the Discount column, and Sage calculates the amount you owe and shows this value in the £ box and in the Payment column.

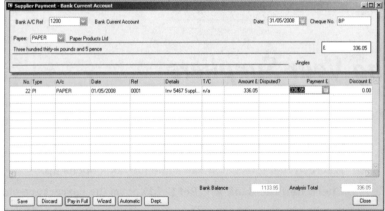

Figure 7-4:
A happy supplier, paid in full.

- **To pay part of an invoice,** enter the amount you wish to pay against that invoice. That amount shows up in the £ box at the top of the screen.

- **To make a payment on account,** enter the amount you wish to pay in the £ box.

You may find that you need to make a payment against a supplier account, but can't specify an invoice to allocate the payment to. You can make a payment onto the supplier account without matching it to a specific invoice.

7. Click Save.

If you make full or partial payments to an invoice, the payment posts to that invoice in the supplier account.

If you make a payment on account, Sage gives you a confirmation message, asking `There is an unallocated cheque balance of £x. Do you want to post this as a payment on account?` Click Yes to accept or No to cancel.

Printing a Remittance Advice Note

You may want to print a remittance advice note to accompany your cheque. A *remittance advice note* simply tells your supplier which invoices you are paying. Alternatively, you can just make a note of the invoice numbers on a compliments slip.

If you selected Always Create a Remittance in your Bank defaults, the system automatically stores a remittance for you. When I loaded my version of Sage, this default was already set, but you can change this default by clicking Bank Defaults. If you uncheck the Always Create a Remittance box, Sage creates a new Create Remittance button on you Payment screen. You can then selectively create remittances.

To print a remittance from the Bank module, click Remittance, and Sage lists all the remittances generated, whether manually or automatic (depending on how you've set your defaults). Highlight the remittances you want to print or select the date range if you have several and click Print. You can preview the remittances or send them straight to your printer.

You can choose from three different remittance advice layouts, depending on your paper size. When you print preview a report, you see a beautifully formatted document, but if you try to print this on plain paper, it looks awful. None of the formatting prints, to encourage you to buy pre-printed Sage paper, which does look very professional.

Chapter 8

Recording Your Bank Entries

In This Chapter:

▶ Looking at the different types of bank accounts

▶ Processing bank receipts and payments

▶ Dealing with bank transfers

▶ Setting up recurring transactions

▶ Keeping track of petty cash

▶ Balancing credit card transactions

*I*f you're the sort of person who likes checking their bank accounts and keeping track of what's been spent on the company credit card, then this chapter is for you! Here I tell you how to process bank payments and receipts that aren't related to sales invoices or purchase invoices. I look at how to process credit card transactions and deal with petty cash (one of the book-keeping jobs that can be a real pain in the backside if not dealt with properly!)

I also show you how you can transfer money between bank accounts – perhaps to take advantage of earning some extra interest (every little helps!). And, as many businesses often have a lot of banking transactions, I show you ways to speed up the processing by using recurring entries.

Understanding the Different Types of Bank Accounts

Clicking Bank shows you the default bank accounts that Sage provides, which include:

- ✔ **Bank accounts:** Current, Deposit and Building Society accounts, for example.
- ✔ **Cash accounts:** For example, Petty Cash account.
- ✔ **Credit card accounts:** These include a Credit Card Receipts account for those of you who receive customer payments via credit card.

You can, of course, add new bank accounts, rename existing accounts or delete accounts you don't think you need – refer to Chapter 3 to find out how.

In the following sections, I show the account number or range of account numbers Sage assigns to each account. These account numbers are the same as the nominal code for that bank account.

Keeping up with the Current and Deposit accounts (1200/1210)

The Bank Current account is the default bank account in Sage, the one that automatically pops up when you enter a bank transaction. Of course, you can choose another bank account if the Bank Current account isn't the right one for your transaction.

Most people use the Bank Current account for the majority of their transactions, although you may have additional bank accounts for different areas of your business. If you have surplus cash that you want to earn a bit of interest on, you may have a deposit account and transfer surplus cash between the current account and the deposit account to take advantage of higher rates of interest. (I talk about transferring money between accounts in the 'Transferring Funds between Accounts' section later in this chapter.)

I know of a number of companies who use a separate deposit account to regularly transfer funds across from their current account to accumulate enough money to pay their VAT bills or PAYE.

Change the name of the Bank Current account to that of your own business current account, and if you have more than one, include the account number within the bank account name – for example, Barclays Current Account 24672376. You can add or amend bank accounts – for more information, refer to Chapter 3.

Sage's Deposit account functions in the same way as the Bank Current account. You can make transfers between Deposit and Bank Current accounts in Sage.

Sage also includes a Building Society account, although I don't know of many businesses that actually have one of those. You can rename or delete it as appropriate.

Counting the Petty Cash account (1230)

Use the Petty Cash account for cash stored somewhere other than a bank or building society – a strong box or safe in the office perhaps (*not* under your mattress!).

You can operate this account in the same way as a normal bank account, although most people don't choose to reconcile it as you don't have bank statements to reconcile to.

You can transfer funds into this account from any of the other Sage bank accounts and make payments accordingly. I give further details in the upcoming 'Dealing with Petty Cash' section.

Handling your Cash Register (1235)

You now have a separate bank account to handle your cash register transactions. Your business may wish to use this cash register function to record receipts of cash and card payments. This type of transaction allows for the sale, supply and payment to happen at the same time. A Cash Register sale can include details of the sale and the method of payment used (cash, cheque or card), the price and VAT (if applicable).

The default bank account is automatically set at 1235. You will need to check your cash register settings in your Bank Default menu. Click on Bank then settings then bank defaults. Here you can select the sales nominal code for your cash register takings, which automatically defaults to 4000 (you can change this). When using a cash register you may find that you have discrepancies between the cash register and actual takings. If so, use the discrepancy account to balance the books – the default code is 8206 (which can also be changed if you wish). There's also a tick box to confirm whether your cash takings are VAT inclusive or not.

For further help in using the cash register function within Sage you can click on 'What's New' on the Welcome screen and follow the guidance for Recording Till Takings.

Managing the company credit card (1240) and credit card receipts (1250)

You can set up a bank account for each individual credit card and manage these accounts as normal bank accounts – reconciling them, for example, with your credit card statements. See 'Paying the Credit Card Bill' later in this chapter for further details about the mechanics of processing credit card transactions.

If you accept payment by credit card, keep a separate bank account for these transactions. You deposit batches of credit card vouchers into your account in the same way that you deposit a cheque. Use the Customer option if you receive money against a customer invoice. The credit card company then deposits the real cash into your nominated bank account, and you can make a transfer between that and the Credit Card Receipts account. You then receive a statement detailing all the transactions, including a service charge, which can be reconciled.

Tracking Bank Deposits and Payments

Your business earns money (which is a good thing, and much better than the reverse!). You need to keep track of how much money you put in the bank and Sage helps you do that in the Bank module. You may also have to make payments to the bank – wages, interest charges, loan payments and dividend payments, for example. Sage makes it as easy to process a bank payment as it does a receipt.

For both types of transactions, start from the Task pane within the Bank module:

- ✔ For receipts, click New Receipt. Alternatively, click the Receipt icon.
- ✔ For payments, click New Payment or use the Payment icon.

In both cases, a new window appears and although the screens are different, they ask you for the same basic information whether you're recording a receipt or payment. Use the Tab key to move across the screen and enter the details Sage asks for:

- ✔ **Bank:** Make sure you select the correct bank account, using the drop-down arrows. Sage automatically defaults to account 1200, which is normally the Bank Current account.

- ✔ **Date:** As usual, Sage defaults to today's date, so ensure that you change this to match the date of the transaction.

- ✔ **Reference (Ref):** If you have a cheque number, payslip reference or BACS (Bankers' Automated Clearing Services) reference, enter it here as it proves very useful when you come to reconcile your bank account.

  When making a payment, be aware that the reference you enter appears on the audit trail in the Reference (Ref) column for that transaction, so use notation you can understand – *DD* for direct debit or *SO* for standing order, for example. If you paid by cheque, enter the cheque number here.

- ✔ **Nominal Code (N/C):** Using the dropdown arrow, select the appropriate nominal code. You can create a new nominal code here if you need to.

✔ **Dept:** Enter the department, using the dropdown arrow. Ignore this field if you don't use departments.

✔ **Project Ref:** Enter your project reference here. When the transaction is saved, your program updates the project activity and analysis information.

And if you're making a payment, enter the relevant cost code.

✔ **Details:** Record any details that may help you with reconciling your account or identifying the transaction.

✔ **Net:** Enter the net amount of the transaction before VAT.

If you aren't VAT registered, put the gross amount here and tax code T0, or T9 if you don't want it to appear on a VAT Return report.

If you only have the gross amount of your receipts or a payment, you can enter this number and then click Calc Net (at the bottom of the Bank Payments/Receipts box) and, provided that the tax code is set correctly, the Sage calculates the net and VAT amounts for you.

✔ **Tax Code (T/C):** Use the dropdown arrow to select the appropriate tax code.

✔ **Tax:** Sage calculates the amount of VAT for the transaction based on the net amount and the tax code selected.

Whatever your business type, all businesses receive monies that have nothing to do with their customers, such as bank interest or grants. Post these payments using the Bank Receipts option.

You can continue to enter receipts or payments in a batch. Figure 8-1 shows a Payment Batch Entry screen. As you enter new transactions, the total in the right corner of the screen increases. Check the batch total you calculated against the total Sage reached in the Total box in the top right of the screen.

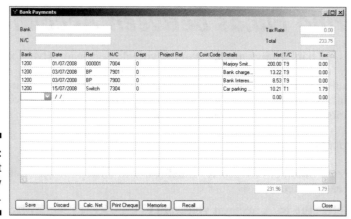

Figure 8-1:
A Payment Batch Entry screen.

Using a template to avoid tedium

If you regularly record the same type of receipts and payments, such as regular receipts of bank interest or regular payments of interest charges, you can set up a template and load it up each time you want to use it. You can change the date and any values or additional information as necessary, without having to enter the tedious details, such as the nominal code and tax information. This not only saves you time, but also reduces the possibility of errors.

To use the Memorise option for a batch of bank receipts or payments, enter the transactions as normal and then click the Memorise button at the bottom of the screen. Select the directory where you want to save your template and enter a filename. (If you're making payments, Sage defaults to an invoices directory, but you can browse to find a more suitable alternative.) Click Save to preserve the template (otherwise, click Cancel) and then click Close.

To recall the template, click Recall from the Bank Receipts or Bank Payments window and choose the directory where you saved the template. Click Open to load the appropriate template. Make any changes necessary and then click Save.

The boxes at the top of the screen show which bank account the receipt is going to, what the nominal code is and the tax rate. A Total box that subtotals all the lines of information in the batch also shows.

When you're happy that the details on the screen are correct, click Save at the lower left of the screen to post payments to the appropriate nominal accounts and bank accounts. If you aren't happy with the information on your Batch Entry screen, simply click Discard and the information clears. To exit the Payment Batch Entry screen, click Close.

Transferring Funds between Accounts

Just as big banks move money around, you may occasionally want to move money from one account to another. For example, when you pay off your company credit card each month, you make a payment from your current account to your credit card account. Create a bank transfer between the two accounts to process this transaction easily.

To process a bank transfer, follow these steps:

1. **From Bank, click Record Transfer in the Task pane (or click the Transfer icon).**

2. **Select the bank account you want to transfer the money from, using the dropdown arrow.**

3. **Select the account you want to transfer the money to, again using the dropdown arrow.**

4. **Complete the information on screen:**

   • **Reference (Ref):** Enter a reference relating to the transaction.

   • **Description:** You have up to 60 characters to describe the transaction.

   • **Dept:** Select a department if applicable.

   • **Payment Value:** Enter the amount of the transaction.

   • **Date**: Enter the date of the transaction. You need to overtype this, as the system uses today's date.

   • **Exchange Rate:** Only use this if you have Sage Accounts Professional and set up a foreign exchange rate. Chapter 14 provides information on foreign bank transfers.

5. **Click Save if you're happy with the information you entered.**

   Sage updates both bank accounts. If you aren't happy, click Discard and the screen clears.

6. **Click Close to exit the Bank Transfer screen.**

Repeating Recurring Entries

Designating recurring entries is extremely useful. Doing so speeds up the processing of data and saves time because you enter the information only once, at the set-up stage, and then process all future transactions with the click of a button. You don't have to re-enter the full details of those transactions again!

You can treat many different transactions as recurring items, although they're typically direct debits and standing orders. The next sections give you an explanation of the different types of transactions you can set up as recurring.

Going for consistency with your bank entries

You probably make regular payments into and out of your Bank Current and Credit Card accounts, as well as doing transfers between accounts on a monthly basis. To set up any of these types of transactions as recurring, follow the steps below.

To view existing recurring entries, from the Bank module on the navigation bar, click Recurring List on the Links list or click the Recurring icon in the Bank module.

1. **From Bank, click New Recurring Transaction from the Task pane (or click the Recurring icon and then click Add).**

   This opens the Add/Edit Recurring Entry box.

2. **Use the dropdown list to select the transaction type.**

   Choose from Bank/Cash/Credit Card Payment, Bank/Cash/Credit Card Receipts or Bank/Cash/Credit Card Transfer.

3. **Fill in the Recurring Entry From/To section.**

   The information you're asked for includes:

   - **Bank A/C:** Select the bank account the transaction is coming from or going to.

   - **Nominal Code:** Enter the nominal code for the transaction.

   - **Bank A/C:** If you're doing a bank transfer, select the account that the transfer is going to.

4. **Enter details of the recurring entry.**

   These details include:

   - **Transaction Ref:** Enter a reference here. Note that Sage already uses DD/SO (direct debit/standing order), which may be sufficient, but you can change it as necessary.

   - **Transaction Details:** Enter details of the transaction. In the example in Figure 8-2, I set up a recurring building insurance payment.

   - **Dept:** Enter a department if applicable.

5. **Determine posting frequency.**

   Make selections about frequency:

   - **Every:** Enter the posting frequency here – daily, monthly, weekly or yearly.

   - **Total required postings:** If you know the exact number of postings to be made, enter the number here. The finish date automatically updates.

   - **Start date:** The date that you want the recurring entry to start (obviously!). The system automatically defaults to today's date, but you can overtype it with the correct date.

   - **Finish date:** If you haven't updated the total number of postings, then this date is blank. This means that the recurring entry continues until you choose to suspend posting or delete the recurring entry.

- **Last posted:** This shows the date of the last posting made. You can't change this date.

- **Suspend posting?** Tick this box if you don't wish to continue posting the recurring entry. The box can be un-ticked after you decide to resume posting.

6. **Type in the posting amount.**

   Break the amount down as follows:

   - **Net Amount:** Enter the net amount of the transaction.

   - **Tax Code:** Select the appropriate tax code, using the dropdown arrow.

   - **VAT:** This displays the VAT amount, determined by the net amount and tax code selected.

7. **To save the recurring entry, click OK. To exit without saving, click Cancel.**

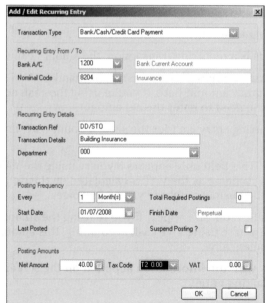

Figure 8-2:
Creating a recurring bank payment.

Repeating customer and supplier payments

If a customer pays you regularly (and I hope they do!) or you pay your suppliers regularly (ditto!), set up these recurring payments as follows, particularly if it's for the same amount each time (although it doesn't have to be the same).

1. **From Bank, click New Recurring Transaction from the Task pane or click the Recurring icon.**

2. **Enter the requested account information.**

   Fill in the following:

   - **Transaction Type:** Select Customer Payment On Account for a customer payment or Supplier Payment On Account for a supplier payment.

   - **Bank Account:** Select the account the payment is to be deposited into, or the account that it's to be paid from if you're making a supplier payment.

   - **Customer/Supplier Account:** Chose the relevant account, using the dropdown arrow.

   - **Transaction Ref:** Enter a reference for your recurring transaction here.

   - **Department:** Select a department if required.

3. **Select the posting frequencies as in Step 5 in the preceding section.**

4. **Enter the posting amount.**

   Even though this is a recurring transaction, the amount can vary:

   - **Net Amount/Amount:** If you're using the standard VAT scheme, enter the gross amount here. If you're using the cash accounting scheme, you need to enter the net amount.

     If the recurring entry isn't for the same amount each time, put a zero here.

   - **Tax Code:** This field only appears if you're using the VAT cash accounting scheme as the VAT is calculated on the cash movements of the business, not the value of invoices.

   - **VAT:** This field doesn't appear if you're using the standard VAT scheme. If you're using VAT cash accounting, this amount is calculated automatically.

5. **If you're happy with the information supplied on the screen, click OK to save the recurring entry.**

   If you click Cancel, you're asked if you want to save the changes. Click No to return to the main screen.

If you use this method to post payments on account to both suppliers and customers, allocate the receipts or payments to the specific invoices as a separate exercise. I don't tend to use this type of recurring option very often because it's quicker to process directly to the invoice in one step: it takes two steps to process a payment on account and then allocate that payment. But every business has different needs and different sets of circumstances, so it may well appeal to you.

Making regular journal entries – if you dare

This option is useful if you have to make an adjustment to the accounts where only a journal is possible. For example, if you make regular payments on a loan, rather than just setting it up as a bank payment, you can set it up as a journal and record both the payment and the interest (the specific journal depends on how the loan has been set up).

I advise using this only if you're confident about using double-entry bookkeeping. If you aren't competent with your bookkeeping, it's dangerous territory! (I offer a brief explanation of double-entry bookkeeping in Chapter 16.)

1. **From Bank, choose New Recurring Transaction from the Task pane.**

   The Add/Edit Recurring Entry box appears.

   Although you enter your debit and credit transactions separately, you need to ensure that your journal entries balance, otherwise you get an error message. So, for every debit entry, you need to make a credit entry of the same amount.

2. **Enter the transaction information in the boxes.**

   You need to enter:

   - **Transaction Type:** Select either Journal Debit or Journal Credit.

   - **Nominal Code:** Using the dropdown arrow, select the nominal account to use. The name of the nominal account appears in the box next to the code selected.

3. **Complete the transaction details, posting frequency and amounts fields, as shown in Steps 4 through 6 in the previous section, 'Going for consistency with your bank entries'.**

4. **Click OK if you're happy with the journal details or Cancel if you're not.**

Your newly created recurring entry now appears on the Recurring list.

Processing and posting recurring entries

After you've set up recurring entries, every time you start up Sage, you're asked if you want to process your recurring entries. In the main, answer no at this stage, as it's better to process them in a controlled manner.

You can turn off this reminder by selecting the No Recurring Entries At Start Up check box in the Parameters tab of Company Preferences (click Settings and then Company Preferences).

You normally process your recurring entries just prior to reconciling your bank account so that they're ready and waiting to be reconciled.

To process your recurring transactions, you need to:

1. **From Bank, click Recurring List in the Links list.**

2. **Click Process.**

   The Process Recurring Entries box displays the message: `Show recurring entries up to:`.

3. **Enter the date you want to process recurring entries up to.**

   Normally, use the month-end date. For example, if you're about to reconcile the bank account to 30 April 2009, put in that date.

   After you enter the date, Sage shows you the recurring entries due to be posted up to the chosen date.

4. **Click Post.**

Sage doesn't post recurring entries with a zero value. Cancel the Posting screen and go back and edit the recurring entry so that a value is entered or choose to suspend the item.

Dealing with Petty Cash

Petty cash, funds kept in the office for incidental expenses, can often be an absolute pain to administer. Normally a company has a petty cash tin, which usually contains a small amount of cash and is stuffed full of receipts. As members of staff are given money from the petty cash fund, they exchange the money with a receipt. If you count up the amount of cash and receipts, the total of both should equal the value of the petty cash float. Unfortunately, some people request £20 from petty cash to buy some stationery, return with the receipt, but forget to return the change! The following sections tell you how to keep the petty cash tin in order.

Funding petty cash

Normally, you write a cheque out for petty cash or take the cash out of the bank and put it into the petty cash tin. To account for this within Sage, you can easily show this transaction as a bank transfer.

To do this, follow the instructions in the 'Transferring Funds between Accounts' section earlier in this chapter. Make sure that the Bank Current account is selected as the *account from* and the Petty Cash account is selected as the *account to.* If you wrote a cheque out for petty cash, you can use the cheque number as a reference.

Making payments from the tin

Make one person solely responsible for the petty cash tin. They can then ensure that if someone returns and doesn't have the correct change and receipts, at the very least an IOU goes into the tin for the money owed. That individual must get the money returned to the tin as soon as possible.

When a payment is made from the petty cash tin, make sure that a receipt replaces the money or use a petty cash voucher to record where the money has been spent. This ensures that all payments are correctly recorded and should also ensure that the petty cash tin balances to the agreed float amount.

To record a payment made from petty cash in Sage, follow the instructions for bank payments in the previous 'Tracking Bank Deposits and Payments' section, but select the Petty Cash account instead of the Bank Current account.

Reconciling the petty cash tin

Periodically, you need to reconcile the petty cash tin. The best time to do this is when you decide to top up the petty cash tin.

To do this, follow these steps:

1. **Extract all the petty cash receipts, batch them up and total them.**

2. **Give this batch a unique reference number, such as PC01 – you can use PC02 for the next batch and so on.**

   You can use this reference in the Reference field for recording the petty cash bank payments.

3. **Count the remaining petty cash.**

   The sum of this with the total from Step 1 should equal the petty cash float.

   If the petty cash float doesn't balance, check to see if anyone is holding back any petty cash receipts or if anyone has been given cash to do something and hasn't returned all the change or the receipts.

4. **Write a cheque for cash for the value of the receipts and use this to top up the petty cash float.**

For all you teccies out there, this method is known as the Imprest system – you only replenish what you've spent.

Paying the Credit Card Bill

Many businesses use credit cards as a convenient way to purchase goods and services. And, just like other financial accounts, you need to include credit card payments in the monthly processing of transactions – after all, they can amount to quite significant amounts of money.

Making payments

After you receive the credit card statement, you need to match up the invoices and receipts with the statement:

✔ **Invoices:** If you paid a supplier using your credit card, you received an invoice, which has probably already been entered and filed away. In order to process this payment, just treat it as a supplier payment (refer to Chapter 7), but make sure you insert a reference to the method of payment somewhere. For example, in the Cheque No field use the reference *CC* for credit card. Alternatively, use a unique reference number for each credit card statement, particularly if several employees have their own cards. In this case, give the statement sheet for each individual its own unique reference number, such as *CC001*. This makes it easier to find the supporting papers for a transaction.

✔ **Receipts:** You may not have a proper invoice, just a till receipt for something purchased using the company credit card. In this instance, attach the receipt to the credit card statement and record the transaction as a bank payment. Make sure you select the Credit Card account as the account from which the payment is to be made. Also, make sure that you're careful with the VAT element of the payment; the amount of VAT attributable to a transaction isn't always obvious.

Reconciling the credit card statement

After you enter all the transactions from the credit card statement onto Sage, you are then in a position to reconcile the Credit Card account in the same way as a normal bank statement. (Chapter 15 talks about reconciling your bank account if you need a reminder.)

The only thing to remember when entering the credit card statement balance is that it is a negative figure, because it's money that you owe the credit card company.

The statement is usually paid via a direct debit from your bank account on a monthly basis, and you can treated it as a bank transfer between the Bank Current account and the Credit Card account, as described in the 'Transferring Funds between Accounts' section earlier in this chapter. You can reconcile the statement in the same way as any other bank account. Provided you enter all the transactions and set the statement balance to a negative figure, you can't go too far wrong!

Chapter 9

Maintaining and Correcting Entries

· ·

· ·

1 think it's fair to say that everyone makes mistakes. Sage understands this and makes it very easy for you to correct any mistakes. You can completely delete an item, change elements of a transaction, such as the date or tax code, or find an item in order to check something.

In this chapter, I show you how to make changes confidently to your data and correct mistakes where necessary.

Checking and Maintaining Your Files

You need to explore the file maintenance options. From the main toolbar, click File and then Maintenance. The File Maintenance box appears, as shown in Figure 9-1.

The File Maintenance screen may look a little daunting, but you probably need to use only the Check Data and Corrections options with any regularity. I look at each function in the following sections.

Checking data

This facility allows you to check your data to make sure that it's not corrupt. It's a good idea to do this if your machine switches off in the middle of using Sage. Power cuts aren't unusual, and if you don't have an alternative power supply, Sage closes without being shut down properly, which can sometimes lead to corruption of data.

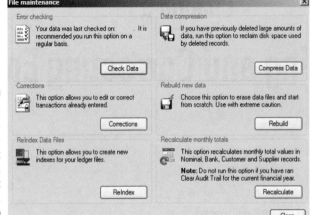

Figure 9-1:
File main-
tenance
options let
you check
and correct
your data.

You'll sometimes experience data corruption when using Sage (but not often, I hope!) In the event that you incur any loss of monthly totals in your Nominal, Bank or Supplier records, you can use File⇨Maintenance⇨ Recalculate monthly totals option to allow Sage to recalculate the monthly totals from your Audit Trail.

If you have used your Clear Audit Trail function at any point, do not use the recalculate monthly totals option, as it will not include any data prior to the Clear Audit Trail date.

To check no errors are present, perform a Check Data routine, following these steps:

1. **From the main toolbar, click File and then Maintenance.**

2. **Click Check Data.**

   The system checks each file, and if there are no problems, Sage gives you a message confirming that there are no problems to report.

3. **Click OK to return to the File Maintenance screen.**

4. **Click Close to exit the File Maintenance screen.**

Interpreting messages

If Sage finds any problems with your data, it brings up a box with several tabs that you can click for more information:

✔ **Comments:** The least serious messages, Comments simply alert you to the fact that your data may have inconsistencies. The Comments tab shows you which accounts you need to look at. Comments are usually insignificant and don't require data correction.

✔ **Warnings:** Similar to Comments, in the sense that they often don't require data correction, Warnings alert you to problems that may require further investigation.

✔ **Errors:** An Error message indicates a problem with the data. You have the facility to fix these errors, but you must make a backup before you do this.

Personally, I'd be very concerned if I had errors in my data and would be tempted to restore my data back to a point where I knew the data was fine. (The 'Restoring Data' section later in this chapter tells you how to restore from a backup.)

Fixing data

You can correct most data problems showing errors via the Fix option. However, the corrective action used to rectify problems can be quite complex. If you're uncertain about the consequences of running the Fix option, seek help from Sage Customer Support, using the telephone number given to you when you took out SageCover.

Making corrections

Probably the most used of the file maintenance options, the Corrections button is a godsend to anyone who makes the odd mistake (including yours truly!).

Be warned that all actions you take are recorded in the audit trail, so your accountant can see how many corrections you've made. From an audit point of view, transactions need to be traceable even if you've made mistakes. Unfortunately, any deletions or changes to data are highlighted in red on the audit trail, so if you make wholesale changes to your data they stick out like a sore thumb!

Sage makes corrections to the individual transactions themselves, so it's important that you identify the precise transaction that needs correcting. You can find details on how to find transactions in the 'Finding Ways to Find Transactions' section later in this chapter.

You can't correct journal entries using the File Maintenance method. You can only correct journal entries by using a reversing journal from within the Nominal Ledger module. See Chapter 16 for details on how to do this.

To make a correction to a transaction, you can delete the whole transaction or correct a part of the transaction. Just follow these steps:

1. **From the File Maintenance screen, click Corrections.**

   This brings up the Corrections screen. Essentially, this screen shows a list of all your transactions in transaction number order.

2. **Find the transaction you want to correct.**

   You can click Find or use the up and down arrows to scroll the data.

3. **Choose how to make the correction and make it.**

   You have the following two options:

   • **Edit Item:** Choosing this option opens the Making Corrections screen (shown in Figure 9-2), which looks different depending on the transaction type. On the first screen, any item in black type can be changed. Click the Edit button to change greyed out items. You then have the option of changing most other parts of the data. Make your changes and click Save. Sage asks `Do you wish to post these changes?`. Click Yes to save or No to return to the Making Corrections screen. Click Close and Sage asks `Are you sure you wish to exit?`. Click Yes to return to the Corrections screen. Click Close and return to the Welcome screen.

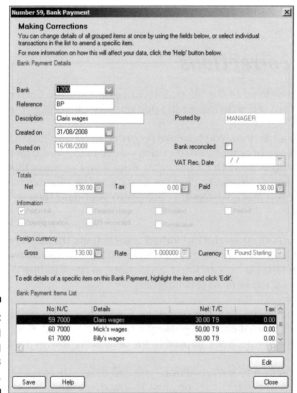

Figure 9-2:
Viewing
the Making
Corrections
screen.

- **Delete Item:** If you know you want to delete an item, highlight it and click the Delete Item icon. The Deleting Transactions window appears. You can click the View button to see more of the transaction. If you are happy to delete it, click Delete. A confirmation message appears asking if you wish to delete the transaction. Click Yes to continue the deletion and No to take you back to the Deleting Transactions window. You can then click Close to return to the Corrections screen. Click Close again to go back to the Welcome screen.

That's how easy it is!

Re-indexing data

Sage recommends using the Re-indexing option only under the guidance of Sage Customer Support. When Sage recommends something like this, it's usually pretty serious! I can safely say that I've never had to do this, so I can only emphasise what Sage says: contact Customer Support if this need arises.

Compressing data

Compressing data files is also pretty serious stuff and outside the scope of this book. Briefly, this function basically constructs a new set of data files whilst removing deleted records, thereby reducing the file sizes. The files are compressed to create more disk space. As the compression procedure is irreversible, you need to take data backups beforehand, just in case any problems occur.

Rebuilding data

You need to tread carefully when using this part of the system because you can end up wiping all the data off your machine! (Mind you, if you take backups, which I explain in the 'Backing Up Data' section later in this chapter, you can restore it all fairly easily.)

You can chose to create new data files for all or part of the Sage Accounts system.

Click the Rebuild button, and the Rebuild Data Files window opens, with all the boxes ticked. A tick indicates that you don't want to create new data files for that part of the system. Removing the ticks tells Sage which parts of your software you want to create new data files for.

If you type **rebuild data files** into the Help menu, Sage guides you through the process of rebuilding your data files. However, have Sage Customer Support on standby, just in case anything goes wrong, so that they can talk you through the issues.

Use the Rebuild tool with extreme caution and always take a backup prior to attempting to do this.

Finding Ways to Find Transactions

Sometimes you need to find a transaction in order to correct or delete it. To find a transaction, you can use the Financials module, the Bank Reconciliation screen or the Corrections screen (in File Maintenance).

I demonstrate from the Financials module. Follow these steps:

1. **Using the navigation bar, click Company and then choose Financials from the Links list.**

2. **Click the Find button at the bottom of the Financials screen.**

   This brings up the Find box, shown in Figure 9-3, which, plainly enough, is what you use to find the transaction.

Figure 9-3:
The Find
box.

Find	
Find What:	[ ]	Find First
Search in:	Transaction Number ▾	Find Next
Match:	Any ▾ ☐ Case sensitive	Cancel

3. **Enter details into the boxes.**

   Tell Sage what to find and where to look:

   - **Find What**: The information entered here is dependent on what is shown in the Search In field (see the next point). For example, in Figure 9-3 the Search In field reads Transaction Number. So the entry in this Find What field should be a transaction number.

   - **Search In:** A dropdown box gives you different variables that you can search with. The default variable is Transaction Number, but you can choose other alternatives. Your other choices are: Account Reference, Reference, Details, Date, Net Amount, Bank Account Reference, Nominal Account Reference, Ex Reference, Tax Amount, Amount Paid and Date Reconciled.

   - **Match:** You don't have to search using the exact data; you have the option to select how close a match you can make.

     Any: Finds all transactions that contain the details you entered anywhere in the field you are searching on. For example, if you're searching for an account reference and you enter RED, Sage finds references such as RED, REDMOND and CALLRED.

Whole: Finds the transaction that contains the exact details you enter in the Find What field. In this instance, when searching for account references, it brings up the RED account transactions.

Start: Finds all transactions that begin with the details you enter. So in the example, Sage would find transactions beginning with RED, such as RED or REDMOND, but it doesn't find CALLRED.

- **Case sensitive:** Check this box if you want Sage to find transactions that contain exactly the same upper and lower case letters as those entered in the Find What field.

4. **Click Find First.**

If a transaction is found, Sage highlights it in blue. If this isn't the transaction that you're looking for, click Find Next.

Note: You may need to cancel the Find box in order to see the transaction properly.

If no transactions are found, a message to that effect appears. Click OK to return to the Find window so that you can enter new search details.

Searching For Records

You can search for records on Sage using the Search button in the Customers, Suppliers, Company, Products, Projects and Financials modules. The Search button is simply another method of tracing transactions.

I tend to search from the Financials module, as Sage performs a search on all the transactions from this module. If you search from the other modules, Sage limits the search solely to the information in that one module – which may be precisely what you want to do, in which case, have at it.

To perform a search from Financials, follow these steps:

1. **From Financials, click Search.**

The Search box opens.

2. **Choose the variables to perform the search.**

Your choices are:

- **Join:** From the Join dropdown list, choose the Where option, which is the only option available. (And as Sage doesn't explain the connection between Join and Where, I can't either. It's just one of Sage's mysteries.)

- **Field:** Click the Field column and select the variable you want to search by. In Figure 9-4, Total Amount Paid is selected.

• **Condition:** Click the Condition column and choose a condition, such as *is equal to* or *is greater than*.

• **Value:** Enter the value you want to search for.

You can enter *wildcards,* which are special characters you can use to represent a line of text or an individual character. Click F1, the Help function key, whilst in the Search box, and Sage explains how to use wildcards.

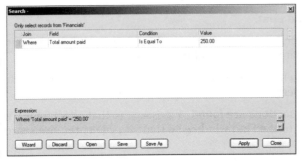

Figure 9-4:
Searching
for – and
finding! –
£250.

Figure 9-4 shows a search for a transaction for the amount of £250. The screen behind shows that Sage found one transaction matching the search details.

3. Click Apply.

Sage identifies all transactions that meet the conditions you selected. If Sage can't find a transaction, nothing comes up.

You can save a search so that you can find records with the same criteria later. Just follow the first two steps in the preceding list and then click Save instead of Apply. Enter a suitable filename and then click Save again. To access this saved file, open up the Search box, click Open and select the chosen file.

Backing Up Data

Performing regular backup routines is extremely important. If your data becomes corrupt or you need to reinstall Sage for whatever reason, you then have a backup that you can restore onto your machine, allowing you to continue working with the least amount of disruption.

To back up your data, follow these steps:

1. **From the toolbar, click File and then Backup.**

   A message asks if you want to check your data. Sage recommends that you check your data, which normally takes a matter of seconds, depending on how may records you have. Click Yes to check or No to continue with the backup.

2. **Make adjustments on the Backup window that comes up.**

   The Backup window contains three tabs:

   • The Backup Company tab, shown in Figure 9-5, displays the filename Sageback, today's date and the .001 file extension.

     Amend the filename with one that has meaning for your business. For example, the filename 'Jingles end of day Sageback 28-02-2009.001' indicates a backup of the Jingles card company's data as at close of business on 28 February 2009.

     Choose a location that you can find easily if you need to restore the data. Use the Browse button to change the location if you're not happy with the location Sage chooses.

   • The second tab, Advanced Options, allows you to choose how much you back up. For example, you can include only data, or data plus reports, templates and so on. At the very least, back up your data files.

   • The Previous Backups tabs holds – you guessed it! – previous backups.

3. **Click OK.**

   The backup starts, and when it's finished you get a confirmation message saying that the backup was successful.

Make sure that each backup has a different name. Sage makes this easy by adding the date to the file name, but if you perform more than one backup in a day, you have to change the name slightly, or otherwise a backup with the same name overwrites the first set of data.

Take backups at least at the end of every day, but if you're doing a large amount of processing, you may want to back up more often so that if you have to restore data you don't have to re-process too much information. Many people use a different disk, CD or pen drive for each day of the week, naming the backup disk Monday, Tuesday, Wednesday, Thursday, Friday. You can then restore information back to any day in your current week.

Figure 9-5:
The Sage
Backup
screen.

Restoring Data

Restoring data means that you erase the current data on the machine and replacing it with data from your backup disks.

Hopefully you won't need to run this routine, but if you do, follow these steps:

1. **From the main toolbar, click File and then Restore.**

   Sage tells you that it can't run this without closing windows. Click Yes, and the Restore window appears.

2. **Click Browse and select the file that you want to restore.**

3. **Click OK.**

   A message appears saying that you're about to restore and the process overwrites any data currently on the machine. Click Yes to continue or No to exit.

After successfully restoring your data, use the Check Data facility in the File Maintenance screen to check for errors. Refer to the 'Checking Data' section earlier in this chapter for advice on how to do this.

Part III
Functions for Plus and Professional Users

'Take me to your Financial Controller!'

In this part . . .

I take day-to-day transactions to the next level. Most of the chapters in this part are only for people who have Sage 50 Accounts Plus or Professional versions. I look at sales and purchase order processing, stock control, project costing and foreign currency.

This is pretty meaty stuff! You may dip into this part only occasionally, but all the information is here if you need it.

Chapter 10

Processing Sales Orders

. . . .

. . . .

Sales order processing is available only if you have Sage Accounts Professional. If you don't have this version, you can skip this chapter. However, the first section on quotations also applies to Sage Accounts Plus, so Plus users may want to read this section.

Sales orders occur when a customer requests some of your goods or services. In this chapter, I walk you through the steps you follow to process a sales order, from the moment a quote is confirmed through to allocating and despatching the stock and then finally issuing an invoice to the customer.

Giving a Quote

I don't mean that your words are recorded for the enlightenment of the masses! In the business sense, a *quotation* is what you prepare when a potential customer asks for a price for a product or service that you offer. You can create a quotation within Sage that you can ultimately convert into an order if the customer accepts your price.

Amending your invoice and order defaults

As an Accounts Plus user, even though you don't have Sales Order Processing as an option, you can still double-check the Invoice/Order defaults to ensure that your quotations raised are going to convert to a Sales invoice. Follow the instructions outlined here, but make sure that in Step 2 the Convert Quotes To field is set to Invoice.

Accounts Professional users also need to amend the Invoice/Order defaults. Whilst this may sound a bit scary, you're simply telling the system exactly how you want it to operate. For example, you can tell Sage exactly what number you want invoices and orders to start from – especially useful if you're continuing on from a previous system. Click the Options tab of the Invoice/Order defaults to make these changes in Sage.

To amend your Invoice/Order defaults, follow these steps:

1. **From Customers, click Invoice/Order Defaults from the Links list.**

2. **From the General tab, ensure that the Convert Quotes To field is set to Sales Orders.**

   You can create an invoice later, which I explain in the 'Invoicing Your Customers' section later in this chapter.

3. **Click OK to accept any changes you made.**

Creating a quotation

After you check your defaults, you can create a quotation by following these steps:

1. **From Customers, click New Quotation from the Task pane.**

   The quotation window looks very similar to the Product Invoicing screen.

2. **Enter the account for which you want to create a quotation by using the dropdown arrows.**

   You can enter an expiry date, but it isn't essential.

3. **Continue to enter the details of the quotation, including the product code and quantity.**

   Figure 10-1 shows a sample quotation.

4. **When you're happy with your quotation details, click Save.**

   The quotation is saved to the Quotations list.

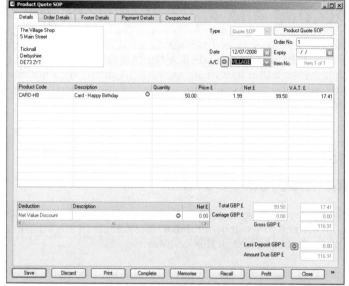

Figure 10-1:
A quotation Jingles created for the Village Shop.

Access the Quotations list through Customers by clicking the Quotations list from the Links list. If you want to edit the details of any quote, from the Quotations list, highlight the quote you want to edit, click New/Edit, make the necessary amendments and click Save.

Sage can list quotations using the following status categories. Generally speaking, the status of the quote is assigned automatically, unless another company gets the business, in which case you have to amend the status yourself.

- ✔ **All quotes:** All quotes of any category.

- ✔ **Quotes won:** A quotation is automatically won when you convert it to an order or invoice.

- ✔ **Quotes lost:** You can amend a quote to give it Lost status. To do this, highlight the quote and click the Lost icon.

- ✔ **Open quotes:** An existing quote that doesn't have an expiry date.

- ✔ **Expired quotes:** A quotation expires after it's been open for a time-out period longer than your specified expiry date. You can re-open an expired quotation by changing the expiry date.

You can change the status of a quote by highlighting and right-clicking a quote from the Quotations list. Use the Set As options to change the status of a quote to open, won or lost.

Allocating and amending stock for a quote

You can allocate stock to an open quotation if you want. To allocate stock, simply select the quotation and click Allocate and then click Yes to the confirmation message that follows. If you want to amend the allocation of stock, select the quotation and click Amend. You can now adjust the amount of stock allocated.

Converting a quotation to an invoice or order

Depending on your Invoice/Order default settings, you convert your quotation to an invoice or to an order. I use the example of an order in the action steps throughout the rest of this chapter.

Accounts Plus users and those Professional users who don't want to convert a quotation to an order can convert it to an invoice instead. Follow the same steps as described in the next paragraph, but provided your Invoice/Order defaults are set to *Convert quotes to an invoice,* an invoice is created when you click Convert. You can look at the new invoice on your Invoice list (click Invoice List from the Links list within the Customer module).

From the Quotations list, select the quote that you want to convert and click Convert. Sage then asks you if you're sure that you want to convert the selected quote. Click Yes.

The status of the quote changes to *won,* and the quotation type becomes an *order.* A sales order is also created in the Sales Order list.

Creating a Sales Order

You can create a sales order in one of two ways: you convert a quotation as described in the preceding section, or you create a new order by clicking Customers from the navigation bar and selecting New Sales Order from the Task pane.

If you use the quotation method, you can access the new sales order after converting your quote by clicking Customers on the navigation bar and then the Sales Order list on the Links list. Highlight the order and then click the New/Edit icon.

Alternatively, if you clicked New Sales Order, the Product Sales Order window opens, which consists of six tabs:

✔ **Details:** This screen allows you to enter the main sales order details, including customer, dates, items ordered and prices.

✔ **Order Details:** You can amend the delivery details and add any notes about the order here.

✔ **Footer Details:** Use the Footer Details to enter information about carriage charges and use of couriers. It also includes a section on settlement terms and discounts.

✔ **Payment Details:** You can record a payment on the Payment Details tab. You can enter details of deposits already received or payments on account.

✔ **Despatched:** This tab shows the order status and details of any goods despatched notes. It only updates after you record a delivery of goods.

A *goods despatched note (GDN)* is essentially the paperwork assigned to stock as it is despatched to your customers. The GDN shows the date that the goods were despatched, the customer to whom the goods were sent and details of the products, quantity ordered and quantity despatched. I talk about GDNs in more detail later in this chapter in the 'Using goods despatched notes' section.

The main body of the Despatched tab shows the goods despatched note number, the customer's GDN and the date that the goods were despatched. It also shows *Y* if the GDN has been printed and *N* if it hasn't. The Despatched tab also contains the following information:

- **Order Status:** The status of the order appears here automatically. It may be *full, part, cancelled* or blank. If the status is blank, it's complete or has no stock allocated to it.

- **Despatch Status:** This box shows the despatch status of the order and can be *part* or *complete.* If no items have been despatched for this order, the box remains blank.

- **Invoice Status:** If you've raised an invoice for this order, the box contains *Y* for Yes. If you haven't yet raised an invoice, the box contains – you guessed it – *N* for No.

- **Complete:** If the order is complete, *Y* appears in this box. If the order is not yet complete, *N* appears here. (I'll let you figure out what *Y* and *N* stand for.)

- **Due Date:** You can enter an estimated despatch date here. However, if the sales order is complete, you can't amend this field.

- **Intrastat**: This box only appears if Intrastat reporting is enabled in the Invoice/Order defaults. The box displays the Intrastat declarations status of the order. *Intrastat* is a system for collecting statistics on the movement of goods between member states of the European Union. (I address Intrastat more fully in Chapter 17.)

✔ **Invoices:** The last tab on the sales order shows which invoices are raised against an order. If you want to see the full details of the invoices, double-click the invoice from the list.

Entering the sales order details

As mentioned earlier, you can create a sales order from a quotation, but not everybody wants to issue quotations. If you want to create a sales order without first creating a quotation, follow these steps:

1. **From Customers, click New Sales Order from the Task pane.**

   The Details tab for a product sales order opens up.

2. **Enter the header details.**

   You're asked to select or provide information:

   - **Type:** Using the dropdown arrow, select Sales Order or Proforma Sales Order.

   - **Order Number**: Sage automatically assigns each order a sequential number after the order has been saved.

     The first order is given the number 1, the next the number 2 and so on. If you want to start from a different number, change the number on the Options tab on Invoice/Order defaults.

   - **Date:** Enter the date of the order. The system defaults to the current day's date, unless you change it.

   - **Invoice Reference:** When you update your sales order to match an existing invoice, the last invoice number relating to the sales order appears.

   - **Account**: Enter the customer account reference here.

   - **Item Number:** The number of the item that's currently highlighted on the order. For example, if there are five item lines, and the cursor is currently on the second line, the box says Item 2 of 5.

3. **Complete the main body of the order by entering the product items that have been sold.**

   Enter the basic information about the products:

- **Product Code:** Using the dropdown arrow, select the product code required. If you don't have a specific product code to use, you can use a special product code. (See Chapter 6 for more details on special product codes.)

- **Description:** This field automatically updates when you select a product code. However, you can edit the description by pressing F3. Refer to Chapter 6 to find out more about using the F3 button.

- **Quantity**: Enter the quantity of stock that the customer has ordered.

- **Price:** The unit price from the product record appears here.

- **Discount:** The customer discount amount for the item displays here.

  A discount appears only if it's been selected within the Invoice/Order defaults. You can apply discounts from the Discounts tab on the Invoice/Order defaults. Find this on the Links list within Customers.

- **Discount percentage:** The percentage discount that the customer receives displays here.

- **Net:** The net amount is calculated automatically. You can't change this value.

- **VAT:** The VAT amount calculates automatically, and you can't change the value.

- **Total:** The order is totalled at the bottom, showing the net value, an addition for carriage charges if they're applicable, the amount of VAT and finally, a gross amount.

- **Deposit:** This new feature has a smart link to the Payment tab of the order, allowing you to record any deposits received against the order. In addition, Sage 50 Accounts now gives you the option to Pay by Card, but you need to have registered for Sage Payment Solutions to use this feature.

  You can find out more about Sage Payment Solutions by clicking Weblinks from the main toolbar and selecting Sage Payment Solutions. For more information, click Help from the main toolbar and type **Sage Payment Solutions**.

- **Deduction:** This is also a new feature. Here, Net Value Discount offers a drilldown arrow in the Description box which, when clicked, reveals an Edit Item line. You can enter information referring to the discount and a discount value, and then press Tab – Sage then automatically calculates the percentage discount. If you enter a discount percentage, Sage calculates the value instead.

4. Click the Order Details tab to add a delivery address or any notes to the order.

Some information is pulled through from the customer record, such as telephone number and contact. A Sales Order Status section shows if stock's been allocated to the order and the delivery status of the goods. You can enter an estimated despatch date for the sales order if required.

5. Click the Footer Details tab to add carriage details.

The information requested includes assignment numbers and courier details:

- **Carriage terms:** You may want to assign carriage costs to the order as you may have postal or courier costs. You can set up specific nominal codes for charging the carriage costs. If you've set up departments, use the dropdown list to select the appropriate one. You can also add the consignment number and courier details and track your parcel by accessing the courier's website.

    To find out how to set up a courier, click Help from the main toolbar on your Footer Details tab. Use the Contents and Index option and type **couriers**.

- **Settlement Terms:** Some information may already be present in these boxes, depending on what details you entered on your customer record. You can enter the number of days during which an early settlement discount applies, if any. You can see the discount percentage applied, if any. Settlement terms also shows you the total value of the invoice.

- **Global:** This section allows you to apply global terms to the whole order. If you choose to use this option, only one line is added to the audit trail. However, carriage is always shown as a separate line.

    You can choose to apply a global nominal code to the whole order. This global code is posted to the nominal ledger when you update the invoice that is eventually generated from the order. You can enter global details to accompany the posting to the nominal ledger. This information appears on all reports that show the Details field. Up to 60 characters are available for you to use.

    You can also apply the same global option to your tax code and your departments (if required).

- **Tax Analysis:** The tax analysis for each product item is shown at the bottom of the Footer tab. The list shows a breakdown of all the VAT into the separate VAT codes (assuming the Global Tax option hasn't been used).

6. Click Save when you're happy with the details you've entered.

The Sales Order screen then reverts to a blank order. Please don't panic! Sage has saved your order, which now shows on the Sales Order list. You can find the Sales Order list from the Links list within Customers.

Dealing with cash sales

Some orders are completed at point of sale, particularly if you have over-the-counter sales. The customer pays for the goods and takes them away immediately. You can receive payment for cash sales online by using the Sage Payment Solutions wizard. (Type **Sage Payment Solutions wizard** into the Sage Help facility to find out more.)

Instead of manually completing each element of the Sales Order life cycle from stock allocation through to ledger update, you can automate the whole process by choosing the Cash Sales option when you're creating the sales order.

To activate the Cash Sales option, enter the sales order details, as shown in Steps 1 through 5 in the preceding 'Entering the sales order details' section. Then click the Cash Sales button at the bottom of the order on the Details tab. A confirmation message asks if you wish to complete this order as a cash sale. Click Yes to continue or No to return to the order. If you click yes, the system completes all stock allocations, creates an invoice and creates a bank transaction for the receipt of cash.

You must have sufficient stock levels to satisfy the whole order, although you can set Sage to allow negative stock values: the order then goes through regardless of stock levels.

You can limit the order paperwork produced for a cash sale to only those documents that you actually need. To select the documents that you need for a cash sale, follow these steps:

1. From Invoice/Order defaults, click the Cash Sales tab.

2. Select the documents you want generated for a cash sale.

You can choose sales order, goods despatched note or sales invoice.

3. Add a message to the invoice if you like.

You may want to type something like 'Cash Sale – paid in full', as shown in Figure 10-2. If not, you can take the tick out of the box and it doesn't print the message.

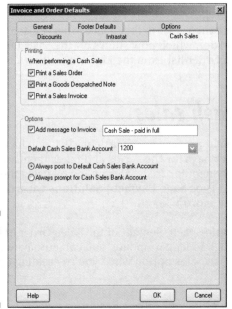

Figure 10-2:
Selecting
the docu-
ments for a
Cash Sale.

4. **Using the dropdown arrow, select the Default Cash Sales Bank Account to which you want the value of the cash sale applied.**

5. **To save your changes, click OK, or to exit without saving, click Cancel.**

To complete the order, Sage generates and allocates a sales receipt to it.

Editing your order

If you decide to change something after you create an order, you can easily amend the details of your order as follows:

1. **From Customers, click Sales Order List from the Links list.**

2. **Select the sales order that you want to amend and click the New/Edit icon at the top of the screen.**

3. **Amend any part of the order you like, and when you're happy with it, click Save.**

Putting sales orders on hold

You may find that you need to put an order on hold while you check out the credit status of a new customer or see if you have enough stock. Just follow these steps:

1. **From Customers, click the Sales Order List from the Links list.**

2. **Select the sales order you want to put on hold and click Amend.**

3. **From the Amend Allocations screen, click Off Order.**

   The Order Status window appears.

4. **Click Held and then OK.**

5. **Close the Amend Allocations screen.**

   You're then returned to the Sales Order Processing screen, where you can see that the status of the order is now *held*.

If you want to take the order off hold, highlight the order, click Amend and then click Order. Close the Amend Allocations screen. You've cancelled the on-hold status.

Duplicating a sales order

You can use the Duplicate facility to copy an existing order with the same details as those that you wish to enter for a new order. I use this time-saving device a lot when processing data.

To duplicate a sales order, follow these steps:

1. **From Customers, click Sales Order List from the Links list.**

2. **Select the sales order you want to copy from the Sales Order Processing screen.**

3. **Click Duplicate.**

   A new sales order opens that's an exact copy of the previous order. Notice that it has a heading showing that it's a duplicate order. After you save the duplicated order, it acquires an order number of its own.

4. **Check that the details of the order are correct and amend any parts where necessary.**

5. **To save the new order, click Save.**

6. **To close the order and return to the Sales Order Processing screen, click Close.**

   The Sales Order List screen appears, showing the new order.

Printing the order

The print facility in Sage allows you to print as many copies of the order as you want. Follow these steps:

1. **From Customers, click Sales Order List from the Links list.**

2. **Select the sales order that you want to print by highlighting the order on the list. Click Print.**

3. **Select which layout you require and the method of output.**

   You can choose to preview, print, send to a file or email.

   I tend to preview the report first to ensure that the details are correct and that I'm happy with the layout.

4. **Click Generate Report.**

   If you choose to preview the report, you still have the option to print or email from the Preview screen. Simply select your desired output from the toolbar.

Allocating Stock to an Order

After you create your sales order, you need to allocate your stock to it. If the order has already been despatched and you've completed the order, Sage automatically allocates the goods for you. Otherwise, the next sections describe how to apportion stock automatically and manually.

Going on automatic

Sage automatically allocates as much stock as possible to your orders, so the amount of *free stock* (stock available to fulfil orders) decreases and the amount of *allocated stock* (items earmarked for specific orders) increases.

To allocate stock automatically, follow these steps:

1. **From Customers, click Sales Order List, highlight the order to which you want to allocate stock and click Allocate.**

2. **Click Yes when Sage asks if you want to allocate all stock to the order.**

   If you don't have enough stock to allocate to the order, Sage lets you know.

   The Sales Order Processing window reappears, and the order shows the word *full* in the Allocated column. If there isn't enough stock to allocate to the order, the column reads *part*.

Assigning stock yourself

Allocating stock manually gives you greater control. For example, if you have two orders, each for ten boxes of cards, but you have only ten boxes in total, you can manually allocate five boxes of cards to each order and tell each customer that the balance of the order is to follow.

To manually allocate stock, follow these steps:

1. **From Customers, click Sales Order List from the Links list.**

2. **Highlight the order and click Amend in the Sales Order Processing screen.**

3. **From within the Amend Allocations screen, manually add the number of units to allocate to this order.**

4. **To save your changes, click Close.**

   The word *part* now shows in the Allocated column against that order.

Sage then reduces the amount of free stock and increases the amount of allocated stock in the same way that it does if you automatically allocate stock. Figure 10-3 shows a partially allocated order.

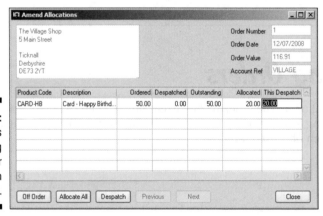

Figure 10-3: The results of allocating stock for part of an order.

Amending the allocation of stock

If you've allocated stock to an order but haven't despatched it, you can still amend the order and reallocate stock. Simply select the sales order from the Sales Order list and click Amend. You can then change the amount of stock you've allocated to that order.

Using the shortfall generator

Sage is an extremely intelligent program and can tell you if you don't have enough stock to fulfil all the orders raised.

To check your stocks, select the orders from the Sales Order list and click the Shortfall icon on the Sales Order Processing toolbar. The Shortfall Generator window shows a list of any products that have a stock level less than the quantity required for the order, as shown in Figure 10-4. If you click Create Order, you can generate a purchase order for the specific products you're running short of.

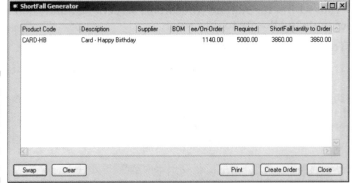

Figure 10-4: Predicting a shortfall is another handy Sage tool.

Despatching Orders

After you allocate the stock to the order, you're then ready to despatch the goods, using any one of the four methods Sage offers. The next sections explain each of these methods.

Completing an order

You complete your order when the goods have already been sent to the customer. In completing the order, Sage allocates stock to it and marks the order as being despatched. To complete an order, you need to highlight the order from the Sales Order list, click Edit to view the order and then click the Complete button (at the bottom of the Details tab). Depending on stock availability, your order is then marked *complete* or *part complete*.

Using goods despatched notes (GDNs)

This option automatically records the despatch of goods and provides maximum traceability because you can view all the GDNs on the Despatch tab for each order.

Before beginning to use GDNs, you need to set up your GDN options in the Options tab of Invoice/Order defaults. You have the following choices:

- ✔ **Generate for all despatches:** The default option. Sage gives you the choice of printing a GDN now or later.

- ✔ **Prompt at each despatch:** Sage prompts you each time you record a despatch as to whether you want to generate a GDN now or later. If you don't generate the GDN, Sage doesn't store the GDN in the Despatched tab of the Sales Order, so you can't view or print the note later.

- ✔ **Do Not Generate:** If you select this option, Sage updates your sales order and your stock level but doesn't produce a GDN.

Sage issues a GDN depending on the default options you select. You can raise a GDN by clicking the Despatch button, or you can click the GDN button. Details of both methods are outlined in the next sections.

Using the despatch facility

You can use the Despatch facility to record complete deliveries of orders to your customers. Follow these steps:

1. **From Customers, click Sales Order List from the Links list.**

2. **Select the orders from the Sales Order Processing screen and click Despatch.**

   Sage then generates a GDN (if this option is selected in your defaults), creates a product invoice and updates the stock level for each product on the order.

Recording a despatch manually

If you're not despatching the whole order, you can manually record the delivery of the stock you're sending. You need to use the Amend facility to record complete or part despatches; just follow these steps:

1. **From the Sales Order Processing window, click Amend.**

2. **Edit the quantity shown in the This Despatch column from within the Amend Allocations window.**

3. **Click Despatch to update the product records.**

   A prompt message comes up, shown in Figure 10-5, asking if you want to create invoice details, update stock and record the despatch for the previous order. Choose an answer:

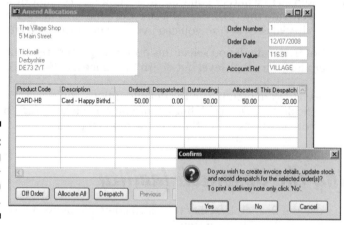

Figure 10-5: Recording a part despatch of an order.

- **No:** Prints a delivery note only (according to the options chosen).

- **Cancel:** Returns you to the Allocations screen, which you can close if you want to.

- **Yes:** Allows you to continue with the despatch of the goods. Sage automatically generates an invoice, which shows on the Invoice tab of the order.

Invoicing Your Customers

After you allocate and despatch all stock relating to your order, you need to print the invoices created from your order and update the ledgers to complete your sales order cycle.

When you despatch an order, Sage 50 Accounts automatically generates a product invoice for each order or partial order. The program also updates your stock levels at the same time.

You can check that Sage has raised an invoice by looking at the Invoice tab for your order to see the invoice number. You can view the invoice from the Invoice tab and then print it. Alternatively, you can print the invoice by using the following method:

1. **From Customers, click the Invoice list.**

2. **Choose the invoice you want to print from the list that appears.**

3. **Click Print and select the layout you prefer.**

4. **Click Generate Report.**

When you're ready to update your invoices, from Customers, click the Invoice list. Select the invoices you want to post and then click Update. Sage posts the invoices to the sales and nominal ledgers.

Deleting and Cancelling Sales Orders

You can delete cancelled or completed orders as necessary and flat-out cancel orders as well.

To free up disk space on your computer, remove fulfilled or cancelled orders by compressing your data.

Before deleting orders, make sure that you carry out a backup in case you change your mind about the deletion and need to restore your data. I give details on how to do a backup in Chapter 9.

To delete an order, follow these steps:

1. **From Customers, click Sales Order List from the Links list.**

2. **Select the order that you want to delete and click Delete.**

    A confirmation message appears asking you to confirm that you want to delete.

When you delete an order, Sage deletes any goods despatch notes associated with that order. You need to be sure that you don't require GDN information before you delete the order.

3. To continue with the deletion, click Yes.

You can cancel sales orders, as long as they don't have the status of *complete* in the Despatched column of the Sales Order Processing window.

After you cancel an order, it still remains on the Sales Order list, but its status changes to *cancelled.* Any stock that was allocated to that order reverts to free stock again.

To cancel a sales order, follow these steps:

1. From Customers, click Sales Order List from the Links list.

2. Select the order that you want to cancel and then click Amend.

3. Click Off Order when the Amend Allocations window appears.

The Order Status window appears.

4. To cancel your order, click Cancel Order. Click OK to confirm the cancellation, or if you decide you *don't* want to cancel the order, click Cancel.

When you cancel a sales order the Off Order button changes to Order. If you want to put a cancelled order back on order, click the Order button from the Amend Allocations window.

When you cancel an order, Sage cancels all the items in that order. If you want to cancel only a specific item on an order, choose the New/Edit icon from the Sales Order Processing window. Delete the unwanted item from the order, or press the F8 key to delete specific lines on the order.

Chapter 11

Processing Purchase Orders

. . . .

In This Chapter

▶ Making up a purchase order

▶ Giving goods *on order* status

▶ Finishing up the purchase order process

▶ Accepting delivery of goods against your order

▶ Generating an invoice

▶ Cancelling and deleting purchase orders

. . . .

*I*f you have Accounts Professional, Sage helps you process your purchase orders. If you don't have this version of Sage, you can skip this chapter.

You raise purchase orders for goods that you place on order with your suppliers. The purchase order processing system (POP) is directly linked to other parts of your system: it updates stock records and project records if you're using these parts of your system.

In this chapter, I cover the stages that a purchase order goes through.

Creating, Changing and Copying a Purchase Order

When you order supplies, materials, widgets or similar, you need to create a paper trail – or at least an electronic trail – that you can send to your supplier to tell them what you need, how much of it you need, by what date and for what price. This paper trail is called a purchase order, or PO for short. Sage Accounts Professional has the perfect process for conveying this information.

Creating a purchase order

Creating a purchase order basically consists of completing information requested in four tabs; just follow these steps:

1. **From Suppliers, click New Purchase Order from the Task pane.**

2. **Fill in the information requested in the Details tab.**

   You're asked to provide basic information such as:

   - **Order Number:** Sage automatically issues each order a sequential number, although you don't see it until you save the order.

     The first order is given the number 1, the next the number 2 and so on. If you want to start from a different number, change the number on the Options tab on Invoice/Order defaults.

   - **Date:** Enter the date of the order. Keep in mind that the system defaults to the current day's date, unless you change it.

   - **Account:** Enter the supplier account reference here.

   - **Project Reference:** This reference only shows when you've switched on Project Costing. Use the dropdown arrow to link the order with a specific project if so required.

   - **Cost Code:** Again, this code only shows when you've switched on Project Costing. You can use the dropdown arrow to select an appropriate cost code.

   - **Reference:** You can enter an additional reference here if you like.

   - **Item Number:** This field shows the number of the item that is currently highlighted on the order. For example, if you have five item lines and the cursor is currently on the second line, the box says `Item 2 of 5`.

   - **Rate:** The rate only appears if you've enabled the Foreign Currency option.

3. **Complete the main body of the order.**

   List the details of the product items that you want to purchase:

   - **Product Code:** Using the dropdown arrow, select the product code required. If you don't have a specific product code to use, you can use a special product code. Refer to Chapter 6 for more details on special product codes.

   - **Description:** The description updates automatically when you select a product code. However, you can edit the description by pressing the F3 key.

   - **Quantity:** Enter the quantity of stock that you want to order.

   - **Price:** The unit price from the product record appears here.

- **Net:** This amount calculates automatically. You can't change this value.

- **VAT:** This amount also calculates automatically, and again, you can't change the value.

- **Total:** The order total appears at the bottom, showing net, VAT and any carriage charges applied.

4. **Click the Order Details tab to add a delivery address or any notes to the order.**

   Sages then pulls certain information from the supplier record, such as the supplier's telephone number and contact information.

5. **Click the Footer Details tab to add carriage details.**

   You can include assignment numbers and courier details here:

   - **Carriage Terms:** You may want to assign carriage costs to the order, or postal or courier costs. You can set up specific nominal codes for the carriage costs to be charged to. If you've set up departments, use the dropdown list to select the appropriate one. You can also add the consignment number and courier details and track your parcel by accessing the courier's website.

   Click Help from the main toolbar to set up a courier on your Footer Details tab. Using the Contents and Index option, type **couriers** to find out how to enter the appropriate details.

   - **Settlement Terms:** Some information may already be present in these boxes, depending on what details you entered on your supplier record. You can enter the number of days during which an early settlement discount applies, if any. You can see what discount percentage is applied, if any, and the total value of the invoice.

   - **Tax Analysis:** The tax analysis for each product item appears at the bottom of the Footer Details tab. The list shows a breakdown of all the VAT into the separate VAT codes.

6. **Click Save to preserve the order.**

   The Purchase Order screen then shows a blank order, but don't panic! Sage has saved your order and is ready for the next one.

As soon as you close the Purchase Order screen, you can view a copy of your order on the Purchase Order list.

Editing your order

If you decide to change something after you've created your order, you can easily amend the details of your order as follows:

1. **From Suppliers, click Purchase Order List from the Links list.**

2. **Select the purchase order that you want to amend and click the New/Edit icon at the top of the Purchase Order Processing (POP) screen.**

   You can then amend any part of the order.

3. **Click Save when you finish editing the purchase order.**

Duplicating a purchase order

You can copy an existing order with the same details as those you want to enter for a new order. I use this duplicate feature a lot when processing orders – it speeds up the entry time. To use it yourself, follow these steps:

1. **From Suppliers, click Purchase Order List from the Links list.**

2. **From the POP screen, select the purchase order that you want to copy and click Duplicate.**

   An exact copy of the previous order opens, as shown in Figure 11-1. Notice that the heading proclaims that it's a duplicate of the original purchase order.

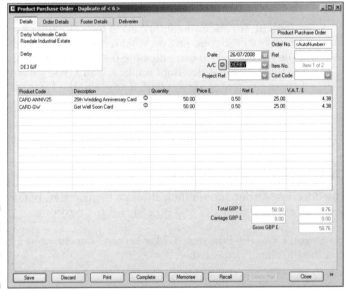

Figure 11-1: Cloning a PO is easy and helpful.

3. **Check that the details of the order are correct and change anything that needs to be different.**

4. **To save the new order, click Save.**

5. **To close the order and return to the POP screen, click Close.**

   The Purchase Order list appears, showing the new order.

Placing the Goods On Order

After you create a purchase order and are about to send it to your supplier, you need to put it on order with Sage as well.

Ordering via the conventional method

In the following steps, you change the status of the order to *on order* and update your on-order stock levels for the appropriate product codes. To do this:

1. **From Suppliers, click Purchase Order List.**

2. **Select the order that you want to place on order by clicking the Order icon in the POP screen.**

   A confirmation message appears, asking if you want to print the order. Click Yes if you want to print or No if you want to continue without printing.

3. **To place the goods on order, click Yes when asked if you want to place all selected items on order.**

   The POP window then reappears, showing the status of the order as *on order.*

Now, when the goods come in, you can receive them properly.

Manually placing goods on order

An alternative method of placing your goods on order lets you view the order again prior to placing it on order – something the method described in the previous section doesn't allow. If you want to double-check the items on the order, follow these steps:

1. **Select the order from the Purchase Order list.**

2. **Click the Amend icon.**

   You see all the product records contained within your order, one line per product.

3. **To put your purchase order on order, click Order. The full order quantity then appears in the This Delivery column.**

In Figure 11-2 note that the This Delivery column is currently zero on both the product lines. As soon as you place the goods on order, the value changes.

Figure 11-2: Manually placing goods on order allows you to check the order beforehand.

Product Code	Description	Project Ref	Cost Code	Ordered	Delivered	Outstanding	This Delivery
CARD-GW	Get Well Soon Card			50.00	0.00	50.00	0.00
CARD-HB	Card - Happy Birthday			50.00	0.00	50.00	0.00

Amend Deliveries

Derby Wholesale Cards
Risedale Industrial Estate
Derby
DE3 6JF

Order Number 2
Order Date 23/07/2008
Order Value 58.76
Account Ref DERBY

Order | Deliver | Previous | Next | Close

4. **Click Close to return to the POP window.**

The purchase order now shows on order.

Completing Your Purchase Order

Completing your order is necessary only if you've already received your goods. The process of completing your order means that Sage saves the order, completes the order and records the delivery of stock immediately.

If the order is linked to a project, Sage automatically allocates the goods to the project and then applies the costs. Sage applies actual costs at different stages, depending on the type of item ordered:

- ✔ **For a stock item:** Sage applies actual costs when the stock item is issued to the project.

- ✔ **For a non-stock or service item:** Sage applies actual costs when the invoice is recorded for the purchase order.

To complete your order, follow these steps:

1. **From Suppliers, click Purchase Order List from the Links list.**

2. **From the POP window, select the order that you want to complete and click the New/Edit icon.**

   This takes you into the Details screen of the order.

3. **Click Complete at the bottom of the screen and then click Yes when you get the confirmation message saying that you've selected to complete the order in full. Click Yes to continue.**

4. **Click Yes again when a further confirmation message appears, asking if you want to update stock and record delivery of the order.**

   Sage then generates a goods received note and asks if you want to print it now or later. Make your choice and then decide whether to print the purchase order as well.

5. **Close the Purchase Order screen.**

   The screen returns to the Purchase Order list and the status of your order shows as *complete*.

If you look on the Deliveries tab of you order, you see that Sage has generated a goods received note (GRN). You can view or print the GRN from this screen.

Printing Your Purchase Order

You can print or spool a copy of one or more purchase orders so that you can send them out to the suppliers or keep a hard copy for your records (although going paperless as much as possible is greener for the planet and cheaper for your company).

Print spooling refers to the process of transferring data to a temporary holding place (a buffer, usually an area on a disk). The printer can pull the data off the buffer when required, leaving you free to carry out other computer tasks while the printing is done in the background.

Printing POs in batches makes sense, if only because you can put the correct stationery in the printer.

To print a batch of purchase orders, follow these steps:

1. **From Suppliers, click Purchase Order List on the Links list.**

2. **Select the purchase orders that you want to print. Click Print.**

3. **From the Layout list box, select the layout you require for your purchase orders.**

   You're presented with a multitude of layouts, dependant on your Purchase Order stationery paper size. Alternatively, you can choose to email the purchase order from this list of options, which has to be better for the planet!

4. Select the output you require.

You can choose to print, preview, file or email.

- **Print:** Choosing this opens the Print window. Select the pages you want to print and change your printer settings if required. You can print orders as many times as you like!

- **Print Preview:** The Print Preview window shows the first purchase order in the batch. If you're happy with it, you can send it directly to the printer by choosing the Print option from the File menu.

- **File:** The Save As window appears. Select a directory to store the file in and enter a filename.

- **Email:** This opens your email system, where you can send the purchase order as an attachment. Just follow the prompts on the screen.

5. To print your purchase orders, click Generate Report.

Getting the Goods In

After you send a purchase order, you typically receive goods after a reasonable amount of time. (If you don't, you need to pursue the issue with the supplier!) When the goods arrive, you need to book them into Sage.

If you placed the order for a project and completed the PO as described previously in this chapter, Sage automatically records the stock as delivered and allocates it to the proper project.

In the following sections, I cover three alternative ways of recording the delivery of goods.

Using goods received notes (GRNs)

A quick and easy way of recording the delivery of stock, GRNs allow you to record deliveries against more than one order at the same time. Sage keeps a record of all GRNs raised against each order. You can view and print these by going to the Deliveries tab of each order.

Setting GRN defaults

To adjust the settings for GRNs, follow these steps:

1. From Suppliers, click Invoice/Order defaults and then click the Options tab.

2. **Amend the default setting for GRNs as needed by using the dropdown arrow.**

   Your options are:

   - **Generate for all received:** The default option. Sage generates a GRN for each delivery, but gives you the option to print now or later.

   - **Prompt at each received:** Each time you record a delivery, Sage asks whether to generate a GRN or not. If you choose not to generate the GRN, Sage doesn't store a copy of it, so you can't view or print it later.

   - **Do not generate:** Sage updates the purchase order and stock levels, but doesn't produce a GRN. The GRN option doesn't appear on the Purchase Order Processing toolbar.

3. **Click OK.**

Generating the GRNs

If you selected the Do Not Generate GRNs option, ignore this section, as the GRN icon doesn't appear on your toolbar. If you want to process your GRNs, then read on:

1. **From Suppliers, click Purchase Order List and select the order for which you want to raise a GRN.**

2. **Click GRN.**

   Note: You can only use the GRN option if the status of the goods is *on order.*

   The Goods Received Note window opens.

3. **Enter the date and supplier information in the boxes provided.**

   As soon as Sage identifies the supplier, all the outstanding items from the selected purchase order appear, as shown in Figure 11-3.

   You may want to enter the supplier's GRN if you have it.

4. **Check the details. If the delivery is all there, click Receive All.**

   If not all of your order was delivered, enter the actual quantities received in the Received column.

   The Received column then changes from zero to the value of the items received.

5. **To save the goods received information, click Save.**

   A message appears saying:

   ```
   A goods received note has been generated for this order
   and stored under the Deliveries tab of the order. You can
   print this goods received note now, or continue process-
   ing and print it from the Deliveries tab of the order.
   ```

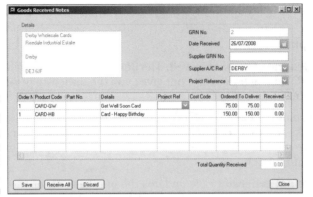

Figure 11-3:
Entering
your goods
received
information.

You can, if you want, tick the Do Not Show This Message Again box to deselect it.

If you don't want to save the goods received information, click Discard.

6. To return to the Purchase Order Processing window, click Close.

The status of the order changes to *complete* on the Purchase Order list, or to *part* if you received less than your full order.

Accepting delivery of everything

If everything on your purchase order comes in, you can use the Deliver function to record that, as long as you've already placed the PO on order (see the 'Placing the Goods On Order' section earlier in this chapter).

To accept delivery, follow these steps:

1. From Suppliers, click Purchase Order List.

2. From the Purchase Order Processing window, select the order you want to process and click Deliver.

You receive a confirmation message asking if you want to update stock and record delivery of the items. Click Yes to continue.

Depending on which GRN options you selected (see 'Setting GRN defaults' earlier in this chapter), you may get a message asking whether you want to print a GRN. Print as required.

The Purchase Order window reappears, showing the status of the order as *complete*.

Taking in part of an order

You can use the Amend facility to manually record delivery of a complete or partial order. You have a chance to check the order line by line against what has been delivered instead of automatically updating and recording stock. Also, you can choose to process part or complete deliveries instead of being forced to record complete deliveries only.

Before you can amend your order, you must place it on order.

To use the Amend tool:

1. **From Suppliers, click Purchase Order List.**

2. **Highlight the order you want to change and then click Amend.**

   The Amend Deliveries window appears, showing the full order quantity in the This Delivery column.

3. **To record a partial delivery, amend the actual quantity received in the This Delivery column.**

   If you want to record a complete delivery, move to Step 4 without amending the This Delivery column.

4. **Click Deliver to update the product records with the new delivery information.**

   A confirmation message appears asking if you want to update the stock and record delivery of the items. Click Yes to continue or No to return to the Amend Deliveries screen.

   Depending on the GRN options you chose, you may be asked to print your GRN.

5. **Click Close to return to the Purchase Order list.**

   If you received a partial order, the Purchase Order window now shows the new status of the order as *part*.

Creating an Invoice from an Order

As part of the life cycle of the Purchase Order process, ultimately you want to match the invoice received from the supplier to the order that you raised in Sage. Sage allows you to do this by converting the purchase order to an invoice by using the Update icon. This icon allows you to mirror the information from the invoice received from the supplier. You also save time, as you don't have to type in all the supplier invoice details, because most of it has already been entered at the order stage.

The purchase order has a Posted column. If it's blank, the order hasn't been posted to the purchase ledger. If the order's been updated, you see a *Y* in the column. When the order is updated, it posts to the purchase ledger and the nominal ledger.

You can update part-delivered orders. Each part creates its own invoice, so you may have more than one invoice relating to the same order.

To create a purchase invoice for a partially or fully delivered order, follow these steps:

1. **From Suppliers, click Purchase Order List.**

2. **Highlight the order(s) against which you want to raise an invoice and click Update.**

   If you've enabled transaction email and linked the selected orders to a supplier record that's marked `I send orders to this supplier electronically`, a prompt appears asking you whether you want to send the orders now.

   The Purchase Order Update window opens.

3. **Edit any of the details shown in the Purchase Order Update window by highlighting the lines you want to change and clicking Edit.**

   Make any changes that you require.

4. **Click Save. If you decide that no changes are necessary, click Close.**

5. **Select the components of the order that you want to update and click Update.**

   The Batch Supplier window appears, showing the details of your purchase invoice.

6. **Match the actual invoice received from your supplier with the details shown on the Batch Supplier window.**

   You need to add the supplier's invoice number in the Ex Ref field or the Details field. You also need to enter your sequential number for your purchase invoice in the Ref field. You can overtype the order number that automatically pulls through in the Ref field.

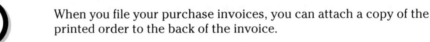

   When you file your purchase invoices, you can attach a copy of the printed order to the back of the invoice.

7. **To update the purchase ledger and create an invoice from the details, click Save.**

   The Purchase Order list now shows a *Y* in the Posted column for the invoice you just updated.

Deleting, Cancelling and Un-Cancelling Orders

Sometimes you need to delete or cancel an order. Sage knows the realities of the business world and accommodates them. And sometimes, you think that you need to cancel a purchase order only to find out that you need it after all. Sage accommodates these human foibles as well.

Deleting

You can delete purchase orders from the Purchase Order list. However, if you try to delete an order that's neither complete nor cancelled, Sage issues a warning message asking if you really want to delete this.

Note that when Sage deletes a purchase order, it also deletes any associated goods received notes, so if you need to keep copies of GRNs, take copies prior to deleting the orders.

After you delete the purchase orders, you can use the Compress Files facility found in File Maintenance to remove deleted orders from the data files and make the unused disk space available.

To delete purchase orders, follow these steps:

1. **Take a backup.**

   Just in case things go pear-shaped, and you need to restore a clean set of data.

2. **From Suppliers, click Purchase Order List and select the order that you want to delete.**

3. **Click the Delete button at the bottom of the screen.**

   A confirmation box appears asking you to confirm that you want to delete the items highlighted. Click Yes to continue or No to halt the process.

Cancelling

With Sage, you have the ability to cancel orders. Just follow these steps:

1. **From the Purchase Order List, select the order that you want to cancel and click Amend.**

The Amend Deliveries window appears, showing the details of the order, with one line per product.

2. Click Off Order.

Clicking the Off Order button cancels the whole order. If you want to cancel one line from an order, choose the New/Edit icon from the Purchase Order List window and delete the required row from the order by using the F8 key.

The status of the PO needs to be *on order* before you can cancel it. Otherwise, when you click Amend, the Off Order button isn't available.

3. To return to the Purchase Order list, click Close.

The status of the order shows as *cancelled.*

Putting a cancelled order back on order

If you change your mind and decide that a previously cancelled order needs reinstating, follow these steps:

1. From the Purchase Order List, select the order that you want to place back on order. Click Amend.

2. Click Order in the Amend Deliveries window.

The button changes to Off Order.

3. Exit the Amend Deliveries window by clicking Close.

The status of the order now shows as *on order.*

Chapter 12

Keeping Track of Your Products

. . . .

In This Chapter

▶ Recording a stocktake

▶ Building a Bill of Materials

▶ Processing stock returns

▶ Assigning stock

. . . .

A lot of money is often tied up in stock, and having proper control over your stock procedures makes good business sense. In this chapter, I give you the tools to do this.

I cover recording a stocktake, which you can do with any version of Sage, in the first section of this chapter; I then explore the added features available only in Sage Plus and Professional versions.

Taking Stock

Every business should undertake a stocktake periodically – once a year at the very least – so that the year-end accounts show an accurate stock position. However, actually carrying out a stocktake can prove a logistical nightmare, particularly if you have a vast array of products.

Usually, recording a stocktake is best undertaken when the factory or office is closed for normal business. Many a time, I've rolled out of bed on a Saturday to help do stocktakes! Whilst Sage doesn't allow you the luxury of a weekend lie-in, it does help you organise your stocktake methodically.

To record a stocktake using Sage, follow these steps:

1. **From the navigation bar, click Products.**

   Ensure that the screen is displaying the Products view and not the Products dashboard (which shows graphs). Use the Change View button to switch the display if necessary.

2. **Select the products for which you want to do a stocktake. Click Stk Take to display the Stocktake window, which shows the product lines you selected.**

   Figure 12-1 shows a sample Stocktake window.

Product Code	Details	Date	Ref	Actual	Cost Price	In stock	Adjustment
CARD-ANNIV25	25th Wedding Anni...	27/07/2008	STK TAKE	100.00	0.50	100.00	0.00
CARD-GW	Get Well Soon Card	27/07/2008	STK TAKE	125.00	0.50	125.00	0.00
CARD-HB	Card - Happy Birthday	27/07/2008	STK TAKE	1170.00	0.50	1170.00	0.00
PAPERGOLD	A4 Sheets of Gold c...	27/07/2008	STK TAKE	50.00	0.25	50.00	0.00
PAPERHAND	A4 handmade paper...	27/07/2008	STK TAKE	100.00	0.50	100.00	0.00
PAPERSILVER	A4 sheet of silver co...	27/07/2008	STK TAKE	50.00	0.25	50.00	0.00

Figure 12-1:
A Stocktake window for Jingles.

3. **Print the stocktake information and use it as the basis of your stocktake.**

   As you go around counting the items, tick them off on the list and note any stock adjustments that you need to make.

4. **Make adjustments in Sage according to the stocktake information.**

   If you find differences in the quantity of stock items, amend the Actual column, which in turn generates a figure in the Adjustment column – a positive number if the quantity of stock is more than the Actual column shows, and a negative number if the stock is less.

5. **To post the new stock levels, click Save. If you don't want to record your entries, click Discard.**

   You can memorise the changes prior to posting by clicking Memorise and entering a file name where you want to save the information before clicking Save. To open that file at a later time, click Recall and select the appropriate file.

Adjusting stock levels

Apart from the automatic changes made when you generate sales or purchase orders, Sage helps you to adjust stock levels. For example, you may need to return some goods to stock without generating a credit note – a *stock in* movement – or record the fact that you sent some stock out to potential customers as samples – a *stock out* movement. As you're not processing credit notes or sales orders, you need to change the stock numbers manually to reflect the movement in stock.

To make a stock adjustment, follow these steps:

1. **From the Product window, select the product that you want to make an adjustment to. Click In to put stock back into your stores, or click Out to remove items.**

   The Stock Adjustment In/Out window appears.

2. **Enter the adjustment details, using one line per product.**

   Entering a reason for the adjustment in the Reference column is a good idea. You have 30 spaces to enter a description.

   The cost price and sale price automatically appear from the stock record.

3. **To save the details entered, click Save.**

   The stock is automatically adjusted.

If you want to check on stock, simply highlight the product and click the Activity icon. You can see a history of all stock movements for that product item.

Checking stock activity

You can look at a product's activity and view stock movements. The Activity screen records all movement of stock in and out and written off. (I talk about writing off stock in the upcoming 'Processing Stock Returns' section.) You can also look at allocated stock, stock on order, the quantity in stock and the quantity available.

You can use your Activity screen to view stock movements (check the preceding section), but you can also use it to view the precise sales orders and purchase orders responsible for the goods in and out. Click the little grey and white arrow next to the Goods In/Out description, and Sage shows you the order and its current status.

To check product activity, follow these steps:

1. **From Products, select the product that you want to view.**

2. **Click Activity.**

   The Activity screen opens, showing all movements of stock.

3. **You can print a list of activities or click Close to close this screen.**

   You return to the Products list.

Using the stock shortfall facility

You can use the Shortfall facility to see if your stock levels have fallen below the reorder levels you set in your product records. If you use Accounts Professional, you can automatically create a purchase order for those items.

Figure 12-2 shows a Shortfall report, generated because the reorder level for 25th Anniversary cards is set at 125 units and the cards in stock have fallen below that level. Clicking the Create Order button at the bottom right of that screen produces a purchase order for the supplier of those cards.

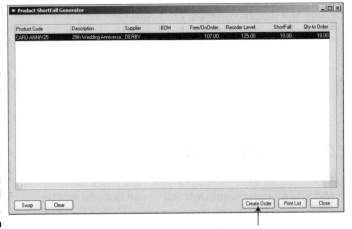

Figure 12-2:
In Accounts Professional you can generate a purchase order from a Shortfall report.

If you have a number of products on your shortfall list, sort the list into supplier order by clicking the top of the Supplier column. Print the list, so you can methodically place orders with each supplier.

If you always buy the same products from the same suppliers, you can enter the supplier reference in the appropriate field within the product record, which makes it even easier to place orders. You simply select all the products that have the same supplier reference and place a bulk order. The Create Order button available in Accounts Professional lets you do this automatically.

To create a product shortfall list, follow these steps:

1. **From Products, click the Swap button at the bottom of the screen.**

   All your product records are highlighted.

2. **Click the Shortfall icon.**

   The Product Shortfall Generator window opens, showing a list of all items that have fallen below the reorder level.

   If you use Accounts Professional, you can automatically create a purchase order from this screen by clicking Create Order.

3. **Click Print List and use the output as a basis for creating your orders.**

4. **Click Close to exit this report.**

Understanding a Bill of Materials

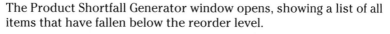

A *bill of materials (BOM)* is best described as a list of products used to make up another product – the component parts of the main product.

You set up each component as a separate product record and link them all together with a BOM; the various levels of components get different names. To help you keep everything straight, look at the following example. I use a Magic Party product that the fictional card shop Jingles offers.

The *product assembly,* or the list of components that make up a product – in this case, a Jingles Magic Party – includes the following elements:

✔ A magician

✔ A box of tricks

✔ Wizard-themed party dishes pack

Each of these three items is a *subassembly* of the product assembly – it may be an individual component (such as the magician) or a group of components that together form the main product assembly, for example, the box of tricks below.

The box of tricks subassembly contains the following *components,* which are the individual items that form assemblies when grouped together:

- ✔ 1 pack of cards
- ✔ 6 feather dusters
- ✔ 6 silk scarves
- ✔ 1 box of party poppers
- ✔ 1 pack of blow-up balloons

The BOM shows the levels of components and subassemblies, and the number of assemblies or subassemblies to which each component belongs – known as the *link*.

Creating a bill of materials

Jeanette, Jingles' owner, needs to create a product record for each subassembly – and each of their components. Fortunately for her, creating a bill of materials is a relatively simple process – a bit like making a shopping list. You essentially create a new product, the BOM, from other products that you hold in stock.

You need to create a product record for the new product, and then use the BOM tab on the product record to build up the list of products required to make it!

To set up a bill of materials:

1. **From Products, choose the product record that you want to create a BOM for and click Record.**

   This opens up the Product Record screen.

2. **Click the BOM tab on the top of the screen.**

   The BOM information table appears, which is blank to start with.

3. **Enter the product code and quantity required of each item needed for the BOM.**

Figure 12-3 shows the BOM for the Magic Party's components, which include:

- **Product code:** Select the product items required for your main product.

  In the case of this Magic Party, the items include a box of tricks, a magician and a party dishes pack.

- **Assembly level:** This field shows how many levels of components and subassemblies are below this component. Sage automatically generates this number.

- **Link level:** This is the number of assemblies or subassemblies to which this component belongs. Each product can be a component of more than one assembly or subassembly.

  Sage automatically creates a link count for each component on the BOM.

- **Available to make up:** This field shows the number of units that can be made with the current stock levels.

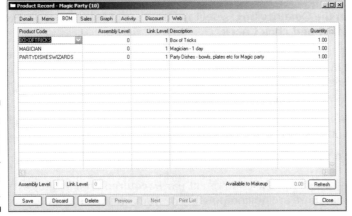

Figure 12-3: Jeanette has created a BOM for a Magic Party.

Before Jeanette sets up a BOM for the Magic Party, she needs to decide what the subcomponents are. She decides upon a magician, a box of tricks and a party dishes pack. At this point, she needs to set up a product record for each of these subcomponents before she can select them for her Magic Party BOM. Whilst she is setting up her box of tricks product record, she can click the BOM tab and select the list of products required to make a box of tricks. She also needs to do the same exercise for the party dishes product record and list the component parts on the BOM tab.

After the subassemblies are set up, Jeanette can click her BOM tab for the Magic Party and select the relevant subassemblies. As soon as she enters Box of Tricks, the assembly level becomes *1* rather than *0*. The number one indicates that Box of Tricks is a subassembly of the main assembly. The magician, however, remains as assembly level zero, because there are no further subcomponents.

Checking stock availability for a BOM

You can use the Check BOM option to see if you have enough stock available to assemble the main product. Follow these steps:

1. **From the Product module, click Check BOM.**

   The Check Stock Make Up window appears.

2. **From the Product Code dropdown list, select the code of the assembly that you want to check.**

   The description of the assembly appears in a text box. You can't edit this information.

3. **In the Quantity box, select the number of assemblies you want to make and click Check.**

   If you don't have enough of an item of stock, a message appears saying how many assemblies you're short of. Click OK to find out what items you need to order. If you have enough components in stock, a confirmation message appears saying that.

   You can create a purchase order automatically by selecting the items you're short of and clicking Create Order.

4. **To print a Component Availability report, click Print.**

Figure 12-4 shows the component parts required for a Magic Party. Sage says that there are no components in stock and gives a list of products that Jeanette needs to order.

The Check BOM screen only shows product items, not service items, so if a BOM includes a service as well as products, you need to deal with the service element separately.

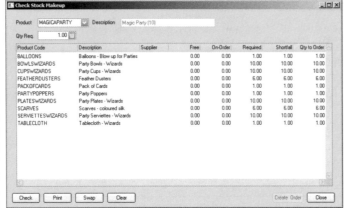

Figure 12-4:
Checking
component
parts for
a Magic
Party.

Transferring stock for a BOM

When you use the Product Transfer facility, Sage automatically calculates the cost of the product assembly by adding together the cost of the component parts.

To complete a product transfer:

1. **From Products, click Transfer.**

   The Product Transfer screen appears.

2. **Insert the details for each transfer in the lines provided, using one line per transfer.**

   Each transfer must involve a product assembly. So in the example, Jeanette selects a Magic Party, a box of tricks and party dishes. She enters a quantity of *1* and Sage transfers the necessary component parts into those items of stock, as shown in Figure 12-5.

3. **As soon as you're happy with the information, you can click Save or Discard to cancel. Click Close to exit the Product Transfer screen.**

Stock Transfers								
Product Code	Details	Date	Ref.	Quantity	In stock	On order	Allocated	
MAGICAPARTY	Magic Party (10)	03/08/2008		1.00	0.00	0.00	0.00	
BOXOFTRICKS	Box of Tricks	03/08/2008		1.00	0.00	0.00	0.00	
PARTYDISHESWI...	Party Dishes - bowls, pla...	03/08/2008		1.00	0.00	0.00	0.00	
		/ /		0.00	0.00	0.00	0.00	

Save   Discard   Close

Figure 12-5:
Transferring
stock to
BOMs.

When you carry out a stock transfer, Sage carries out the following postings:

✔ Increases the in-stock quantity of the finished product by the quantity entered. This transaction is recorded as a *Movement In (MI)* on the product activity file.

✔ Reduces the in-stock quantity of each individual component type. The transfer is recorded as a *Movement Out (MO)*.

✔ Updates the product activity file with each transfer made.

✔ Updates the cost price of the finished product in the product record.

Processing Stock Returns

You may have stock returned for a variety of reasons – the customer just didn't like it (their bad taste is their problem!), the item didn't fit, or didn't fit their needs, or was the wrong colour, size or whatever. When this happens, you have to adjust your stock levels. You can adjust your stock levels by issuing a credit note and updating the system (which in turn updates the stock levels) or by making an *adjustment in* to stock.

The Stock Return option isn't available if you selected the product code as a non-stock or service item. Refer to Chapter 3 for more information.

If the returned items are damaged or faulty, you use a different method to process the stock return to accommodate the ultimate destination of the defective goods:

✔ **Damaged goods returned to you (damages in):** No, you're not taking in what used to be called wayward girls, you're accounting for products that customers are returning to you because they – the products, not the customers – are damaged or don't work. Because you can't just add faulty items back into your stock and sell them again, you create a record of the stock return that doesn't increase the in-stock quantity. Figure 12-6 shows such a return.

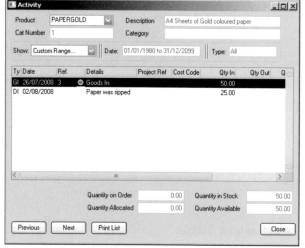

Figure 12-6:
Part of a Product Activity screen showing how damaged stock is recorded.

✔ **Damaged goods you're returning to your supplier (damages out):** Again, as the goods are being returned for repair or replacement, you don't update the quantity in stock, sales value or sales quantity figures.

✔ **Write off:** Use this option if you need to *write off* the stock, which means determining that it has no value and you can't sell it. Sage makes an adjustment to the stock levels in the same way that an adjustment out does.

At least once a year, you have to value your stock for accounts purposes. Any written off stock reduces the value of the stock in the accounts. You can obtain a Product Writeoff Details report from the Product Reports window, in a subsection of Product Damage and Writeoff Reports. This report can help you identify the value of stock to be written off in the accounts. I advise talking to your accountant about processing this type of adjustment in your accounts.

To record a stock return, follow these steps:

1. **From Products, select the product you want to record a return for.**

2. **Click the Returns icon in the Products toolbar.**

   The Stock Return window appears, as shown in Figure 12-7.

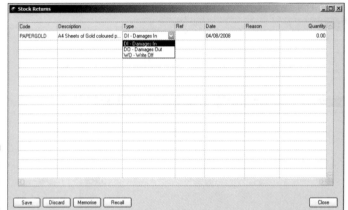

3. **Enter the stock return details.**

   The boxes include:

   - **Code:** Change the product code by using the dropdown arrow if necessary.

   - **Description:** This field automatically comes up when the record is selected.

   - **Type:** Click this box to reveal a dropdown arrow and select Damage In, Damage Out or Write Off.

   - **Reference:** Enter a reference if required.

   - **Date:** Change the date if you don't want to use the current day's date.

   - **Reason:** Enter a reason for the return.

   - **Quantity:** Note the quantity of stock being returned.

4. **To post the stock return, click Save. Otherwise, click Discard.**

If you want to, you can click Memorise to temporarily save the stock return details and then post the items at a later date. You can access the memorised information next time by clicking the Returns icon and then Recall. Open the saved file to bring up your previously memorised items, which you can then save and post.

Allocating Stock

If you run Plus or Professional versions of Sage, you can manually allocate stock for general use or project use and allocate it to a project by way of a purchase order. Both manual and purchase order stock allocations affect the committed costs of a project. *Committed costs* are costs allocated to a project. Committed costs are not formally charged to a project until the stock allocated to a project is issued. See the upcoming 'Issuing allocated stock' section.

When you record a stock allocation, you can't allot more than the amount of available stock, called *free stock*, unless you set your program to allow negative stock. After you assign stock, it's no longer free and can't be used for other sales orders.

To allocate stock, follow these steps:

1. **From Products, click the Allocate icon.**

   The Allocation window appears, with the Allocate Stock option highlighted.

2. **Click OK.**

   The Stock Allocation window appears.

3. **From the Stock Allocation window, enter the stock allocation details.**

   Using the dropdown arrows, enter the product code, the project reference and the cost code, if required. Figure 12-8 shows allocation information for Jingles. Jeanette has decided to allocate 27 sheets of handmade A4 paper to an order. Sage has calculated that 100 sheets are available.

   Sage automatically shows the amount of free stock, but you need to enter the quantity of stock you want to allocate.

4. **To print a copy of the stock information you've entered, click Print List.**

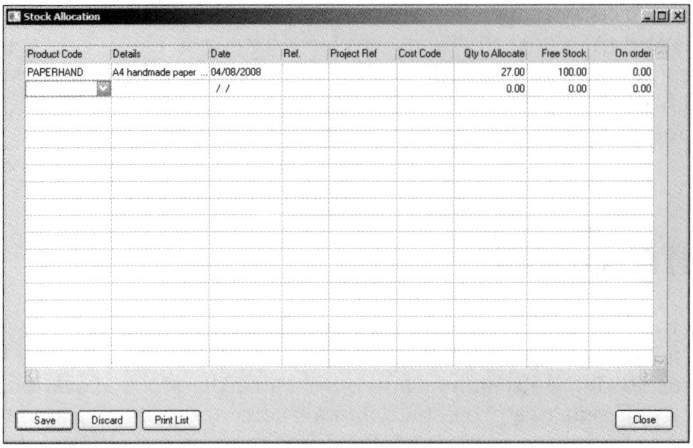

Figure 12-8:
Jeanette decides to allocate some handmade paper to a customer's order.

5. **To save the allocation, click Save. If you don't want to save the information, click Discard. Click Close to return to the Products window.**

You can view how much stock is allocated by looking at the bottom left corner of the product record, as shown in Figure 12-9. The record shows how much of that item is in stock, how much of it is allocated and how much is free stock.

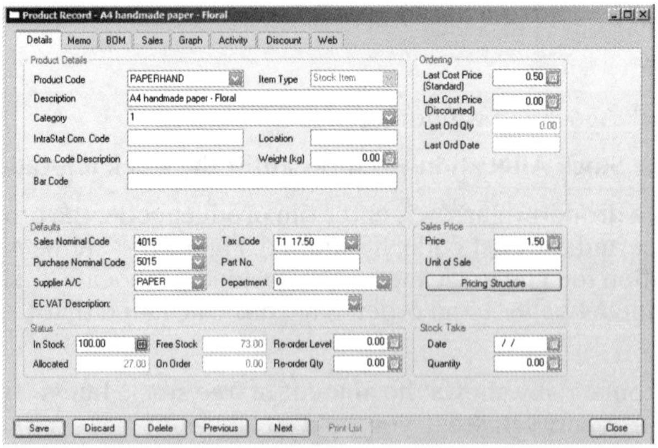

Figure 12-9:
The product record after stock is allocated.

Changing stock allocation

You can amend any previous allocations you made to stock by following these steps:

1. **From Products, click Make Allocations on the Task pane (or click the Allocate icon).**

   The Allocation window appears.

2. **Select View/Amend Allocations and click OK.**

3. **Select the product you want to amend or delete by using the dropdown arrow and click OK.**

4. **Change the allocated quantity by overtyping.**

   You can only change the quantity.

   Press **0** (zero) to remove a product allocation. By removing a product allocation, you increase the amount of free stock available for that product and reduce the allocated amount.

   For example, you may want to do this if a big order came in for a valued customer and you needed to ship it quickly. You can decide to take stock that had been previously allocated to another customer and reallocate it to your priority order.

5. **To generate a copy of the stock allocation information, click Print List.**

6. **To save the details of the stock allocation, click Save. If you want to clear the allocation, click Discard.**

If any of the stock was allocated to projects, the costs become committed to the project and you can view this stock on a committed costs report.

Issuing allocated stock

After stock has been allocated, it needs to be issued. By issuing stock, you update your stock records and stock allocation records. When issuing an allocation associated with a project, the value of the issued stock is applied to the cost of the project. In other words, Sage converts *committed costs* to *actual costs* for the project.

To issue stock, follow these steps:

1. **From Products, click Make Allocations from the Task pane or click the Allocate icon.**

2. **Click Issue Allocations and then click OK.**

   The Issue Allocations window opens, as shown in Figure 12-10.

3. **Use the dropdown arrow to select the product that you want to issue.**

   The product must be allocated before it can be issued (see the preceding section).

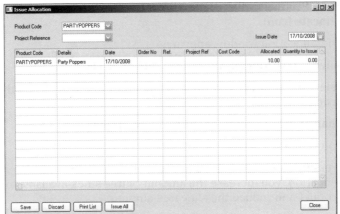

Figure 12-10:
Issuing allo-
cated stock.

4. **Enter the quantity of stock you want to issue and click Save. Alternatively, you can click Issue All.**

   You can choose to issue less than the whole quantity of stock. Only the stock you choose to issue is allocated and charged to the project; the balance remains as committed stock.

5. **To print a list of the stock allocation information, click Print List.**

6. **To issue the stock, click Save. To clear the information, click Discard.**

You need to be aware of the following rules when issuing allocated stock:

✔ When issuing stock to a project, you must ensure that the status of the project allows postings.

✔ You can't change the details of a stock allocation, such as the project reference or cost codes, during a stock issue. You can only change the stock quantity.

✔ A stock issue can't exceed the allocation amount, regardless of the negative stock setting.

Chapter 13

Managing Projects

. . . .

In This Chapter

▶ Assigning status and costs to a project

▶ Managing project resources

▶ Recording project costs, including purchase order processing

▶ Analysing project costs

▶ Charging project costs to your customers

▶ Completing a project

. . . .

Sage's Project Costing tool, available to users of Accounts Plus and Accounts Professional, enables businesses large and small to successfully manage a project.

In Chapter 3, I describe how to set up a project by using a blank record. You can follow that process or access the Project Record wizard by clicking New Project from the Projects Task pane. After you set up the project, the information in this chapter comes into play, because here I tell you how to manage projects.

With Sage, you can track costs and ensure that you capture every expenditure associated with a project. You can then charge the client a fee that produces a profit for your company. You can evaluate future projects more accurately and target your business towards more profitable ventures.

Appointing a Project's Status and Costs

Project status helps you track a project's progress. You can set the status to allow or disallow postings. Sage has five status categories for you to use according to where the project is in its life cycle.

Each status has its own rules as to whether you can make postings to it or not. Postings that assign costs to a project are usually allowed when a project is in full swing, but postings are no longer allowed in a project's later stages. You can also decide at which point in the life cycle to change a status or even when to delete the project record.

Only two statuses don't allow postings: when the project is complete and you're not expecting any more costs to come in; and if the project has been suspended.

As every project is specific to each individual business, only you determine if the status of a project needs changing. For example, when an active project comes to an end, you give it the status of *complete*. You don't want additional postings being made (even in error) to a finished project. To be absolutely sure that a completed project doesn't incur further costs, you can delete the project record after you change the status to complete. Personally, I think deleting the project record is a bit extreme; only consider deleting the project record if you no longer require any analysis information for the project.

Assigning status

- ✔ **Active:** This status indicates that a project is open and ongoing. You can make postings to the project, but you can't delete the record.

- ✔ **Snag:** Although completed, the project remains open so that you can still make final postings. You can't delete the record.

  A snagged project may be a building project, for example, at a stage where the project is essentially finished, and you've charged major costs. Now comes working out the wrinkles to rectify minor defects. During this snag phase, you can assign additional costs to the job.

- ✔ **Completed:** The job is closed and you can't post to the project. You can delete the record if you want to.

- ✔ **Suspend:** The project has been suspended. You can't post to the project or delete the record. This status usually indicates a problem with the project.

- ✔ **Initial:** The project is at a preacceptance stage. Although you can make postings to the record, you can't delete it. You can use this status for very new projects that are just getting off the ground. You may decide to start recording the costs in case the project gets the official go ahead. If it doesn't, no harm is done, but if it does go ahead, you've begun the process of recording costs and can monitor the project effectively.

You can access the Configuration Editor and change the names of the status categories to ones that suit your business better. See the 'Changing status and costs' section later in this chapter.

Looking at costs – types and codes

You give each project a project reference and use that reference when recording costs to the project by using cost types and cost codes:

- **Cost type:** A label that describes an activity or resource. Labour and materials are examples of cost types.

  A cost type on its own is meaningless – it must be associated with a cost code.

  The default cost type is *other.* This *other* cost type is linked to the default cost codes in the next point.

- **Cost code:** A *cost code* is a way to further differentiate cost types. For example, you can further divide the cost type *labour* into plumbers, carpenters, bricklayers and so on. You can create the cost code yourself, according to the needs of your business. You have just eight characters to name your cost codes, but you don't have to use all eight, so if you can get by with four characters, shorter is better. The default cost codes are labour (LAB1), materials (MAT1), overheads (OHD1) and mixed (MIX1).

A cost type can link to many cost codes, but a cost code can link to only one cost type.

You can view cost types and cost codes in the Configuration Editor, as shown in Figure 13-1.

You can set up budgets for a project against each cost code. When you apply costs to a project, it's the cost *code* that records the charge, not the cost *type*. For example, when entering a purchase invoice, you have a column for the project reference and then one for the cost code. There is no cost type column; instead, the cost codes are linked to the cost types in the Configuration Editor.

Changing status and costs

If you're using the default status set, the only time you want to change the status of the project is when it gets to a different stage in its lifecycle. For example, all projects start at the default status of *Active,* but when that project is complete, you no longer want to accept costs against that project. You need to change the status, as outlined in the last section in this chapter, 'Completing Your Project'. However, you can also change the default project status names to better describe your business needs. This section is all about how to make these changes. You can make the same name changes to the cost types and cost codes, so if you want to know how to personalise them, read on.

You can amend the project status, cost code or cost type by using the Configuration Editor window:

1. **From the main toolbar, click Settings and then click Configuration.**

   A message appears saying that this option can't be run with any other windows open. Click Yes to close all other open windows. The Configuration Editor appears.

   Alternatively, from the Projects window, you can click Project Defaults within the Links list.

2. **Click the Project Costing tab, as shown in Figure 13-1, which also shows the types of field that you can change.**

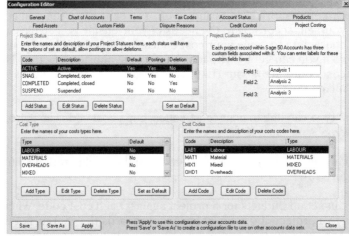

Figure 13-1: Changing your status, cost types and cost codes with the Configuration Editor.

3. **Amend the project status, cost type and or cost codes by clicking the Edit button for the relevant section and changing the necessary details.**

   For example, if you want to edit the cost codes, click Edit in the cost code section. The Edit Cost Code window appears, and you change the description or cost type and then click OK.

4. **Click Apply to use this configuration on your accounts data.**

5. **Click Close. A message appears asking if you want to save the changes. Click Yes and then click Close again.**

   The Apply button greys out when you click Yes. After clicking Close the second time, you return to the Welcome screen.

You can edit and apply your own project status names, using titles that may be more meaningful to your business.

Managing Project Resources

To undertake work on a project, you need manpower, resources and equipment. Plant and machinery, computer equipment and people cost money, and you need to apply these costs to the project.

The term *resource* applies to any cost applied to a project. For example, you apply people costs via a timesheet. You can use the timesheet to apply labour costs to a project. Machinery has some sort of hire charge or other cost associated with it, which you can also apply to the project.

When you come to record a project charge, you select the type of resource used. You can use the resource information to calculate a total cost for the charge, but you can override this as the charge is recorded.

Creating or amending a resource

You can create as many resources as you want, but each one must have a unique reference.

You can create or amend a resource as follows:

1. **From Projects, click Manage Resources in the Task pane.**

   The Resources box opens.

2. **For a new resource, click Add. To edit a resource, click Edit.**

   If you're adding a new resource, enter the details here. You must give each resource a unique reference number, a name, a unit of measure (such as hour), a cost rate and a cost code (use the dropdown arrow).

   When editing, you can't change a resource's reference number. You can change the name, the unit of measure, cost rate and cost code – but not the reference.

3. **Click OK.**

   Your newly created or amended resource appears in the Resources box.

Figure 13-2 shows Jingles' new labour resource, Megan, who is a specific, though imaginary, person. You can create resources for different people with individual charge rates. For example, you can set up each member of your staff as a resource and charge them to the specific projects they work on.

Figure 13-2:
Adding a
resource
called
Megan.

Add Resource

Reference	001
Name	Megan
Unit of measure	Hour
Cost Rate	20.00
Cost Code	LAB1

OK   Cancel

Deleting a resource

You can easily delete a resource if you find that it's no longer required.

Follow these steps:

1. **From the Projects window, click Resources.**

   Alternatively, click Manage Resources from the Task pane to open the Resources window.

2. **From the Resources window, highlight the resource that you want to delete and click Delete.**

3. **A confirmation message appears. Click Yes to delete or No to return to the Resources window.**

4. **Click Close to return to the Projects window.**

Tracking Project Costs

You can record costs or charges against a specific project as soon as they're incurred. For example, you can apply timesheets to a specific project when they're turned in. The following sections outline the mechanisms of applying costs – project charges, invoices, bank payments and stock issues – to both the accounts and projects.

To be able to apply costs to a project, the project must be set up to allow postings. Refer to the section 'Appointing a Project's Status and Costs' earlier in this chapter to find out about allowing postings.

Sharing out project charges

A project charge applies a cost to the project but doesn't charge the nominal ledger and therefore doesn't affect the accounts. This may sound a bit odd, but let me give you an example: labour costs go through the accounts by way of wages journals, which directly affect the accounts. But you can't post to Projects directly from a journal. So at a later stage, you need to allocate the applicable labour costs directly to the project by way of a project charge.

The types of project charges you can make include:

- ✔ **Labour charges:** You can take these from the rates and hours entered on timesheets.

- ✔ **Costs:** You can include costs that don't affect your stock, such as costs involving non-stock items or service items. You can't issue non-stock items to a project, so the only way to post a charge to the project for items of this nature is to process a project charge. You can only charge service items to a project this way. (Non-stock and service items are discussed in Chapter 3.)

- ✔ **Adjustments or corrections:** You can incorporate amendments to other costs for the project. For example, if you post an invoice to the wrong project, you can do a credit from the project without having to reverse the invoice. You can then put the appropriate charge through to the correct project.

Project charges are shown as transaction type CD (costing debits) in Sage, but you can also issue a cost credit (CC) if you need to make an adjustment to the project cost.

To record a *project only* cost or credit (the *only* indicates that you're only charging amounts to the project, not affecting your nominal ledger), follow these steps:

1. **From the Projects window, select the project for which you want to process a charge.**

2. **From the Projects toolbar, click Charge (or Credit if you need to credit the project).**

   The Project Charge or Project Credit window appears.

3. **Enter the details of the charge or credit in the boxes provided, using one line per charge.**

You must enter a cost code for the cost. If you don't, Sage shows an error message when you try to save the cost.

If you select a resource for the charge or credit, Sage automatically fills in the rate and cost code as the default rate from when you entered it on the resource list. You can overwrite this rate if you require.

When you enter the quantity, the program automatically calculates the total cost and displays it in the Total Cost column.

4. **To save your entries, click Save. Click Discard to exit without saving.**

5. **Click Close to return to the Projects window.**

Figure 13-3 shows a charge for the costs of hiring Claris the Clown for the Fun Day project. Claris has been set up as a resource and given a cost code of LAB1. The Fun Day project is allotted the costs of the number of hours that Claris will work.

Figure 13-3:
Applying a project charge to a project – Claris the Clown is a labour charge to the Fun Day project.

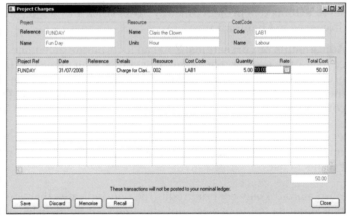

Issuing stock to a project

You often use stock on a project, and sometimes you don't use all of it. You can use the Products module to allocate stock to a project and put returned or unused products back into stock. These stock postings are shown as Adjustments In (AI) or Adjustments Out (AO) on the Product Activity screen. You can find details about allotting stock in Chapter 12. Just remember to select a project reference and ensure that the project status allows postings.

When you allocate stock to a project, that stock is set aside for the use of that project. The cost of the stock becomes a *committed cost* to the project, but it only becomes an *actual cost* to the project when the stock is issued.

Sage uses a *first in first out (FIFO)* method of allocating stock, meaning it uses the oldest stock first. If you order stock specifically for a project and get a special price for it, you have to make a price adjustment to assign the correct price to the stock allocated to the project. Otherwise, Sage uses the stock price of the oldest stock first, which may be different from the price you paid.

Use the Products module to issue the stock, which then shows up in your project reports. (See the 'Integrating POP with project costing' section later in this chapter for more information.)

Figure 13-4 shows the issue of party poppers stock to the Fun Day project. The stock shows as an adjustment out of stock and against the project.

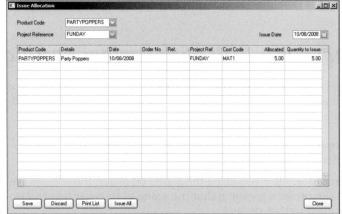

Figure 13-4:
Party pop-
per stock
issued to
the Fun Day
project.

Stock issues are a cost to the project. Usually, when stock leaves your hands, you invoice a customer, the customer pays the invoice and money subsequently flows back into the business. When you allocate stock to a project, you don't get paid for it immediately or directly.

You can use the Clear Stock option as part of your month-end or year-end routine. This option involves removing stock transactions from your product activity record, up to and including a specified date. Note that any project active at the point you clear your stock still holds the details of all the transactions showing in its product activity, so you can maintain a complete history for that project.

Counting costs from a supplier invoice

You can post purchase invoices (PI), purchase credit notes (PC) and bank payments (BP) to a project. By doing so, you update your accounts with the cost and also link the cost to your project. (To see how to post a supplier invoice, refer to Chapter 7.) Just remember to enter the project reference in the Project Reference column and enter a valid cost code in the Cost Code column.

When you post an invoice to a project, you post a value to the project, but not a quantity. The Batch Entry screen for posting invoices doesn't have a quantity column – it just registers an amount. If you need to post quantities of an item to a project, post the invoice without a project reference, and then post a separate project charge to the project.

You can apply costs using bank payments. When making a bank payment, select a project reference and a cost code. That cost is then applied to the project. (For details on how to process a bank payment, refer to Chapter 8.)

Integrating POP with project costing

As Sage is an integrated system, you can link purchase order processing (POP) and projects. The project is updated at various points of the purchase-order life cycle:

- ✔ **Creating an order:** At the time of creating an order, give a project reference and enter a cost code.

- ✔ **On order:** After you place the goods on order, those costs are *committed* to the project, meaning that the value of those goods and services is applied to that project.

- ✔ **Goods received:** After you receive the goods, you can automatically allocate them to stock and then allocate that stock to the project. You can see that the stock has been allocated to the project by clicking the product record and looking at the Stock Allocated box in the lower left corner of the record.

- ✔ **Stock issued:** After the stock is issued, the amount of allocated stock reduces; *actual costs* are applied to the project and committed costs are reduced. The transaction is shown as an AO (adjustment out of stock) transaction type and shows the project reference and cost code associated with that transaction.

   You can look at the Activity tab of the project record to see the transaction.

✔ **Invoice:** For stock items, you apply the actual cost to the project at the point the stock is issued. When stock is issued to a project, the costs convert from *committed* to *actual costs*. You can update the invoice at a later point to ensure that the accounts and supplier ledger have been updated.

You must manually issue the stock to the project by going into the Products module. The purchase order only allocates stock to your project and labels it a committed cost. When you formally issue the stock to the project, the committed costs change to actual costs.

When you update your purchase order, notice that in the Batch Supplier Invoice screen, the project reference and cost code are blank. Do *not* re-enter the project reference and cost code. If you enter the project reference on the Batch Supplier Invoice screen, you post the actual costs for a second time, thus double-counting. Click Save instead. Sage flashes up a warning message about double-counting. Click Yes to continue. You're then returned to the Purchase Order Processing window.

For non-stock items, the actual cost to the project is applied when you generate and update the invoice. When you produce a purchase order for these items, enter the project reference and cost code on the Batch Supplier screen, as it allows you to post the actual costs to the project. When you click Save, a warning message appears, saying:

```
If you have already entered a project reference for these
items on the purchase order, they will automatically
become a realised cost when the stock is issued. You may
be double-counting for these items. Are you sure you want
to continue?
```

Click Yes. As you've created a service invoice, not a stock invoice, you're not issuing any stock and therefore can't be double-counting.

You can review the value of both committed costs and actual costs by looking at the Analysis tab of the relevant project record.

Analysing Project Costs

Sage has several features that help you to track your projects and analyse your costs and revenues. Tracking and analysing gives you the ability to respond to customer enquiries about the projects.

Looking at the project's activity

When you're analysing a project, the first thing you may want to do is look at the Project Activity screen. This screen shows you all the transactions with a specific project reference. You can also filter the transactions by type with the Custom Range button, as explained in the following steps:

1. **From Projects, click the Activity tab or select the specific project and click Activity.**

   The transaction information for the project appears.

   If the project you select is a multi-level project, tick the Include Rolled Up Transactions check box to show all the transactions for all the projects linked with the one you're viewing.

2. **Filter the transactions by clicking the dropdown arrow next to the Show field to select specific calendar months or by clicking the Custom Range button.**

   Clicking the Custom Range option opens up an Activity Range window, as shown in Figure 13-5. You can view the project activity by specific transaction types or display all transactions.

Figure 13-5: Filtering the project activity with the Custom Range button.

Sage remembers the filter that you used, so the next time you view the activity, Sage applies the same filter until you change it.

You can look at the transactions that are recorded against a project. These transactions may include the following types:

✔ **CD:** A project charge (costing debit).

✔ **CC:** A project credit (costing credit).

✔ **AO:** A stock adjustment out of stock into the project.

✔ **AI:** A stock adjustment out of the project back into stock.

✔ **PI:** A purchase invoice, which you can generate from a purchase order if you have Accounts Professional.

✔ **PC:** A purchase credit note may be issued to the project.

✔ **BP:** A bank payment.

✔ **SI:** A sales invoice is issued to charge the customer, as part of the project billing process.

✔ **SC:** A credit note can be issued to the customer in respect of adjustments to the project billing process.

Stock allocations aren't displayed as part of the project activity.

As well as looking at the specific project record, you can also check the customer record associated with the project. Just access the Projects tab from the customer record to view a list of every project associated with that customer. Figure 13-6 shows the customer record for Any Town Parish Council and the Fun Day project associated with it. The record shows the price quoted for the project and the costs billed to date.

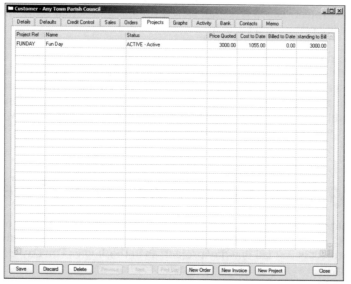

Figure 13-6:
Showing a project associated with a customer – viewed from the Projects tab of the customer's record.

Comparing costs to budget

Comparing actual costs of a project against a budget gives you an indication of how well the project is being managed. Costs at or below budget give a good indication of a well-managed project. Costs starting to exceed the budget indicate that the project is not going as planned and that costs need to be controlled. Each aspect of the project needs investigating to see why costs are exceeding budget.

To assign a budget, follow these steps:

1. **From Projects, select the project you require and click Record.**

2. **Click the Budgets tab.**

   The budget information shows all cost codes currently set up in Sage 50 Accounts.

3. **Select the Budget column for each labour cost and enter a figure.**

4. **To save your entries, click Save. Click Discard if you want to clear data and start again.**

5. **Click Close to exit the project record and return to the Projects window.**

You've now successfully applied budgets to your project.

To see how the project costs compare to the budget, click the Analysis tab on the project record. You can view a summary of actual costs, budgeted costs and committed costs here.

You can run many reports to check the progress of your project. You can run reports showing committed costs for each project; cost transactions by cost code; checking stock issued for a project and a number of day book reports allowing you to see postings to the project by various transactions types. To print a report, simply click Reports from Projects and select whichever report you require from the array of reports available.

Charging Your Customers for a Project

Ultimately, you need to charge your customers for work carried out on your project. If the project is large, you may want to do this on a continual basis. If the project is a small one-day project, as in the Jingles Fun Day example, then you invoice at the end of the project.

Project costing doesn't automatically bill your customers, but the Analysis tab of the project record helps you calculate how much to charge them. You can see how much you've billed a customer already or how much you've quoted a customer and therefore what is outstanding. Sage provides a variety of project-costing reports that can help you decide how much to charge your customer.

Figure 13-7 shows that Any Town Parish Council was quoted a price of £3,000 for a Fun Day and currently no bills have been issued, so Jingles needs to raise an invoice for the full £3,000.

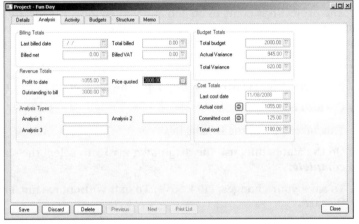

Figure 13-7: Showing the Project Analysis screen to extract data for billing purposes.

After you know how much you're going to charge, you can invoice your customer in a number of ways:

- ✔ Issue a service invoice, showing details of work carried out.

- ✔ Issue a product invoice, using special product code S3 (only if you have Accounts Professional). This product code allows you to issue service charges and product charges on the same invoice.

- ✔ Issue a product invoice, showing non-stock or service items. You can use this type of invoice if your business is service-based, but you use product records to keep track of your services or to produce price lists.

If you overcharge a customer for a project, you can credit your customer by raising a credit note. (Refer to Chapter 6 for how to raise product and service invoices.)

When you enter the invoice, you must ensure that you include the project reference and cost code. When the invoice is posted to the ledger, it updates the project activity information and the Analysis tab.

A number of reports provide you with the information necessary to produce an invoice based on time and materials used. This process isn't automated, so you need to produce your bills manually. Refer to Chapter 6 for details.

Completing Your Project

After the project has come to an end and you no longer have any invoices or transactions to post to it, you need to mark the project as being complete. Changing the status to *complete* ensures that no further postings can be made to it. Change the status of the project by following these steps:

1. **From the Projects window, highlight the project you want to complete.**

2. **Click Record.**

   This takes you to the Details tab.

3. **On the status line, use the dropdown arrow to select the status** *complete.*

4. **To save your changes, click Save. To exit without saving, click Discard.**

You've now successfully completed your project.

If at some time in the future, you no longer need to view this project record and have no need for any further analysis of the project, you may delete the project. You can only do this if the project shows the status as being complete.

To delete a project, simply highlight the project you want to delete and click Delete.

Chapter 14

Using Foreign Currencies

. . . .

. . . .

*T*his chapter is all about getting your head around the foreign currencies element of Sage. I always found this topic a bit scary, so I'm going to go through it step by step and make it as easy to understand as possible.

Discover how to set up foreign currencies in Sage and how to deal with exchange rates. You can take a look at the Foreign Trader facility and see how it fits into the day-to-day working of your business. Then find out how to deal with the paperwork when it comes to your customers, suppliers and your bank. Finally, you get the opportunity to see how you can use the Revaluation wizard.

Most of this chapter is relevant only if you have Sage 50 Accounts Professional, which has the Foreign Trader option and the capacity to process paperwork in a foreign currency. If you only have the odd foreign invoice, it's probably easier for you to process foreign invoices by converting the foreign currency to pounds sterling and processing as normal (Chapter 7 tells you how to process invoices).

This chapter mainly applies to businesses that receive multiple foreign invoices and pay suppliers in foreign currencies. I look at setting up foreign bank accounts and foreign supplier accounts to accommodate this.

Setting Up Foreign Currencies

As you're reading this chapter, you most likely deal with foreign currencies within your business. And, if you deal with foreign currencies, you need to set up those currencies in Sage.

To process an invoice in a foreign currency, you have to convert the foreign currency into your base currency, which you select when you run the Active Set-up wizard, which I cover in Chapter 1. (I assume your base currency is pounds sterling; if not, you need to convert this version of *Sage 50 Accounts For Dummies* into a different currency . . . er, language.)

In order to do the conversion, Sage needs to have exchange rates in place, but you probably already know that these are always fluctuating. Make it a point to agree a rate or set a time to check the current rate with your customers and suppliers. For example, you may agree with your supplier to use the exchange rate issued by HM Revenue and Customs (HMRC) on the first day of each week for a month, or you may set a rate to use for the whole of that month. Every circumstance is different, and you need to factor the regularity of exchange-rate fluctuations into your decision.

The HM Revenue and Customs website at `www.hmrc.gov.uk` provides useful information in the Rates and Tables section under Quick Links. Clicking the VAT link brings you to exchange rates by year and month. So, if you have a February 2008 invoice from the USA, you can select February 2008 rates of exchange and find the dollar exchange rate. You can then use this rate to convert your invoice to pounds sterling.

Entering the exchange rate for a currency

One of the best places to find exchange-rate information is the HMRC website at `www.hmrc.gov.uk`. You can enter the rates from this website into Sage so that you can utilise the foreign currencies options. To register the exchange rate, follow these steps:

1. **From the main toolbar, click Settings.**

2. **Select Currencies.**

   Pounds sterling is displayed as the base currency – the currency you selected when you first set up Sage. (Refer to Chapter 1.)

   The Currencies box opens, showing a list of all currencies available in Sage, along with the currency code and symbol (for example, US dollars is USD $). If you need to add a new currency or edit an existing one, then do it here.

Converting currencies with F5

Function key F5 works as a currency converter when you press it if you're in any numeric field. This nifty function comes in handy when you're processing your invoices in pounds sterling and converting the foreign invoice value prior to entering invoices into Sage.

Using F5 is easy: press the F5 key and a currency converter box appears. Type in the amount of foreign currency and specify which currency it is (for example, US dollars), and Sage converts it to your base currency.

Note: You need to set up the exchange rate you want to use to convert the currencies in your Currencies table. See the 'Entering the exchange rate for a currency' section later in this chapter for help on how to do this.

3. **Select the currency for which you want to enter an exchange rate.**

   The currency you select appears at the bottom of the currency screen and shows an exchange rate of zero (if you haven't already entered an exchange rate).

4. **Enter the exchange rate you want to use.**

   You can enter exchange rates for as many currencies as you require.

5. **Click Close to exit the Currencies screen and save the exchange rate details.**

You can now use the currency converter!

Amending the Countries table

The Countries table may conjure up all sorts of images, but it isn't a table of the four-legged variety with a map of the world draped on it! Instead, it consists of a list of countries and their country codes, including the current members of the European Union (EU), which are indicated by a tick in the EU column.

The Countries table doesn't link to exchange rates; it's used for the purposes of Intrastat reporting. *Intrastat* is a system that collects data about the movement of physical goods between member states of the European Union. You may have to amend the Countries table as and when countries join the European Union.

Intrastat has been in operation since January 1993 and replaced the customs declarations. The supply of services is excluded from Intrastat, which is closely linked with the VAT system. Companies who are not VAT registered have no obligations under the Intrastat system.

To amend your Countries table:

1. **From the main toolbar, click Settings and then Countries.**

   This opens up the Countries table, which has three columns showing the country, the country code and a tick box that indicates with a green tick if the country is a member of the European Union.

2. **To add a country, click Add and type the country name in the Add/Edit Country Details box that opens. To edit the details for a country, highlight its name and click Edit.**

   Figure 14-1 shows how easy it is to add a country to the Countries table. Sage automatically generates the country code.

Figure 14-1:
Adding a country to the Countries table is almost as easy as filling in the blanks.

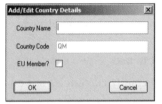

Tick the EU Member box if you're adding a country that is part of the EU. If you're editing countries, you can change EU status by clicking the EU Member box to add or remove the tick.

3. **Click OK to save the changes or Cancel to exit without saving.**

   Sage returns you to the Countries table.

4. **Click Close to exit the Countries table and return to the Welcome screen.**

Tailoring the Foreign Trader Tool

Basically, the Foreign Trader facility is the crux of the foreign currencies part of Sage. When activated, this facility can process customers and suppliers based in a foreign currency; allow you to use foreign currency bank accounts; and process invoices, credit notes, bank payment and receipts in different currencies.

A foreign currency checklist

This checklist can help guide you through the maze of working with Sage 50 Accounts and foreign currency.

❏ Activate the Foreign Trader Set-up wizard.

❏ Enter exchange rates for all currencies you use.

❏ Set up new customer accounts for those that use foreign currencies. If you have customers who are likely to pay you in more than one currency, you must use a separate customer account for each currency.

❏ Set up new foreign currency supplier accounts – and a separate account for each currency.

❏ Set up bank accounts for each foreign currency.

Two important points:

✔ After you activate the Foreign Trader option, you can't switch it off!

Activating this option causes numerous changes to the mechanics of Sage, so press F1, type **Foreign Trade** into the Help box and read the Help sheet called 'How Foreign Trader affects Sage 50 Accounts'.

And although turning Foreign Trader on is a choice, if you trade using foreign currencies, you have to activate Foreign Trader, so it's an easy decision to make!

✔ You can't use this facility if you use VAT cash accounting.

You can easily set up the Foreign Trader option by using the Foreign Trader Set-up wizard, and you can't operate the foreign currencies feature of Sage unless you use the wizard. Here's how:

1. **From the main toolbar, click Modules and then Wizards. Select the Foreign Trader Set-up wizard.**

   A warning message appears, saying that you can't run this wizard with other windows open. Click Yes to close all other windows.

2. **The wizard is split into four screens, which you deal with in turn (see the Foreign Trader screen in Figure 14-2). After you complete each screen, click Next.**

   • **The Welcome screen:** This screen explains that you need to use a nominal code to handle exchange-rate variances and to choose how you want to update exchange rates – decisions you make later in the process and which I cover later in this list.

Figure 14-2:
Welcome to
the Foreign
Trader
Set-up
wizard.

- **Currency Revaluation:** Choose the nominal code you want to use to post all your currency variations. You need this account to accommodate invoices issued with one exchange rate and paid when a different rate is in effect. The difference in rates can result in a slight over- or underpayment of that invoice. Sage recommends that you use the default nominal code of 7906. Click Next to continue.

- **Exchange Rate Update Method:** Choose the method by which you update your exchange rates. Sage recommends (as do I) that you use the default Always Prompt To Save Exchange Rate Changes, although you can choose to automatically update the currency record whenever you change an exchange rate or never to save any exchange-rate changes.

- **Finished!:** After you click Finish, Sage makes the necessary file changes to enable the Foreign Trader facility. Sage recommends that you now use the Settings, followed by Currencies menu option to check your currency codes and exchange rates that you want to use.

    If you need to make any changes, click Back. If you don't want to proceed, click Cancel. Otherwise, click Finish to activate your Foreign Trader option.

When you run the Foreign Trader option, a Currency Exchange Rate box appears in the Invoice defaults on the General tab. Using the dropdown arrow, you can choose a different exchange-rate change method from the default setting of Always Prompt To Save Exchange Rate Changes.

Keeping Trade Status in Mind when Setting Up Accounts

Getting your customer, supplier and bank records ready for foreign trade is as simple as making sure that you give them a touch of the exotic when you set them up. (Chapter 3 explains basic set-up procedures, so check there for help.)

When you set up customer and supplier records for foreign trade, don't forget to keep the following points in mind for individual records:

- Make sure that you click the correct country when entering the address of your customer or supplier.
- Select the correct currency on the Defaults tab.
- Adjust the tax code accordingly, keeping in mind that if you supply goods to a VAT-registered customer in another EU member state and the goods are moved from the UK to that EU country, your supply may be zero-rated. (Please refer to HMRC Notice 725, 'The Single Market', for more information.) Some supplies of services to overseas customers are zero-rated, but many are standard-rated. Seek advice from your local tax office.

You need a separate bank account for every currency you deal with. For example, if you trade in pounds sterling, US dollars, euros and Japanese yen, then you need four bank accounts. Sage shows you the balance in the original currency and also what it converts to in the base currency. Use these accounts just as you do any other bank account.

Be careful when entering transactions, as after a transaction is entered, you can't delete it or change its currency.

To convert a bank account to foreign currency usage, simply change the currency by using the dropdown arrow of the Currency box on the Account Details tab within the bank account. Figure 14-3 shows an example of an American bank account set-up. Notice that the Account Details tab shows a field for both the US dollar balance and the pounds sterling base currency.

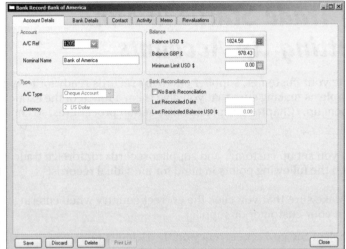

Figure 14-3:
Setting up a
foreign bank
account.

Processing the Paperwork

In the following sections, discover how to raise sales invoices and purchase invoices, using foreign currencies and then how to apply receipts and payments by using foreign currency bank accounts.

Raising invoices/credit notes and orders

You can raise invoices, credit notes and orders in the usual way (I explain the usual way in Chapter 6 for invoices and credit notes and Chapter 10 for orders). The main differences are that when you open a foreign customer record, a Rate box appears under the Address box on the Details screen of both the Invoice and Sales Order screens and the currency symbol changes from pounds sterling to the currency chosen for that customer.

You can change the currency rate in the Rate box by overtyping the current rate shown.

As you know, exchange rates fluctuate all the time, often between processing one foreign invoice and the next. But you can apply a new exchange rate as you enter your sales invoice/credit note or order. As soon as you attempt to change the exchange rate (assuming that you've accepted the defaults for the exchange-rate method), a confirmation message appears, asking if you want to update your currency record with your new exchange rate. Click Yes or No depending on your requirements.

Choosing VAT codes

You must also make sure that the VAT is showing correctly. For example, exporting goods to a customer outside the EU is normally zero-rated. (Read HMRC Notice 703, 'Exports and Removal of Goods from the UK' for confirmation.) When processing a sales invoice/credit note or order to a country that is zero-rated, make sure that the VAT is calculated using the T0 tax code.

You may need to press F3 and edit the information entered on your invoice to ensure that you've selected the correct VAT code. Click OK to apply these changes. Figure 14-4 shows an invoice for goods sold to a business in the United States.

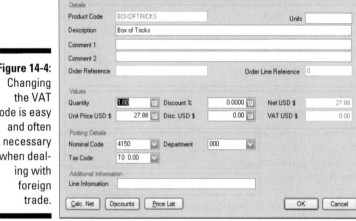

Figure 14-4:
Changing the VAT code is easy and often necessary when dealing with foreign trade.

For VAT-registered customers outside the UK but within the EU, use the tax code T4 (Sales to Customers in the EU) and make sure that you have the customer's VAT registration number on the customer record.

Other useful VAT codes include:

✔ T7 for zero-rated purchases from suppliers within the EU.

✔ T8 for standard-rated purchases from suppliers in the EU.

For EU VAT codes for purchases, Sage allocates a notional rate that's linked to the UK VAT system. For example, T8 is linked to the UK standard VAT rate of 15 per cent.

Figure 14-5 shows an invoice to American Events for a box of tricks, which retails at £15 in the UK. Sage converts this to $27.88 in US dollars.

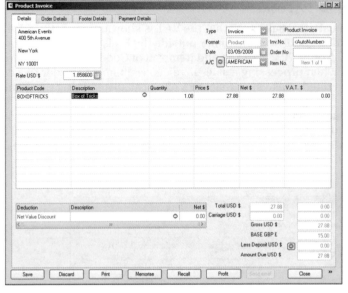

Figure 14-5:
A sales
invoice
raised to an
American
customer.

Converting currencies and viewing invoices

Although you create the invoice in a foreign currency, after you save it the invoice shows on the Invoice list in pounds sterling. So the invoice in Figure 14-5 shows a value of £15 on Jingles' Invoice list, even though the invoice itself is for $27.88 in US dollars.

After you update the invoice to both the nominal ledger and the customer ledger, the balance on the Customer screen shows in pounds sterling, just like all the other balances outstanding. If you double-click the customer record and look at the Details tab, the balance in sterling still shows, but as soon as you look at the Activity tab, you see the foreign currency, as shown in Figure 14-6. The right side of the screen shows the customer balance in US dollars and the turnover YTD (year-to-date) is shown in pounds sterling. The invoice details themselves are also in US dollars, and the balance outstanding is aged in dollars at the bottom of the screen.

Entering batch invoices and credit notes

You can use the batch-entry method of inputting invoices for both customers and suppliers in the currency that appears on their record. For example, if you have a German supplier, you can enter the invoice in euros as it appears on the German invoice.

Figure 14-7 shows an invoice from Tiki Toys in Japanese yen for some fancy-dress costumes for the clowns and the magician to wear at the children's parties that Jingles provides. The Batch Entry screen looks similar to the usual one, but has an additional Currency box showing Japanese yen, as well as the exchange rate used for processing this invoice and the T0 tax code used for zero-rated supplies.

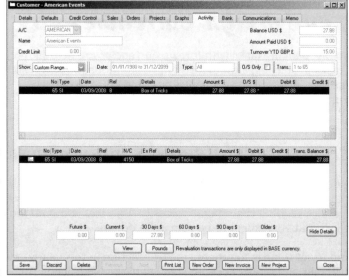

Figure 14-6: Customer activity for an American customer's account.

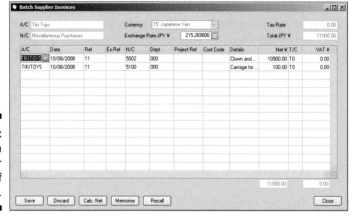

Figure 14-7: A foreign supplier batch of invoices.

After you enter the batch invoice and are happy with the details, you can save the invoice. You can now view the transaction within the supplier's Activity screen. The transaction is shown in yen, the balance on the account is in yen, but there's also a turnover year-to-date (YTD) in pounds sterling. As with the customer Activity screen, the balance outstanding is aged into current, 30 days, 60 days, 90 days and older.

Banking on Foreign Currencies

Essentially, banking tasks with foreign currencies are no different than the same tasks in sterling, although you have additional boxes on some of the screens that highlight the exchange rate, and you see references to the foreign currency.

Customer receipts and supplier payments

When dealing with businesses and customers in foreign countries you expect to receive and send invoices and payments in different currencies. For example, if you're sending customer invoices to America, you send the invoice in US dollars and you expect to be paid in US dollars.

The important thing is to process the transaction in the same currency from the customer or supplier account through to the bank account.

On some occasions, you receive money in a foreign currency that doesn't relate to any invoices you issued. And sometimes, you may need to make foreign currency payments where you have no invoice associated with the payment. To accommodate these invoice-less transactions, follow the procedure explained in Chapter 8 as a bank payment or bank receipt, noting that the Bank Account screen shows the currency along with the exchange rate you entered in the Currency table. You can change this rate if required. Depending on the defaults chosen, you may also be able to update your currency record here as well.

The Net and Tax columns show the currency code associated with that bank account. For example, if it's a US dollar account, you see the $ sign at the top of the Net and Tax columns.

Depositing foreign currencies

You process receipts in a foreign currency in the bank account that you set up to deal with that type of money – Japanese yen in the yen bank account, euros in the euros account and so on. So, when Jingles receives payment from American Events for the sum of $27.88, it's deposited in the US dollar account.

Process a receipt in foreign currency as follows:

1. **From Bank, highlight the bank account for which you're processing a receipt and then click Customer.**

2. **Select the customer account.**

   Outstanding invoices then appear in the main part of the screen.

3. **Enter the date of the receipt.**

   Sage automatically defaults to the current day's date, so change it if you need to.

4. **Enter a reference.**

   Putting a paying-in slip or BACS reference is a good idea.

5. **Make sure that you entered the correct exchange rate in your Currency table and change it as needed.**

   If you used the HMRC website to obtain your previous exchange rate, check that the rate is still valid; if not, you must amend it.

6. **Enter the amount received against the invoice or click Pay In Full in the Receipt box.**

7. **Click Save to process the data or Discard to exit without saving.**

8. **Click Close to exit the Customer Receipt screen.**

   Clicking Close returns you to the Bank screen.

Paying a foreign supplier

Undoubtedly you expect to pay the foreign invoices you receive, and people generally like to receive the currency in which the invoice was sent – you do yourself, don't you?

As an example, look at what happens when Jingles pays Tiki Toys for the fancy-dress outfits. The total amount outstanding on the account is ¥11,000. Jeanette processes this transaction through the Japanese bank account in the usual way (refer back to Chapter 7 for a reminder on how to process supplier payments).

Doing a bank transfer

Bank transfers need to be made to open new accounts in foreign currencies and put in some working capital. In this section, I describe how to make transfers from your base currency to a foreign currency and from one foreign currency to another.

Use the exchange rate shown in the table at www.hmrc.gov.uk and follow these steps:

1. **From Bank, click the Transfer icon.**

2. **Using the dropdown arrows, select the account you want to transfer from and the account you want to transfer to.**

   The Reference and Description fields have details entered already, but you can change these to something more meaningful to you.

3. **Use the dropdown arrow to select a department (if required).**

4. **Enter the date of the transaction.**

5. **Enter the amount that you want to transfer from account to account.**

6. **Enter the exchange rate you want to use if you're transferring from your base currency to a foreign currency account.**

   The Bank Transfer screen for foreign to foreign bank accounts, shown in Figure 14-8, appears slightly more complicated than the screen for transferring from a UK account to a foreign account because Sage needs to calculate the exchange-rate conversion between two foreign accounts.

   If you're transferring funds between foreign currency accounts, you must enter the currency amount that you're transferring from and Sage automatically calculates the value of currency to be received in the other foreign account, which shows in the Receipt Value field. Sage uses the exchange rates shown in the Currency table for the two currencies involved.

7. **Click Save or click Discard to exit without saving.**

Figure 14-8 shows a 5 August transfer of $200 in US dollars from the Bank of America into Jingles' Japanese bank account. Sage calculates the value to be received in yen for the Bank of Japan and deposits the proper sum – in this case, ¥23,164.64 – in the Japanese bank account. Jingles can use the money in this account to pay its Japanese suppliers and receive payments from Japanese customers.

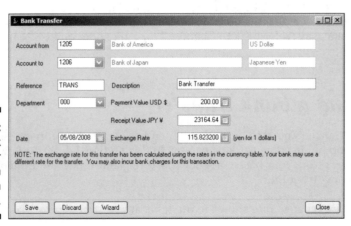

Figure 14-8:
A bank transfer between two foreign accounts.

When you perform bank transfers between foreign accounts and you enter a payment value for a transfer from a particular account, Sage uses the exchange-rate information held within the Currency table to calculate the receipt value in the other account. If you decide to change any part of the information in this transaction, Sage may need to recalculate the figures. The program makes these changes according to the order in which you change the data.

For further information on how Sage deals with a number of different scenarios regarding changes of information on the Bank Transfer screen, type **foreign bank transfers** into Sage Help.

Expecting changing exchange rates

Exchange rates vary from month to month, often from day to day. So it's very likely that the exchange rate changes between the time you receive an invoice and the date that you pay it.

When you're posting invoices and making payments to your ledgers, you do so in the relevant foreign currency. For example, a $100 invoice is likely to prompt a $100 payment in US dollars. That payment clears the balance on the account to zero, which is all well and good, but it doesn't take into account any exchange-rate differences that occurred between posting the invoice and posting the payment. However, Sage is secretly working in the background to make adjustments for exchange-rate fluctuations.

To accommodate exchange-rate differences, Sage cleverly creates a dummy invoice with the reference Reval (short for Revaluation). Sage works out the differences on the two parts of the invoice and posts the necessary adjustment using the 7906 exchange-rate-variance nominal code. If the exchange rate works in your favour so that you pay less than invoiced, Sage posts purchase credit notes to account for the exchange-rate fluctuations.

You can view these adjustments by looking at the nominal activity of account 7906. (See Chapter 20 to see how to access a Nominal Activity report). In addition, opening the foreign supplier record and clicking the Activity tab reveals a button at the bottom of the screen that says Pounds. Click this to see the transactions in pounds sterling and not the foreign currency.

Figure 14-9 shows Jingles' supplier record for Tiki Toys. Between the time Jingles ordered fancy-dress costumes from the supplier and the time the invoice was paid, the exchange rate changed, so that instead of paying £51.09, the ¥11,000 was worth £57.09, so the fancy-dress costumes cost £6 more due to currency fluctuations. Sage automatically posted the necessary adjustments into nominal account 7906, which you can see on the Activity screen with REVAL in the Ref column.

These exchange-rate revaluations go on all the time as you continue to process your foreign currency transactions. For more information on this, type **exchange rate fluctuations** into Sage Help, and it shows you more examples of different types of transactions that are affected by exchange-rate fluctuations.

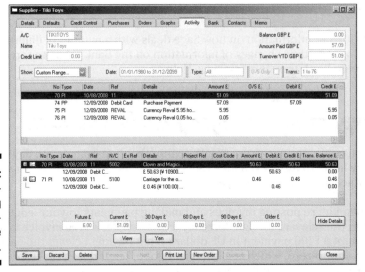

Figure 14-9: Accommodating exchange-rate fluctuations.

Doing Revaluations with the Wizard

The Revaluation wizard is pretty useful for keeping your monthly foreign currency bank accounts straight. Sage does a lot of automatic adjustments in the background, but from a housekeeping point of view, you need to ensure that you update and review all your foreign currency bank accounts on a regular basis. Doing this at the end of the month ensures that your financial reports give the correct figures.

For example, a bank account with a balance of $996.70 at an exchange rate of 1.9967 is £1,000. But at the month-end, if the exchange rate falls to 1.8649, the account has £1,070.67. You need to take account of these fluctuations by running the Revaluation wizard, as shown in Figure 14-10.

To run the Revaluation wizard, follow these steps:

1. **From the main toolbar, click Modules⇨Wizards⇨Foreign Bank Revaluation Wizard.**

   The Revaluation wizard opens with the Welcome screen, shown in Figure 14-10.

Figure 14-10:
Running
the Foreign
Bank
Revaluation
wizard.

2. **Click Next to proceed. Using the dropdown arrow, select the currency you want to revalue. Highlight the accounts that you want to revalue and then click Next.**

3. **Enter the date that you want to revalue. Click Next to proceed.**

   The last day of a month is a good date.

4. **Enter the exchange rate for the foreign currency on the date of revaluation. Click Next to continue.**

5. **Check that the details of the revaluation are correct before clicking Next.**

6. **Select Finish to post the revaluation amount or cancel.**

   The final screen advises you that the wizard is about to post journal transactions (using your revaluation control account nominal code) to revalue your foreign currency bank accounts.

You can check the journals that have been posted by visiting your audit trail in Financials.

You can also check revaluations from the Revaluations tab of the bank record, where you see the date of the revaluation and the exchange rate used. You can make changes to these revaluations. Sometimes you may need to make corrections to the exchange rate used or even reverse the revaluation altogether if you think that an error has been made.

To amend the exchange rate previously used in a revaluation, follow these steps:

1. **From Bank, select the bank account to which you want to make the adjustment and click Record to open up the bank record.**

2. **Click the Revaluations tab.**

3. **Click Show Balances.**

   The information updates to show the foreign balance and the prior base currency balance. The revalued base balance also shows.

   Note that the Edit and Reverse buttons are also activated and available to use. The Reverse button comes in handy when you've made a complete pig's ear and want to reverse the transaction. If you click the Reverse button, Sage automatically reverses the revaluation and creates and posts the appropriate journals to the necessary accounts.

4. **Select the revaluation that you want to adjust and click Edit.**

5. **Change the exchange rate in the Edit Revaluation box.**

6. **Click OK to complete the adjustment or Cancel to take you back to the Bank Record Revaluation tab.**

Part IV
Running Monthly, Quarterly and Annual Routines

'Reading your accounts in the tea leaves
is not really very satisfactory, Miss Jones.'

In this part . . .

You need to perform certain routines regularly – some monthly, some quarterly and some at the end of the year. The chapters in this part look at the procedures that you need to carry out when you prepare monthly accounts and year-end reports.

The VAT return is a key quarterly deadline that VAT-registered businesses have to meet: I give you information on what to do in Chapter 17.

Chapter 15

Reconciling Your Bank Accounts

. . . .

In This Chapter

▶ Valuing the importance of bank reconciliations

▶ Preparing to do your bank reconciliation

▶ Reconciling your bank account

▶ Checking things out when things don't check out

▶ Clearing up items that haven't cleared

. . . .

*A*re you the type of person who likes to know to the penny what's in your bank account? If so, then this is the chapter for you! Reconciling your bank accounts normally forms part of your monthly accounting routine. Running through the bank reconciliation process gives you a thorough review of your bank statements and provides a good opportunity to investigate any unusual or incorrect transactions. As a result, you're fully aware of the financial transactions flowing in and out of your bank accounts.

Recognising Reasons to Reconcile

Performing a bank reconciliation requires you to check that you've matched all the bank transactions in Sage against the entries on your bank statements. Ultimately, you should be able to tick off every item on your bank statement against a corresponding entry in Sage.

Most businesses have at least one current account, a deposit account and possibly a business credit card, as well as a petty cash tin. Each one needs to have statements of one sort or another. Sage assumes that you have all these accounts and provides default accounts for each one, which you can rename or add to as required. (Refer to Chapter 3 for how to amend accounts.) Additionally, Sage includes a Building Society account and Credit Card Receipts account as default accounts, as shown in Figure 15-1.

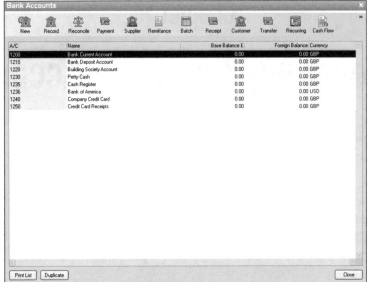

Figure 15-1:
The bank
accounts
Sage
assumes
you to have.

After you reconcile the accounts, you can be sure that the data entered is accurate, as well as any reports run from the information.

You need to reconcile all your bank accounts to ensure the accuracy of the accounting records. Reconciling all bank accounts is important, particularly if you're VAT registered, because in doing so you pick up all transactions that have VAT associated with them. Credit cards transactions in particular can attract a lot of VAT. If you don't reconcile credit card statements, you can miss VAT-liable transactions and render both the accounts and the VAT return incorrect.

When you set up your bank records, you're given the opportunity to determine whether you want the bank account to be a reconciling one or not. If you don't want to reconcile an account, simply click the bank record and put a tick in the No Bank Reconciliation box. However, use this feature with caution! Most bank accounts need to be reconciled to ensure accuracy of information.

Doing your bank reconciliations on a regular basis not only guarantees the accuracy of your information, but also gives you the ability to run meaningful reports that help you manage your business and enable you to make sensible decisions.

Getting Ready to Reconcile

The aim of a reconciliation is to match transactions in Sage with your bank statement, so the process is easier if you've entered as many transactions as possible prior to looking at the bank statement. Before starting a reconciliation, make sure that you've accomplished the following tasks:

- ✔ **Entered all the payments from your cheque stubs for the period you're reconciling**: Refer to Chapter 7 for a reminder on how to process supplier payments and Chapter 8 for all other payment types.

- ✔ **Entered the receipts from your paying-in book, up to and including the date to which you're reconciling**. Refer to Chapter 5 for help with processing customer receipts and Chapter 8 for recording other bank receipts.

Make sure that you enter the cheque numbers and payslip numbers in the Reference field so that you can easily identify those items on your statement.

Have a copy of your bank statements in front of you and check them for any other transactions that aren't yet in Sage, but that you can input before the reconciliation. Items in this last-minute batch may include:

- ✔ Bank interest (both paid and received).

- ✔ Bank charges.

- ✔ Direct debits – to pay suppliers, for example.

- ✔ Direct credits or BACS from customers.

- ✔ Transfers between accounts.

Tick off the items on your bank statement as you enter them onto Sage. That way, you can see if you missed anything that needs to be entered.

Doing the Actual Reconciliation

You need your bank statements in front of you as you work through the reconciliation process, so have them at hand (where they should be if you prepared properly according to the tips I offer in the preceding section).

TIP

If you mark each item with a tick as you enter it onto Sage, you can then put a line through the tick or use a highlighter pen to indicate that you've reconciled that item. Make your mark visible, so that you can easily spot anything that hasn't been reconciled. Figure 15-2 shows an example of a bank statement with marks for items entered and reconciled in this way. The payments are all entered onto Sage and reconciled; the receipts have been entered, but aren't yet reconciled.

BISI BANK LTD
Statement Period ended 30.04.08

Account No: 51235467   Sortcode: 21.45.85

		Payments	Receipts	Balance
01.04.08	Account Opened			£0
01.04.08	100001		£2000 ✓	£2000
01.04.08	Cheque No 1	£100 ✗		£1900
15.04.08	Cheque No 2	£29.38 ✗		£1870.62
15.04.08	100002		£200 ✓	£2070.62
15.04.08	DD Denby DC	£120 ✗		£1950.62
30.04.08	balance carried forward			£1950.62

Figure 15-2:
A bank statement with the different types of ticks.

To begin the reconciliation process, follow these steps:

1. **From the navigation bar, click Bank.**

   Make sure that your cursor is highlighting the bank account you want to reconcile. Sage defaults to account 1200, which is the Bank Current account, so move the cursor if necessary.

2. **Click Reconcile to bring up a statement summary, as shown in Figure 15-3.**

3. **Enter the statement summary information.**

   Your statement summary contains the following fields for you to fill in:

   • **Statement reference:** Give your statement a reference, such as the month you're reconciling through, if you want the reconciliation to be archived into History. Archiving the statement means that you can pull up a copy of that bank reconciliation at any point in the future. Otherwise, you can leave this field blank, and the statement won't be archived. The reference is used to name the PDF document created when archived.

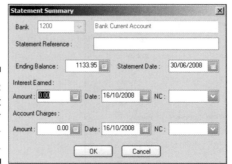

Figure 15-3:
Statement
summary for
bank recon-
ciliation.

- **Ending balance:** Enter the final balance shown on the bank statement for the period you're reconciling.

  Most people reconcile to the end of the month, but I find it easier to reconcile a page at a time: you have fewer transactions to reconcile, which means fewer transactions to check back through in the event of an error (yes, errors happen to the best of us!). To reconcile by page, simply use the balance at the bottom of the statement page and reconcile each item on that single page.

- **Statement date:** Sage automatically defaults to today's date, so change this to the date of the bank statement you're reconciling.

- **Interest earned:** If there's any interest received on the bank statement, enter it here. Alternatively, you can enter any interest as an adjustment in Step 6.

- **Account charges:** Enter any bank charges on this screen, or enter an adjustment on the Bank Reconciliation screen in Step 4.

4. **Click OK to bring up the Bank Reconciliation screen, shown in Figure 15-4.**

   If you click OK without changing any of the information on the statement summary, you still get the opportunity to change both the statement balance and date on the actual Reconciliation screen itself.

   The screen is split into two parts. The top part shows all the transactions currently entered in Sage that need to be matched against the bank statement (up to and including the statement-end date, shown at the top of the screen). Items move to the bottom part of the screen after you match them against the bank statement. The bottom screen also shows any account charges or interest earned if you entered it on the statement summary, as well as showing you the last reconciled balance. If it's the first time a reconciliation has been performed, the last reconciled balance is zero. Otherwise, the balance from the previous reconciliation shows.

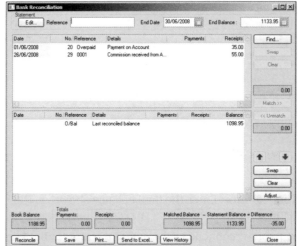

Figure 15-4:
The Bank
Recon-
ciliation
screen.

Sage only brings up transactions posted to the system up to the statement-end date that you enter on the Summary screen.

In Figure 15-4, the end date is 30 June, so only items dated on or before that date appear. If you didn't specify a date on the Summary screen, Sage brings up *all* transactions posted to the system date, which is the current day's date, so you're looking at quite a few transactions!

You can change the statement-end balance and the date whilst in the Bank Reconciliation screen by overtyping the date and end balance at the top of the screen.

5. **Match items on Sage against the bank statement.**

   Match each item on your bank statement against the same item in the top part of the Bank Reconciliation screen.

   To match an item, double-click the item in the top box, or highlight it and click the Match Transaction button to the right of the screen. As soon as you match an item, it moves to the bottom part of the screen and the values of the Matched Balance and the Difference boxes at the bottom right of the screen change accordingly.

   As you double-click each item in Sage, make a corresponding mark on the bank statement. If you ticked items on the statement, put a cross through the same tick or highlight the item. You can then identify anything not reconciled at the end.

   If you move a transaction to the bottom section in error, just double-click the transaction or highlight the transaction and click Unmatch Transaction, and it moves back to the unmatched items at the top.

The three boxes at the bottom right corner of the screen keep track of the balance between the transactions you match and what your statement says. If you get everything to agree, the Difference box contains a zero.

6. **Click the Adjust button (above Difference at the bottom right of the screen) to make any adjustments.**

   You may find that you missed inputting an entry that's on the bank statement. If the transaction is a customer BACS receipt or a supplier direct debit/switch payment, you need to save the bank reconciliation (see Step 7) and use the Customer Receipt or Supplier Payment option. But you can enter most other entries directly, using the Add Adjustment feature, as shown in Figure 15-5.

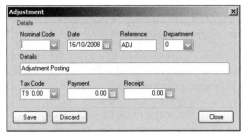

Figure 15-5: Adding an adjustment directly to your bank reconciliation.

Complete the following boxes:

- **Nominal Code:** For example, bank interest is 7900.

- **Date:** Enter the date of the transaction.

- **Reference:** Sage automatically uses ADJ for adjustment, but you can change this.

- **Department:** Use a department number, as applicable.

- **Details:** For example, something like, 'bank interest to 15 Feb 09'.

- **Tax Code:** Choose VAT standard, exempt or otherwise – T9 for bank interest.

- **Payment/Receipt Amount:** Use Payment if it's interest paid.

Take care when completing the last box. You can easily post a bank payment rather than a bank receipt, as this is the first box you come to.

When you're happy with the information input, click Save to post the adjustment automatically to the reconciled items section at the bottom of the screen.

7. **Save the reconciliation.**

Ideally, you work through the bank reconciliation until you've matched all your items from the bank statement. However, life isn't like that. Your phone may ring, or someone walks into your office for a chat. Save the work you've done so far by clicking the Save button, near the bottom left of the screen, and then click OK.

When you're ready to continue reconciling, click the Reconcile icon. A pop-up screen asks whether you want to use the saved statement or discard it. Click the Use Saved button, and Sage takes you back to the point where you left off.

Clicking Discard Saved wipes out your previous work, and you have to start your reconciliation again.

8. **Reconcile your bank transactions.**

All your transactions match, and the Difference box reads zero, so click the Reconcile button on the bottom left of your screen.

Sage saves your reconciled statement in a history file (providing you gave your reconciliation a reference on the Statement Summary screen), and you can review it later if you need to.

To access your archived reconciliations, click the Bank Reconcile button and then the View History button at the bottom of the screen. A list of PDF files appears, displaying your historical bank reconciliations, as shown in Figure 15-6. Double-click the one you want to view, and the PDF file opens.

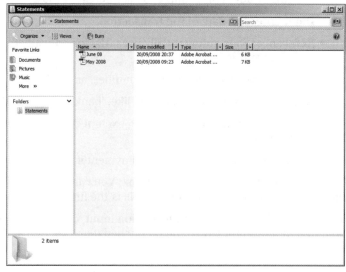

Figure 15-6:
View the historical bank reconciliations.

Troubleshooting when Your Account Doesn't Reconcile

Hopefully, your accounts always reconcile, especially because you've followed my suggestions to the letter. But, if they don't, try these suggestions:

- ✔ See if every item on your bank statement has been ticked off. You may have missed something, which is easy to do when you have lots of transactions on a page or lots of pages in a statement.

- ✔ Make sure that all the items left on the top part of the screen haven't yet cleared the bank account. On a bank statement several pages long, you can easily overlook a transaction, especially if you're going through the statement page by page.

- ✔ As a last resort, check off each item again, perhaps this time circling the items on the bank statement to differentiate your markings. You may have entered and ticked the same entry twice. If you have, double-click the offending item in the matched section of the Bank Reconciliation screen to unmatch it. You then need to find the transaction number of that item and delete it.

After you make sure that your difference is zero, you're in a position to save or reconcile.

If you reconcile a transaction by mistake, you can fix it by going into File Maintenance, clicking Corrections and finding that transaction. Click Edit Item, uncheck the Bank Reconciled box and save the changes. Click Yes to confirm the changes. The next time you open the bank reconciliation, that transaction appears.

Rounding Up Stragglers

You may find that even though the Difference box is zero, you still have some unmatched items in the top part of the screen. Not to worry; this is perfectly normal. It just means that you've entered cheques or receipts that haven't cleared the bank account and therefore don't show on the current bank statement.

For example, if you're preparing accounts to the end of March, you need to ensure that you've entered all cheques up to and including 31 March. However, the 31 March bank statement may not include cheques you wrote on 31 March – or even 30 March or 29 March – because they haven't cleared your bank yet. Your cheque may still be sitting on your supplier's desk, waiting for someone to take it to the bank.

Cheques that show on Sage, but aren't yet on your bank statement, are known as *unpresented cheques.* You may also have an *outstanding lodgement* or two – a deposit paid in toward the end of the month that doesn't appear on your bank statement because it hasn't cleared the banking system.

Listing unpresented cheques and outstanding lodgements

At the year-end, your accountant needs to perform a traditional bank reconciliation and has to know what the outstanding cheques and lodgements are. Figure 15-7 shows an example, using some of Jingles' figures.

You can print a list of unpresented cheques and outstanding lodgements at the end of any month, but the traditional bank reconciliation, as shown in Figure 15-7, is often done only at the year-end.

Figure 15-7:
The bank reconciliation that your accountant likes to prepare.

Bank Reconciliation as at 30th June 2008	
	£
Balance per Bank Statement	1133.95
Less unpresented cheques	0.00
Add back outstanding lodgements	55.00
Balance per Cash book	1188.95

Although Sage doesn't provide a traditional bank reconciliation layout, you can print reports that show the unpresented cheques and outstanding lodgements. Click the Report icon within the Bank module and select Unreconciled Transaction Reports and then Unreconciled Payments or Unreconciled Receipts – or both, one after the other.

If Sage can't find any transactions for the report, it informs you that no trans-actions have been found. If you expect transactions, make sure that you've highlighted the correct bank accounts and run the report again.

Remembering recurring entries

The Recurring Entries feature helps speed up the data-entry process, particu-larly where you have the same type of entries occurring every month. Set up the recurring entries and you no longer have the laborious task of entering them manually each month! Refer to Chapter 8 to find out how.

Entering recurring entries only works when the value is the same each month, but can be used for:

- ✔ **Regular supplier payment on accounts**: You may be paying off a large supplier balance in instalments. Set up a regular payment on account to that supplier by using recurring entries.

- ✔ **Customer payment on accounts**: You may have a customer who pays you a regular amount each month or week.

- ✔ **Bank receipt and payments**: You may have loans that go out of your account on a regular basis, for example, car or equipment loans.

- ✔ **Bank transfers**: You may want to transfer a regular sum of money into a deposit account in order to put money aside for bills, such as VAT or PAYE.

- ✔ **Nominal journals (both Debits and Credits)**: If you're confident with your double-entry bookkeeping, you may have regular journals for the same value that need to be done each month.

Chapter 16

Running Your Monthly and Yearly Routines

. . . .

In This Chapter

▶ Entering accruals

▶ Recording prepayments

▶ Deducting depreciation

▶ Juggling journals

▶ Running month-end tasks

▶ Counting on the cash-flow facility

▶ Carrying out year-end routines

. . . .

*T*he nominal ledger lists all the nominal codes that your company uses. These nominal codes, when grouped together, form the record of your company's assets, liabilities, income and expenditure. They are grouped together in categories identified in your Chart of Accounts, which I talk about in Chapter 2.

Sage uses the accounting principle of *accrual accounting*. Accrual accounting isn't just about accruals (bizarre as it sounds!), but about recording sales and purchases when they occur, not when cash changes hands; you match revenue with expenditure. For example, if you're preparing the accounts for the month of June, you need to make sure that you enter all the sales invoices for June even if you haven't been paid for them yet. You also check that all the purchase invoices relating to June are posted, so that you get an accurate reporting position.

In this chapter, I show you how to run wizards and create journals by using the nominal codes to run the monthly routines and yearly routines. You need these routines to produce timely and accurate reports for management decision-making.

If you leave this chapter with just one tip, I hope you remember that checklists are vitally important to the smooth running of both month-end and year-end processes. You can design your own checklist or use the wizards to guide you through the processes, but either way, you need a routine.

If you're not running Accounts Plus or Accounts Professional, you can't perform some of the steps outlined in this chapter. Instead of benefiting from the wizards, you have to manually process your accruals, prepayments and depreciation by using a nominal journal. If you're not happy dealing with journals, then leave this for your friendly accountant!

Adding Up Accruals

An *accrual* is an amount you know you owe for a product or service you've received, but for which you haven't yet received the invoice. An accrual occurs for items that you pay in arrears, such as telephone bills. To maintain an accurate set of accounts, you post an accrual into your nominal ledger by using the appropriate journals. These journals increase the costs to the business and create an accrual for the value of the outstanding invoice. The accrual is treated as a liability within the accounts as the business owes money. As soon as you receive the bill, you can reverse the accrual.

Charging a monthly amount for a service that's normally paid in arrears has a smoothing effect on company profits. For example, a £3,000 telephone bill that's paid quarterly is accrued in the accounts for the three months prior to receiving the bill, and a charge of £1,000 is put through the accounts each month. Otherwise, the first two months of the quarter show artificially high profits and the third month shows artificially low profits when the full cost of the telephone bill hits the Profit and Loss account in one go. Obviously, the cumulative effect over the three months is the same, but the monthly effect can make the difference between a profit and a loss for that company. So reviewing your accruals and prepayments (which I talk about in the next section) is important for monthly reporting purposes.

If you're confident with your double-entry bookkeeping, you can post a debit to the Cost accounts and a credit to the Accruals account. However, Sage likes to make things easy for you and provides a wizard you can use to set up adjustments for any invoices you're likely to pay in arrears.

To access the wizards and set up the accruals, follow these steps:

1. **From Company, click the Accruals icon.**

   The Accruals window opens up.

2. **Click Wizard to open the Nominal Ledger Accruals wizard.**

3. **Select the code for which you want to set up an accrual. Click Next.**

4. **Enter a description about the accrual. Click Next to continue.**

   For example, 'Telephone accrual for June–Sept 2008'.

5. **Enter the total amount of the accrual. Click Next to continue.**

   In the three-month telephone bill example, you enter £3,000.

6. **Enter the number of months the accrual runs and, if you're using departments, enter the department to which the cost is allocated. Click Next to continue.**

   The telephone bill time period is three months.

7. **Review all the details you've entered and then click Finish to finalise the accrual or Back to change any of the details. If you're not happy with the accrual and want to clear it, click Cancel.**

8. **Click Save after the accrual appears on the Accruals list.**

   A confirmation message appears saying that the accruals will be posted to the ledgers when you run the month-end option.

Alternatively, if you're happy with the accrual process and don't need to be guided step by step with your friendly wizard, you can set up a nominal ledger accrual as follows:

1. **From Company, click Accruals.**

2. **Manually fill in the fields in the Accruals window.**

   Enter the following information:

   - **Nominal Code:** Using the dropdown arrow, select the nominal code affected by the accrual.

     In the telephone bill example, the code is 7502.

   - **Details:** Enter details of the accrual. These details show up in the Nominal Activity reports.

   - **Department:** Enter the department if required.

   - **Accrual Nominal Code:** This field is set to the default accrual nominal code of 2109. Don't change this code, because it's a control account. Of course, if you're not using the Sage default codes and chose a customised set of nominal codes during Active Set-up (refer to Chapter 1), your accrual account may have a different code.

   - **Value:** Enter the total value of the accrual. In the telephone bill example, the amount is £3,000.

- **Months:** Put in the number of months to spread the accrual over, from between one and twelve months.

- **Monthly Amount:** Sage automatically calculates this field after you enter the total amount and the number of months. It shows the monthly amount that's debited when you run the month-end Post Accruals option.

3. **After you're happy with the information entered for your accruals, click Save.**

   A confirmation message appears, saying that these details will be posted to Sage when the month-end option is run. The accrual now appears on the Accruals list.

Unfortunately, if you're using the basic Sage Accounts program, you have to complete a nominal journal for your accruals, as you don't have the luxury of getting Sage to work it out for you. For the telephone costs example, the double-entry is a debit to the cost code (telephone 7502) and a credit to default accrual code 2109.

Counting Out Prepayments

A *prepayment* is basically payment in advance for services you haven't completely received. For example, your business buys a year-long radio advertising programme for £12,000, which is invoiced in March. The invoice is entered in March for the full value of the advertising programme, which is clearly not right as most of this invoice relates to a future period of time. So you create a prepayment for the 11 months of advertisements to come.

Registering a prepayment has the effect of decreasing the cost code in the expenses and increasing the Prepayments account in the debtors ledger because you've paid in advance for services that haven't been supplied in their entirety (effectively, the supplier owes you).

You can set up prepayments in much the same way as accruals. If you want to use the wizard method, follow these steps:

1. **From Company, click Prepayments.**

   The Prepayments window opens.

2. **Click Wizard.**

   The Nominal Ledger Prepayments wizard opens.

3. **Select the nominal code for which you want to set up the prepayment.**

   In the advertising example, you set up an advertising prepayment, using the nominal code 6201.

You can sort the nominal code list into alphabetical or numerical order by clicking the field with the word Name or Nominal Code. But you can only do this whilst in the nominal record. The system doesn't allow you to sort differently whilst trying to set up the code in the Prepayments screen.

4. **Enter the description of the prepayment. Click Next to continue.**

   For example, the advertisement description may read, 'Radio Advertising Prepayment April 08–February 09'. (The prepayment is only for 11 months because the initial payment paid the bill for March.)

5. **Enter the total amount for the prepayment. Click Next to continue.**

   In the advertising example, the total amount is £12,000.

6. **Enter the number of months the prepayment is for and the department, if any, to which you want to allocate the cost. Click Next to continue.**

7. **Review the summary of the prepayment. Click Finish if you're happy with the details or click Back if you want to change some details. Click Cancel to exit without saving.**

   After you click Finish, the prepayment appears on the list of prepayments.

8. **Click Save. A confirmation message appears, saying that the payments will only be posted when you run the month-end option. Click OK.**

   You're then returned to the Nominal Ledger window.

An alternative method of setting up the prepayment is to follow Step 1, but instead of clicking the wizard, simply enter the details directly onto the screen manually (see the example in the preceding 'Adding Up Accruals' section). This method is quicker, as you're not clicking through so many screens. After you use the wizard once, you don't need to continue using it in the future.

Again, if you're using plain Sage Accounts, your nominal journal double-entry is a debit to Prepayments and a credit to the cost code.

Depreciating Fixed Assets

A *fixed asset* is an item likely to be held in the business for more than 12 months. They're usually big and expensive items that have a long useful life, such as machinery, land, buildings, cars and so on.

Because fixed assets last so long, you can't charge the Profit and Loss account with their full value. Instead, you have to *depreciate* the asset, assigning a proportion of the asset to the Profit and Loss account and offsetting that amount against any profits you make.

Depreciation is an accounting method used to gradually reduce the value of a fixed asset in the accounts. (Otherwise known as *writing down your assets*). Depreciation applies a charge through the Profit and Loss account and reduces the value of the asset in the Balance Sheet.

If you have many different types of assets, figuring out individual depreciation amounts can become quite time-consuming. Fortunately, Sage has a Fixed Asset Register that enables you to enter the details of each asset (refer to Chapter 3 for more on assets) and the method of depreciation you intend to use. Each time you run your month-end option, Sage calculates the depreciation due for each asset and automatically posts this to the appropriate accounts.

Writing down your assets

Sage provides two accepted methods of calculating depreciation and a write-off facility; if you use the Fixed Asset Register, Sage calculates the depreciation for you.

Some people prefer to depreciate their assets manually by posting a nominal journal each month. In fact, for those of you who don't have Accounts Plus or Accounts Professional, that is exactly what you have to do, as fixed asset records aren't available in the Accounts entry-level program. (Perhaps you should have spent that extra bit of money!)

You can choose your method of depreciation, but after you have, you must use the same method consistently every year. This method becomes part of your Accounting Policy and is referred to in the Notes to the Accounts section of your year-end accounts if they are prepared by your accountant.

Your accountant can help you decide which of the methods I explain in the next sections is best for you.

Ruling on the straight line method

In *straight line depreciation*, the value of the asset is depreciated evenly over the period of its useful life. For example, an asset depreciated over a four-year period has a quarter of the value depreciated each year (25 per cent). The same amount of depreciation is charged each month. For example, an asset that cost £24,000 and is due to be depreciated over a four-year period is depreciated by £6,000 each year, which equates to £500 per month.

Counting down the reducing balance method

An asset is depreciated by a fixed percentage in *reducing balance depreciation*, but the calculation is based on the net book value (NBV) each year, so the NBV reduces each year. For example, a £12,000 asset with a four-year lifespan, depreciated at 25 per cent by using the reducing balance basis, is depreciated as shown in Table 16-1.

The *net book value* is the cost price of the fixed asset less the accumulated depreciation to date. So at the end of year one, a £12,000 asset has depreciated by £3,000 (at 25 per cent), leaving the net book value as £9,000.

Table 16-1	Depreciation on a £12,000 Asset over Four Years	
Year	*Net Book Value*	*Depreciation Amount*
1	£9,000	£3,000
2	£6,750	£2,250
3	£5,062.50	£1,687.50
4	£3,796.88	£1,265.63

Using the reducing balance method means that the asset never fully depreciates. The amount of depreciation just gets smaller and smaller each year. You're more likely to write off the asset because it's obsolete before the NBV is anywhere near to zero.

Going for the one-time write-off

If you use the *write-off* method, you make a single posting to write off the remaining value of the asset in one go. You may choose to write off an asset if you disposed of it and need to remove the value from the books. Alternatively, if the asset is so old that it's no longer worth the value shown in the books, it's a candidate for write-off.

Posting assets and depreciation

You post the actual capital cost of an asset when you make the invoice or bank payment and you've coded the item to Fixed Assets. You make the depreciation postings when you run month-end routines or if you've chosen to manually post your journals each month-end. You can only make the postings once in a calendar month. For those using the month-end option (which I explain later in this chapter), if you forget to run the depreciation, you need to set the program date back to the month that you forgot to run and post the depreciation.

For those of you posting your depreciation journals manually, the double-entry way to complete your journals is to debit Depreciation (an expense account in the Profit and Loss) and credit Accumulated Depreciation (a Balance Sheet account).

To make sure that you're posting the correct amount of depreciation, you need to check that your Fixed Asset records are up to date. Ensure that you correctly set up the asset and the required depreciation.

Entering Journals

If you don't have Accounts Plus or Professional, pay special attention to this section, as it explains what journals actually do. You need to understand the principles of double-entry bookkeeping to make journal entries competently.

A *journal* is where you transfer values between nominal accounts. You can use journals to correct mistakes where something was posted incorrectly, but you don't use journals just for corrections. For example, you use journals to do your accruals and prepayments if you don't want to use wizards.

You use debits and credits to move values between nominal accounts. The journal must balance, so you need equal values of debits to equal values of credits, otherwise Sage is unable to post it.

I suggest using journals only if you're confident with double-entry bookkeeping. Otherwise, just stick to the wizards, because they perform the double-entry for you.

You may need to update several journals on a monthly basis, including depreciation journals if you're not using the Fixed Asset Register, wages journals and any other journals that you may require to correct items posted to the wrong account (cleverly known as *mispostings*).

To complete a journal, follow these steps:

1. **From the Company module, click New Journal from the Task pane or the Journals icon.**

2. **Enter the necessary information in the Nominal Ledger Journal sheet.**

   You're asked for the following information:

   - **Reference:** For example, 'June 2009 depreciation' if you're manually posting depreciation and not using the Fixed Asset Register.

   - **Posting Date:** The system uses the current day's date, so you need to specify the date on which you want to post the journal.

   - **Nominal Code:** Use the dropdown arrow to select the first nominal code for your journal.

     For example, if you're posting a journal for depreciation, you may show a debit entry for Plant and Machinery (N/C 0020) for the sum of £200. The detail would read 'P&M June Depreciation'. The corresponding credit entry would use Plant and Machinery Accumulated Depreciation (N/C 0021) for the sum of £200, as shown in Figure 16-1.

   - **Name**: The nominal code name automatically comes up on the screen.

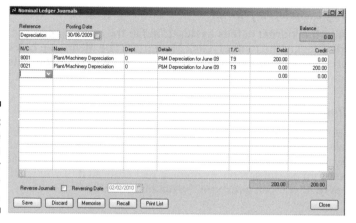

Figure 16-1:
An example
of posting a
journal for
deprecia-
tion.

- **Department**: Choose a department if you need one.

- **Details**: Enter details of the journal to appear on the Nominal
  Activity report.

- **Tax Code**: The system defaults to T9, the code most often used,
  but you can change this if required by using the dropdown arrows.

- **Debit or Credit**: Fill in the appropriate column according to
  whether it's a debit or a credit.

When you finish, the Balance box shows zero and the totals of the debits
and credits is the same.

3. Click Save if you're happy with the journal.

The journal is posted to the nominal codes shown.

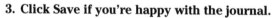

Prior to saving the journal, you have the option to reverse it at a future point
in time. This is particularly useful if you are posting an accrual or prepayment type of journal. Tick the box Reverse Journals and then enter the date
that you want the journal to reverse on. These boxes only show up on your
nominal journal if you have ticked the box Enable Reversing Journals on the
Parameters tab of Company Preferences (accessed from the main toolbar).

Rattling skeleton journals

If you do the same journals on a regular basis, you can take advantage of the
option to create a *skeleton journal,* which you can reuse. After you save a skeleton journal, when you need to use the journal, all you do is recall it, and the
details that you saved appear.

You can only save values in your skeleton journals if you tick the Copy
Skeleton Journal Values box in Settings⇨Company Preferences⇨Parameters.

Creating a skeleton journal

You enter the journal details as described in the preceding section, but instead of saving the journal, click Memorise. The Memorise box opens, and Sage prompts you for a file name and a description of the journals. Type these and then click Save, which saves the journal for reuse another time.

Recalling a journal

When you're ready to reuse your skeleton journal, from Company, click Journals to bring up the Nominal Ledger journal. Click Recall to see a list of memorised journals. Highlight the journal you want and click Load. The journal comes up on the screen, as if you'd just entered it. If you want to make changes to it, you can overtype the details.

Reversing journals

Sometimes you may want to cancel a journal. Making a mistake when you're trying to reverse a journal manually is very easy, especially if you get the double-entry wrong. Sage can help you with the reversing journal option.

The main reason you may want to reverse a journal is because you got the double-entry bookkeeping wrong – maybe you got your debits mixed up with your credits – easily done! As long as you can identify both the debit and the credit that need to be corrected and these have individual transaction numbers, you can reverse them. You may not need to reverse the whole thing; perhaps just two lines of your original journal need reversing.

Before you undertake the nominal journal reversal, take a backup – just in case things go wrong and you need to restore the data.

To start with, you need to know which transactions you want to reverse, and then you follow these steps:

1. **From Company, click Reversals.**

   At this point, Sage prompts you to take a backup and print a copy of the Nominal Ledger Daybook report. Doing this is wise.

2. **Click Print Now to obtain a printout of the Nominal Ledger Daybook report.**

   You can select the date ranges and nominal codes from the usual criteria box.

3. **Click Backup, and the usual Backup screen appears. Click OK. After the backup is complete, you return to the Nominal Reversals screen. Click OK.**

4. **Enter the transaction range your journal appears in.**

   You can find this information on the Nominal Ledger Daybook report that you printed.

5. **Enter the date of the original journal and then click OK.**

   A Nominal Reversal window opens, showing the journal transactions that you want to reverse.

   If the journal you're trying to reverse doesn't come up, check that you used the correct transaction number. Also make sure that the journal you're trying to reverse balances, otherwise Sage doesn't accept the reversal.

6. **Highlight the items for reversal and click Reverse, followed by Save.**

Now that you've reversed the offending journal, don't forget to post the correct one!

The journal you reversed shows on the audit trail with the reference REVERSE and the details say, 'Reversal of transaction XX'.

Carrying Out Your Month-End Routine

Running the month-end process in Sage allows you to automatically run the accruals, prepayment and depreciation journals described in earlier sections. However, you also get the opportunity to clear your customer and supplier month-to-date turnover figures, remove fully paid and reconciled transactions, clear the audit trail and remove stock transactions – although the last two tasks are optional.

The month-end process gives you the opportunity to review your accounts and prepare for the next accounting period. After you post all the journals and run all monthly routines, you can start running reports (which I cover in Chapter 18).

Ticking off your checklist

Having a checklist is probably the easiest way to run the month-end in a controlled manner. Use the following month-end checklist to ensure that you do everything.

Prior to running the month-end, run through these tasks:

❑ Change your program date to the month-end (Settings⇨Change Program Date).

❑ Enter all transactions for the current period.

❑ Process bank recurring entries for the month.

❑ Reconcile all bank accounts (including credit cards).

❑ Post all journals (including skeleton).

❑ Post revaluation journals if you use foreign currency. (Refer to Chapter 14 for more on this.)

❑ Set up prepayments, accruals, fixed assets and depreciation.

❑ Post opening and closing stock journals (use Modules⇨Wizards⇨ Opening Closing Stock Wizard).

❑ Take a backup and label it. For example, 'June 09 month-end'.

As you run month-end processes, be sure to cover these points, as necessary:

❑ Remove stock transactions if required.

❑ Clear audit trail if required.

❑ Take another backup entitled 'After month-end' with the date.

As you work through the month-end processes, be sure to tick off each item, so that you can see which tasks are remaining.

Running the month-end

The month-end procedure allows you to clear down the month-to-date turnover figures on all your customer and supplier records. In clearing the month-to-date turnover figures, Sage zeroes down the sales or purchase value in the Month to Date field, which helps for reporting purposes. And, if you have Accounts Plus or Accounts Professional, you can process your accruals, prepayments and depreciation as well.

You can post transactions beyond the month-end date, and Sage designates them to the appropriate month. Even after you post the month-end, you can still post transactions to any previous accounting period: Sage just slots them into the appropriate month.

To run the month-end, follow these steps:

1. **Click Tools⇨Period End Tools⇨Month End from the main toolbar to bring up the Month End window.**

2. **Select the appropriate options by putting a tick in the relevant boxes in the Month End window.**

   Ticking the Clear Turnover Figures box sets your month-to-date turnover figures for your customers and suppliers to zero.

   You can post prepayments and accruals that you previously set up, as well as the depreciation for assets set up with the Fixed Asset Register.

3. **Click OK if you're happy to run the month-end.**

4. **Click Yes when the confirmation message appears to complete the month-end process.**

Alternatively, you can click Manage Month End from the Company screen, which takes you through the checklist items in the preceding 'Ticking off your checklist' section, using the appropriate wizards.

Clearing stock transactions

Clearing stock transactions is a way of reducing the number of transactions that appear on your product activity ledger. You clear the transactions up to a date you specify. You may decide to do this if your system is beginning to slow down due to the vast number of records it has to process. A year-end is often a good time to clear stock transactions. You don't have to clear the stock transactions, and many people prefer not to, as they like to be able to view a complete history of transactions.

You must print off your Product Valuation and Product Activity reports prior to clearing your stock transactions.

When you run the Clear Stock option, it removes all individual product transactions from each product record, leaving Adjustment In (AI) and Movements In (MI) – records of stock movements – which are brought forward as opening balances.

To clear your stock, follow these steps:

1. **Take a backup before you run the Clear Stock option.**

2. **From the main toolbar, click Tools⇨Period End⇨Clear Stock. A confirmation message appears, asking if you're sure that you want to continue. Click Yes.**

3. **Sage asks for a date to clear transactions up to. Enter the date you want and then click OK to continue or Cancel to exit.**

   Transactions prior to that date are permanently removed from stock transaction history.

Clearing the audit trail

The process of clearing your audit trail actually removes fully paid and fully reconciled transactions from the audit trail up to a date that you choose. You're left with fewer transactions on the screen, which makes it easier to work with and also speeds up the process of running reports and backing up your data.

Taking backups prior to running this process is absolutely essential. Clearing your audit trail is irreversible. Make sure that you print your audit trail, day-book reports, sales, purchase and nominal activity reports, and also any VAT return reports prior to running the Clear Audit Trail option.

You can look at the deleted transactions by clicking Company⇨Financial Reports⇨Cleared Audit Trail Reports (from the Links list).

During the process of removing transactions, Sage posts journal entries to the nominal codes to which the transactions were linked. This posting ensures that the balances on the nominal accounts stay the same as before the Clear Audit Trail process was run. The journals are displayed with the detail opening balance and appear at the end of the audit trail when the Clear Audit Trail process is complete.

To run the Clear Audit Trail, follow these steps:

1. **From the main toolbar, click Tools⇨Period End⇨Clear Audit Trail.**

   The Clear Audit Trail wizard opens, which takes you through the process step by step.

2. **Click Next to work through each screen. On the final screen, you need to click Process to begin the Clear Audit Trail process.**

   A Progress taskbar appears. After the process is complete, the Finished screen appears. This screen tells you how many transactions were removed and enables you to view the cleared transactions. If you want to see the removed transactions, tick the I Would Like To View Details Of The Removed Transactions box to open the Audit Trail Historic List report. You can print or save this report if desired.

3. **Click Finish to complete the Clear Audit Trail process.**

Managing Cash Flow

Have you ever wondered if you have enough money in the bank to pay your suppliers and your wages? I've certainly heard this question many a time. The only way to truly know is to keep an eye on your cash flow.

Sage has a cash-flow facility that helps you to plan your payments and consider what monies are due in, so that you can calculate whether or not you have the cash to carry out your day-to-day banking transactions.

You need to be in the Bank module to run the cash-flow forecast.

1. **From Bank, click Cash Flow. (You may need to click the little chevron sign next to the Recurring icon if the Cash Flow icon isn't visible.)**

   The Cash Flow screen opens, with two boxes at the top of the screen. The box on the left is a summary of the bank balance and notes any regular receipts or payments (recurring entries). It also shows any forecasted receipts and payments and provides a projected bank balance up to the period specified. The box on the right shows bank accounts. The default shows the main bank account only, but you can include more accounts if you want to. The bottom section of the screen shows a list of all outstanding receipts and payments in date order.

2. **In the main body of the cash flow, remove the tick in the Include? column to remove the corresponding transaction from the cash flow.**

   The forecast bank balance adjusts accordingly.

   Figure 16-2 shows the Cash Flow screen with the Include? column.

   To make a manual entry to see what effect a transaction may have on the cash flow, place the cursor on the first vacant line on the main body of the cash flow and enter the details of the manual entry. The forecast bank balance adjusts for the new transaction.

3. **Print the cash flow by clicking Print, or send the cash flow to Microsoft Excel by clicking Send To.**

   Excel opens and you can view the cash-flow details on a spreadsheet. The spreadsheet allows you a lot more flexibility to play around with the figures.

 The layout of the Sage cash flow exported to the spreadsheet may not suit you. Many businesses like to have a much more detailed cash flow, and if the business operates on a very tight cash flow, sometimes you may need to review cash flow on a daily basis. You can choose to design your own spreadsheet layout. Most local high street banks can provide you with examples of cash-flow statements – go and have a word with your friendly business banker.

Figure 16-2:
Posting
a manual
entry onto
your cash
flow.

Additional features on the cash-flow tool include a Manage Payments button (at the bottom of the screen), which opens up the Manage Payments window. This window shows a list of supplier accounts with a summary of their current payment position. You can see which supplier accounts are overdue. You can click the Suggested Payments icon to help you allocate amounts of monies to suppliers, and then make payments to suppliers by clicking the Make Payment button.

You can also click the Chase Debt button to open up the Chase Debt window. This window displays a list of customers and the amount of monies overdue on each. By clicking the Communications icon, you can access the customer record and see details of debt-chasing conversations that you've had with the customers.

You can find more details about both the Manage Payments and the Chase Debt options by pressing the F1 key and typing **manage payments** and **chase debt** into the Help field.

Doing a Year-End Routine

The year-end procedure is principally a financial accounting process. You must run your month-end for the last month of your accounting year, which takes care of the usual journal routines (although you are probably a little more careful at checking things like accruals and prepayments at the year-end).

The year-end procedure clears down the Profit and Loss accounts to zero and transfers any current-year profit or loss to the Retained Profit account. You carry forward the balances on the Balance Sheet to the new year and transfer any future-dated transactions into the relevant months for each nominal record.

As regards budgets, you transfer the actual values for the current to the prior year, so that you can make comparisons in the new financial year.

You must make sure that you take a backup before you run this process (Sage recommends taking two, so that if one is lost or damaged, you always have another copy). You also need to check that you've run all the reports that you require for your accounts and that you've adjusted your system date to the same as your year-end date (Settings⇨Change Program Date).

Check that your Chart of Accounts doesn't contain any errors, although you should notice these sorts of mistakes when you run your Profit and Loss and Balance Sheets for the year.

To run your year-end, follow these steps:

1. **From the main toolbar, click Tools⇨Period End⇨Year End.**

   The Year End window appears.

   Alternatively, you can select the Manage Year End option on the Company toolbar. This wizard takes you through the process step by step.

2. **Select Copy Current Year Budgets for both your nominal and departmental budgets and also your stock budgets.**

   You can increase your budget by a percentage increase if desired.

3. **In the Postings box, enter the date you want on your year-end journals.**

   Your financial year-end date appears here automatically, but you can change it if you want to.

4. **Decide what method of output you want for your year-end updated audit trail – you can print or save it to a file.**

5. **Choose whether to archive the closing year's data. To archive, select the Archive Company Data Before Year End check box.**

6. **After you're happy with the details that you've chosen, click OK.**

   Sage now continues with your year-end.

You may want to take a backup and label it 'After the year-end'. You can also check the data.

Before you begin the next financial year, check that the financial year start date is correct (Settings⇨Financial Year). Click OK if the details are correct.

You've now completed your year-end!

Chapter 17

Running Your VAT Return

*T*he letters VAT (which stand for Value Added Tax, of course) usually have a profound effect on people, from grown men turning a pale shade of green to a pure state of panic if a VAT inspection suddenly looms! You can avoid all this by keeping proper accounting records with a system such as Sage and running your VAT returns in a systematic, methodical manner.

The actual running of a VAT return takes seconds, due to the integrated nature of the Sage software.

In this chapter, I take you through the two different VAT schemes that you can operate within Sage, as well as how to switch VAT schemes if required. I also cover fuel-scale charges and Intrastat reports.

Understanding Some VAT Basics

You only need to worry about VAT if your business is VAT registered. After you register, you can reclaim VAT on certain purchases, but you also have to charge and pay VAT across on your sales.

Your company can voluntarily register for VAT and should if you can reclaim VAT on a significant proportion of your purchases. VAT registration is mandatory if you exceed certain VAT thresholds – currently, you must register if your annual sales reach £67,000 or above.

A basic knowledge of what you can claim VAT on and what you can't pays off (literally!). You can find many books on this subject, and the VAT office also provides plenty of publications for specific industries. A quick look on the HM Revenue and Customs (HMRC) website at `www.hmrc.gov.uk` gives you a list of all publications. You can find the main VAT rules and procedures in Notice 700.

Knowing your outputs from your inputs

VAT inputs and outputs have nothing to do with the Hokey Cokey. I wish they were that enjoyable!

Output VAT is just a fancy name for the VAT element of your sales. *Input VAT* is the opposite; it represents the VAT element of your purchases.

Basically, a VAT return compares the total of your VAT inputs and outputs, and subtracts one from the other. If the outputs exceed the inputs, you owe the Revenue, and if the Inputs exceed the Outputs, then the Revenue owes you a refund! Yes, it does happen. . . .

Cracking the codes

When you enter invoices, credit notes or orders (whether for your customers or suppliers), you need to know which tax code to use. Sage automatically provides you with a list of UK tax codes, or T codes:

- ✔ **T0:** Zero-rated; VAT is not payable on zero-rated supplies. Examples include books, children's clothes and some items of food.
- ✔ **T1:** Standard rate; currently 17.5 per cent.
- ✔ **T2:** Exempt from VAT. For example, postage stamps.
- ✔ **T4:** Sales to customers in the European Union (EU).
- ✔ **T5:** Lower-rate VAT, usually 5 per cent; this applies to the purchase of energy-saving materials and, for example, reclaiming VAT on DIY building work.
- ✔ **T7:** Zero-rated purchases from suppliers in the EU.
- ✔ **T8:** Standard-rated purchases from suppliers in the EU.
- ✔ **T9:** Transactions not involving VAT. For example, wages.

For unexplained reasons, Sage doesn't use T3 or T6, but you have eight other codes to use.

Comparing Sage's VAT accounting methods

Sage supports two types of VAT schemes: the standard VAT accounting scheme and VAT cash accounting. The Inland Revenue provides some helpful information about other VAT schemes on its website; if you want to find out more, go to www.hmrc.gov.uk.

Set up your accounting method before you enter any transactions onto Sage. The Active Set-up wizard I talk about in Chapter 1 includes the accounting method as one of its steps. If you're not sure which method you chose, click Settings⇨Company Preferences and then click the VAT tab. If you have cash accounting set up, the VAT Cash Accounting box has a small tick. If you're operating standard VAT accounting, then this box is greyed out, as shown in Figure 17-1. The next sections explain the two methods.

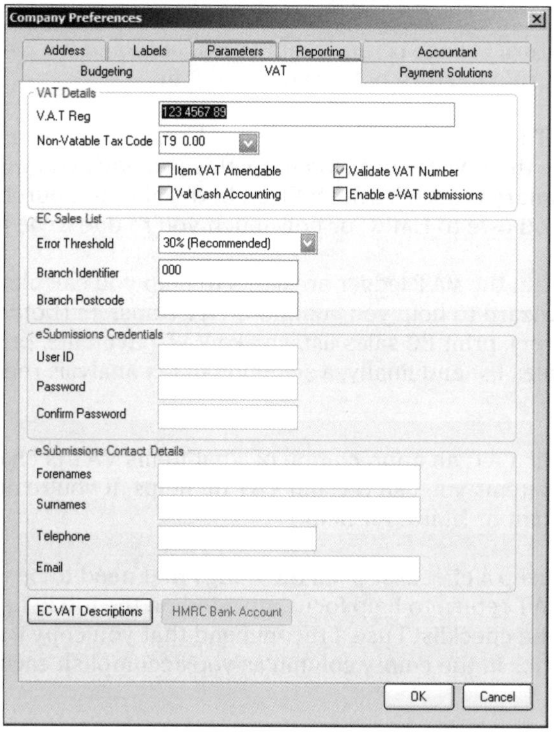

Figure 17-1: Checking your VAT scheme.

Setting the standard scheme

In the standard VAT scheme, Sage calculates the amount of VAT based on when an invoice is issued. Therefore, as you raise each invoice, you're liable to pay the VAT on it when your next VAT return is due. However, you can reclaim the VAT on invoices sent to you from your suppliers, regardless of whether you've paid them or not.

Considering cash accounting

VAT cash accounting calculates the VAT based on when your customer pays an invoice and when you pay your supplier. You benefit if your customers are slow to pay, as you don't need to pay the VAT across until they pay you.

VAT cash accounting in the Republic of Ireland is slightly different. Sometimes known as the *monies received* scheme, you calculate your VAT on the money you actually receive from customers and on the invoices or credits you receive from your suppliers. Sage 50 Accounts has the ability to operate both the UK scheme and the Republic of Ireland scheme.

Running the VAT Return

Running a VAT return in Sage is remarkably easy, *but* – and it's a big but – you have to check your VAT return before you send it in.

To access the VAT ledger, from Company, click Manage VAT from the Task pane. You can see the VAT Return icon here; this provides you with both detailed and summary reports of the VAT on both sales and purchases, and calculates what you owe to HMRC or how much you're due to be refunded.

Also included within the VAT ledger are icons to help you calculate your fuel-scale charges, a wizard to help you complete VAT transfers (both outlined later in this chapter), print EC sales lists, make VAT payments, produce a reverse charge Sales list and finally, a selection of tax analysis reports that you can run.

When figuring your VAT, an appreciation of what items VAT is charged on and what types of items you can reclaim VAT on helps. If you're unsure, contact your accountant or HMRC for help.

I find it useful to keep a checklist of all the things that need to be done prior to and during a VAT return to help focus my mind on the job in hand. Table 17-1 is a copy of the checklist I use. I recommend that you copy it and use it yourself. Place a tick in the empty column as you accomplish each task.

Table 17-1	VAT Return Checklist
Task	**Accomplished**
Post scale charges if you have company cars.	
Calculate and print the VAT return for the appropriate quarter.	
Check the VAT return:	
Print the VAT report.	
Print the Nominal Transaction report for Sales and Purchase Tax control account.	
Make sure that the preceding reports are for the same quarter as the VAT return.	
If you use VAT cash accounting, print the necessary nominal, cash and bank daybook reports.	
Make any adjustments to your VAT return as necessary.	
Reconcile your VAT transactions.	
Enter the details onto your hard copy of the VAT return or submit your VAT return online.	
Clear down your VAT control accounts.	

The sections throughout this chapter explain each task in the checklist.

Calculating your VAT

Before you start figuring out your VAT return, make sure that your books are up to date for that period. By this, I mean enter all sales invoices and purchase invoices and all receipts and payments, and reconcile all the bank accounts and credit card accounts to ensure that you've accounted for all elements of VAT.

The first step of running your VAT return is to calculate the amount owing or owed. Using the new VAT ledger that made its debut in Sage 2008, this calculation becomes very easy; just follow these steps:

1. **From Company, click Manage VAT in the Task pane to open up the VAT window.**

    Alternatively, you can click Financials from the Company Links list and then click VAT from the Financials screen.

2. **Click the VAT Return icon.**

   The VAT form opens up. This form looks like the manual VAT return that you get from HMRC.

3. **Enter the period that the VAT return relates to.**

   For example, 01.06.08 to 31.08.08.

4. **Click Calculate.**

   Sage tells you how many transactions were found for this VAT return, as well as how many transactions are dated before the specified period but haven't been reconciled. You can choose whether you want to include them or not. If you choose not to include them, they remain as unreconciled items in the audit trail and appear again when you do your next VAT return.

5. **Click OK to continue.**

   As soon as you click OK, the VAT Return fills with figures, and you can see how much Sage thinks you owe the Inland Revenue or vice versa.

Figure 17-2 shows a VAT return for Jingles. Sage found 42 transactions, including nine unreconciled transactions before the specified period. In the example, these unreconciled item are included as they form part of the set-up of the company and need to be accounted for. Sage calculates that Jingles owes £221.51 to HMRC.

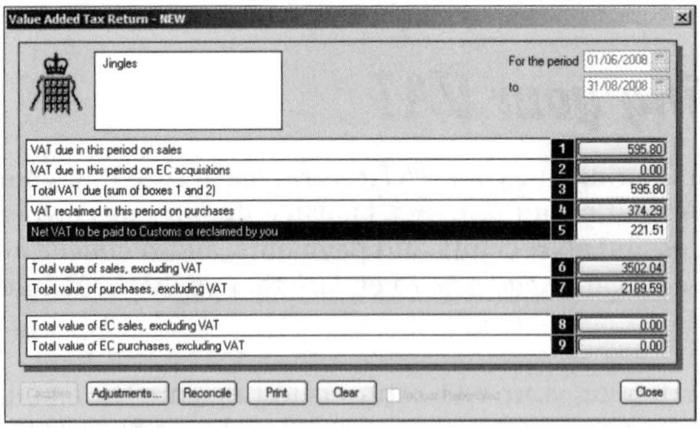

Figure 17-2: A VAT return for Jingles.

Checking Your VAT Return

You may think that the job is done after Sage calculates your VAT. However, the information is only as good as the person who entered it, so you need to check it against the information held in the nominal ledger. The checks are different depending on which VAT scheme you operate. I look at each scheme in turn and examine which reports you need to check to ensure the accuracy of your return.

Checking under the standard scheme

Your Sales Tax and Purchase Tax control accounts must agree with the boxes on the VAT return. To make sure that they do, print the VAT return, a detailed VAT report and the Nominal Activity report for both the Sales Tax control account and the Purchase Tax control account. These documents identify all elements of VAT on sales and purchases. Make sure the Nominal Activity report is run for the same quarter period as the VAT return.

Printing out the VAT return and a detailed report

The main screen of the VAT return is the place to go to print VAT reports. Just click Print and a VAT Return Report window opens. Tick both the VAT Return and Detailed boxes and then click Run. Sage previews both reports on the screen, one behind the other. The screen behind the VAT return has a white background and has lost the green colour – don't worry, this is normal. Print a copy of both reports.

The detailed VAT report provides a breakdown of all the transactions behind each number on the VAT return. And, if you use the VAT standard accounting scheme, the detailed VAT report shows each sales invoice and credit note, and every purchase invoice and credit note.

Sage groups the transactions on the report according to the box they belong in on the VAT return. For example, you can see each individual transaction contained within VAT box 1.

Getting a hard copy of the Nominal Activity report

You need to check that the net value of the Sales Tax control account and Purchase Tax control account on the Nominal Activity report agree with box 5 of the VAT return. To check, print the nominal activity for codes 2200 and 2201, the Sales Tax control account and the Purchase Tax control account.

If the net value of the tax control accounts doesn't agree with box 5, do the following checks:

> ✔ Make sure that you selected the same dates for the Nominal Activity report as you have for the VAT return. That way, you select data for the same period and it should agree, unless you've said Yes to any unreconciled items from a previous quarter.

> ✔ Check if the VAT control accounts include any totals for tax codes that aren't included in your VAT return. For example, T9 by default isn't included in your VAT return.

> ✔ Check that your Clear Down journals have been correctly posted from the previous quarter. (I talk about these journals in the 'Clearing Down VAT' section later in this chapter.)

✔ See if any journals were posted to the VAT control ledgers. Journals don't normally need to be posted to the control accounts, so if they are, you need to fix that error.

✔ Check the audit trail. You can check which items have already been reconciled by looking for *R* for reconciled in the V (VAT) column. Those with an *N* in the column haven't been reconciled and need checking as part of the current VAT return.

✔ If you still can't find the discrepancy, print the Customer daybook reports and the Supplier daybook reports and manually tick off each item to the tax control accounts. This last-resort check can be extremely time-consuming, but it does usually work.

✔ If you still have a discrepancy after all this, print the daybooks for your bank, cash, credit receipts and payments, and check these reports to find the error.

Checking with cash accounting

If you're operating the VAT cash accounting system and working from a cash-based system instead of an invoice-based one, you need to print several reports. First, print your detailed VAT report as described in 'Printing out the VAT return and a detailed report' in the previous section. Then follow these steps:

1. **From the navigation bar, click Company⇨Financials from the Links list.**

   The Financials window opens.

2. **Click the Audit icon and select Detailed. Click Run.**

   The Criteria box opens.

3. **Select the same quarter period as your VAT return and then click OK.**

   Your report appears in Preview format. Click Print for a hard copy.

   Transactions that have an *N* in the V (VAT) column haven't yet been reconciled and are the transactions that you include in your current VAT return. Items with an *R* in this same column have been reconciled for VAT purposes and aren't included in the VAT return.

4. **Make sure that you use the same date range as your VAT return to print nominal reports.**

   The reports you print are:

   • **Nominal Ledger Daybook reports:** From the navigation bar, click Company, click the Reports icon and double-click Nominal Daybook Reports. Select Day Book: Nominal Ledger and the Criteria Value box opens. Select the same dates as your VAT quarter and click OK.

- **Customer Receipts and Supplier Payments:** Print these reports from Bank reports. These are all bank and cash accounts. (If you're using the Republic of Ireland VAT accounting scheme, you don't need to print the Supplier Payments report.)

- **Customer Invoices and Credits Daybook reports**: Print these reports from Customers.

- **Supplier Invoices and Credits Daybook reports:** Print these reports from Suppliers.

5. **Make sure that your VAT return is correct by checking it against all the reports you print in Steps 2, 3 and 4.**

Analysing Your VAT Return

After you calculate your VAT return, you can analyse it.

If you look at your green stripy VAT return, you can see the numbers 1 to 9. Each number represents a line on the VAT return. By clicking each box with a pound value in it, you can drill down the VAT return and obtain a breakdown of all entries made to each tax code, indicating if each entry is a sales invoice, credit note, journal, receipt or payment. You can also see any manual adjustments that have been made.

If you want even more detail, you can double-click any of the numbers on the VAT Breakdown screen and view all the transactions that make up that total. You can click Print List to obtain a detailed VAT breakdown. Click Close to return to the VAT Breakdown screen and Close again to exit the screen.

Making Manual Adjustments to Your VAT Return

Sometimes you miss something from your VAT return from a previous quarter and you need to make an adjustment. In the past, you had to get your biro and calculator out and make an adjustment on the face of your VAT return prior to sending it to HMRC, but now you can do it within Sage. Just follow these steps:

1. **From the VAT Return, click Adjustments.**

   The VAT Manual Adjustments screen opens, as shown in Figure 17-3.

2. **Click the arrow in the Adjustments column, and, in the screen that appears, enter some text describing why you're making the adjustment.**

Figure 17-3:
Making
manual
adjustments
on your VAT
return.

For example, your notation may be something like, 'prior quarter adjustment'.

3. Click Save.

You're returned to the previous summary screen, where you can now see your adjustment.

4. Click Close.

The VAT Return screen appears. The total amount owed to the Inland Revenue has now been revised for the manual adjustment that you just made. Sage posts the manual adjustments to the nominal default code 2204.

If you make an adjustment but close the VAT return without reconciling, the adjustments aren't saved.

5. Click Close again to return to the Financials screen.

Reconciling Your VAT Transactions

After you're happy with the information in your VAT return, you need to flag each individual transaction for VAT so that an *R* appears in the VAT column of the audit trail and it doesn't appear again in future returns, unless you ask to include previously reconciled transactions. This process is known as *reconciling your VAT return*.

To do the reconciliation, you must first calculate the VAT return for the correct VAT quarter. When you can view the VAT Return screen, click Reconcile. A confirmation message appears, asking you if you want to flag the transactions for VAT. Click Yes and then click Close.

To check if the transactions have definitely been reconciled, try to calculate the VAT return again for the same period. A message appears saying that you've selected a date range that's already been reported on. Click Yes to continue. Sage then confirms that no transactions were found for that period; evidence that the transactions have been reconciled. You can also check that the individual transactions have been reconciled by viewing the Audit Trail screen and looking for an *R* in the VAT column.

When you reconcile the VAT return, a copy of it is archived in Sage. The reconciled and archived VAT return is then listed on the VAT ledger window. It is given a return number as a method of identification. The listing shows the period of the return, the amount and has a Paid column that shows an *N* if the return hasn't yet been submitted to HMRC.

You can view a saved return by highlighting the return you want to view from the VAT ledger and clicking View. If you want to, you can delete the VAT return from Sage by highlighting the return and clicking Delete. However, you more than likely want to keep a copy of your VAT return on Sage. I recommend that you keep a hard copy of all your VAT returns and keep them in a file somewhere safe. You must keep copies for the purposes of any VAT inspection for at least six years.

Submitting Your VAT Return

When you've reconciled your VAT return, you're ready to submit it to HMRC. You must keep a copy of all your reports, just in case you're inspected at a later point in time – HMRC has six years to do so.

Sending it in by hand

If you haven't elected to send your VAT returns electronically, follow this procedure:

1. **From the VAT ledger, highlight the VAT return you want to submit and click View.**

   The VAT return opens up.

2. **Print the VAT return and keep a hard copy in your file.**

   Your VAT return is archived after you have reconciled, so you also have an electronic copy.

3. **Enter the figures from the VAT report in Sage onto your manual VAT return.**

   If the value in box 5 is negative, then you have a VAT reclaim, and HMRC actually owes you money! If the figure is positive, you owe the amount to the Revenue and must pay it across.

4. **Post your refund or payment in Sage.**

   To post a VAT refund, post a Bank receipt to the VAT Liability account (2202), coded to T9.

   If you're required to make a VAT payment, you must select the VAT quarter from the VAT ledger and click Payment. The Bank Payment screen opens up. Sage has already completed most of the fields for you, but you must make sure that you select the correct date, as Sage automatically picks the current day's date. When you're happy that the information is correct, click Save.

   As soon as you save the bank payment, the Paid column changes from *N* (No) to *Y* (Yes) on the VAT ledger list of returns.

5. **Put a copy of the VAT return in the mail and send payment to HMRC.**

Posting your return online

The 2007 Budget announced that most companies (with the exception of small traders and newly registered VAT traders) would be required to file their VAT returns online and pay electronically from April 2010 at the earliest – e-VAT, as it were. You can make electronic payments before you're required to however, and Sage helps you do this.

You must have a Government Gateway account to make e-VAT payments. Go to www.hmrc.gov.uk for details on how to obtain one.

You must also enable e-VAT submissions on your VAT preference settings – click Settings⇨Company Preferences⇨VAT tab and tick the e-VAT Submissions box.

To send your online VAT return, follow these steps:

1. **From the VAT Ledger screen, highlight the VAT return you want to send.**

   The return's status must be pending or partial.

2. **Click Submit Return.**

   Assuming your VAT preferences and e-submission credentials are set up correctly, the Sage Internet Submissions wizard guides you through the process.

Clearing Down VAT

If you're wondering what on earth clearing is all about, don't worry, it's quite straightforward. Essentially, *clearing* is transferring the values from your Sales Tax and Purchase Tax control accounts to your VAT Liability account.

The balance created in your VAT Liability account should agree with the amount due to HMRC, or in the case of a reclaim, it should equate to the refund due.

After you make the VAT payment or refund (and post it to the VAT Liability account), the balance on the Liability account becomes zero.

If you're thinking that this sounds rather complicated, then panic not, as Sage has a wizard to help you!

To run the wizard, follow these steps:

1. **From the VAT Ledger screen, click the VAT Transfer icon and then click Yes to confirm that you've closed all other windows so that the wizard can run.**

2. **Click Yes at the next message if you've fully reconciled and printed your VAT return. Click No if you need to print any reports.**

3. **Follow the wizard as it guides you through the steps necessary to complete the VAT transfer.**

4. **Check that the amounts the wizard wants to transfer are correct.**

   Sage then provides you with the double-entry bookkeeping necessary to clear down each of the control accounts.

5. **Click Finish to post those entries.**

After you transfer the values to the VAT Liability account and the VAT payment or refund has been received and posted to the account, the balance on that account is zero until the next clear down.

Changing VAT schemes

Can you change from VAT cash accounting to standard accounting or vice versa? The answer is yes, you can, but you have to prepare carefully for the change.

Going from standard to cash accounting

You need to switch methods at a month-end or quarter-end, after reconciling the VAT on standard accounting.

Always take a backup of your data, just in case anything goes wrong and you need to restore. Label the disk something like, 'Prior to VAT cash accounting transfer'.

After you take a backup, follow these steps:

1. **From Company, select Financials and then click VAT.**

2. **Calculate and reconcile the VAT return.**

   Refer to the 'Reconciling Your VAT Transactions' section earlier in this chapter.

3. **Post the VAT Clear Down journal.**

   The preceding section 'Clearing Down VAT' tells you how.

4. **Double-check that the reconciliation flags have been set by running the VAT return again for the same period and checking that it finds no transactions.**

After you're happy that you've reconciled all your VAT transactions, you're ready to transfer to the VAT cash accounting system by following these steps:

1. **From Company, click Settings. Click the VAT tab and tick the VAT Cash Accounting box.**

   If you have transactions that haven't been VAT reconciled, a warning message appears. You can't change your VAT scheme until you calculate and reconcile all the items for your final VAT standard accounting return.

   If there are no unreconciled items and Sage can change the VAT scheme, a message appears prompting you to check your recurring entries before you process them.

2. **Click OK.**

   The Sage desktop now appears.

3. **Change the VAT codes so that you don't reconcile the VAT that you reconciled under the old VAT standard scheme a second time under the VAT cash accounting scheme.**

   The next section tells you how.

Changing VAT codes

To make sure that the VAT reconciled under the old standard scheme isn't reconciled again under the new scheme, you change VAT codes so that you don't include the old ones in the VAT return (see Figure 17-4).

To change the VAT codes:

1. **From the main toolbar, click Settings and then Configuration. Select the Tax Codes tab.**

   A list of all tax codes appears.

2. **Select the tax code that you want to change and then click Edit.**

   The Edit Tax Code window appears.

3. **Amend your current tax codes so that they don't appear on your VAT return. You need to clear the green tick from the Include In VAT Return box.**

4. **Click OK.**

   You're then returned to the list of tax codes.

5. **Repeat Steps 1 through 4 for each tax code from T0 to T8 and remove them from the tax return.**

6. **Edit tax codes T10 to T18 and select the Include In VAT Return box.**

   Use these tax codes when entering transactions from now on. Sage uses these new codes to calculate your VAT return.

Figure 17-4: It's important to change VAT codes when you change VAT accounting schemes.

Table 17-2 shows what your new UK tax codes should look like.

Table 17-2		Altered VAT Codes
New Code	Tax Rate	Category
T10	0%	Zero-rated transactions
T11	17.5%	Standard-rated transactions
T12	0%	Exempt transactions
T14	0%	Sales to VAT-registered customers in the EU
T15	5%	Lower rate
T17	0%	Zero-rated purchases from suppliers in EC (link to T10)
T18	0%	Standard- rated purchases from suppliers in EU (link to T11)
T19	0%	Non-VATable tax code

If you want to see which codes to use for the Republic of Ireland, press F1 for the Help screen, click Index and type **switching**. The Help screen for switching to VAT cash accounting appears, and you can follow the links for more information about the Republic of Ireland.

Making the switch from VAT cash to standard accounting

Make sure that you run the changes after the month-end or quarter-end for VAT purposes, and always take a backup before you make any changes. Label the backup something like 'Backup prior to changing to standard VAT accounting'.

Then get ready to switch schemes by taking the following steps:

1. **Reconcile all unreconciled VAT transactions.**

2. **Post the VAT Clear Down journals.**

   The 'Clearing Down VAT' section earlier in the chapter tells you how.

3. **Check that the reconciliation flags have been set properly by running a VAT return again for the same period and making sure that it doesn't find any transactions.**

After you reconcile transactions that were included in your last VAT cash accounting return, you can turn your hand to actually switching the system, by following these steps:

1. **From the main toolbar, select Settings followed by Company Preferences and then click the VAT tab.**

2. **Clear the tick from the VAT Cash Accounting box and click OK.**

   A warning message appears, saying that if you have any transactions that haven't been VAT reconciled, you won't be able to change VAT schemes.

   To make sure that the VAT reconciled under the VAT cash accounting scheme isn't reclaimed a second time with the standard accounting scheme, produce and reconcile your VAT return again and set the reconciliation flags.

   Following the rules of the standard accounting scheme, the VAT amount remaining on the Sales Tax and Purchase Tax control accounts becomes liable for payment.

3. **Post a journal entry from the control accounts to the VAT Liability account when you're satisfied that the values are correct.**

   If you're not sure about the amounts, you need to reconcile the values remaining, which I tell you how to do in the next section.

Reconciling the sales tax and purchase tax control accounts

When you're changing from VAT cash accounting to the standard VAT scheme, you need to be sure that the items of VAT currently sitting in both the Sales Tax control account and the Purchase Tax control account are valid. They should be for genuine sales and purchases for which the VAT hasn't been paid across because the cash had not been received for them. However, now that the scheme has changed, this VAT becomes payable, so follow these steps:

1. **Take a backup, as you need this data to restore later.**

   Label the backup something like 'Backup prior to reconciliation of VAT'.

2. **From the main toolbar, select Tools⇨Period End⇨Clear Audit Trail.**

   This opens up the Clear Audit Trail wizard.

3. **Work through the wizard step by step, clicking Next to proceed through each screen.**

4. **Enter the date up to which you want to remove all fully paid and reconciled transactions.**

   This is the date from which you are transferring to the new system.

5. **The final screen warns you that you're about to remove the transactions from your audit trail up to the date you've entered. Click Process to remove the transactions or Cancel to exit the wizard.**

6. **Print the customer invoices, customer credits, supplier invoices and supplier credits daybooks.**

   Any transactions shown on these reports become liable for VAT under the standard VAT accounting scheme.

   You may find that the VAT control accounts don't match the VAT shown in the daybooks. This may be due to one of the following reasons:

   • Part-paid invoices show the full amount of the transaction on the daybook, but show the reduced amount on the VAT control account.

   • If you use the Automatic Write Off option, the VAT isn't removed from the VAT control account, but the invoices are marked as being paid in full and are removed during the Clear Audit Trail. You therefore still have the amount showing in the VAT control accounts but the invoices don't show on the daybooks.

   • If you've made payments on account on a customer or supplier account, you won't have a record of the invoice. Sage enters the VAT into the VAT control account but no invoices are entered and consequently they don't show on the daybooks.

7. **Reconcile the remaining VAT amounts with the outstanding invoices and credit notes. Make a note of these amounts.**

8. **Restore the data from the backup taken in Step 1.**

9. **Post a journal to enter the values from the relevant tax control accounts into the VAT Liability account.**

10. **Create a new nominal code called VAT Discrepancies if you have a remaining value in the Sales Tax or Purchase Tax control accounts. Clear the values from the tax control accounts into this VAT Discrepancies account.**

After you complete all these steps and are happy with the outcome, you're then ready to enter transactions under the VAT standard accounting scheme.

Posting Scale Charges

Fuel-scale charges occur when company vehicles are subject to private use. According to HMRC, if fuel is bought by employees for business use and that vehicle is also used privately, the business must account for output tax on the private use by using scale charges.

If you use scale charges, you can claim back all the VAT charged on road fuel without splitting your mileage between private and business use. The calculations are based on the CO_2 emissions of the vehicle plus the engine size.

Scale charges only apply to cars and not to commercial vehicles.

Thankfully, Sage has made claiming back VAT much easier with a wizard that guides you through the process:

1. **From the main toolbar, click Wizards and select Scales Charges Wizard.**

2. **Sage confirms that the Scales Charges Wizard can't be run without closing all other windows. Click Yes to continue.**

   Before you continue with the wizard, you need to calculate the scale charge for each vehicle. The HMRC publication Notice 700/64 helps you do this. You can get a copy from the HMRC website at www.hmrc.gov.uk.

3. **Click Next to continue.**

   Sage confirms the use of nominal code 7350 as the default nominal code for scale charges.

4. **Enter the gross scale charge and a reference, if you like. Then click Next.**

   Sage calculates the VAT element and the net charge. The wizard confirms the journals it's going to post for your scale charges.

5. **Click Finish.**

   Sage makes the postings, and you can view the entries on your VAT return.

Reporting Intrastat

Intrastat is concerned with collecting statistics surrounding the physical movement of goods around the European Union. It's closely linked with the VAT system, and if you're not VAT registered, you don't have any obligations under the Intrastat system.

However, if you exceed the so-called assimilation threshold in the amount of goods you supply to customers in the EU, you're required by law to submit certain details about your trade to HMRC. You can find details about Intrastat in HMRC Notice 60 – 'Intrastat General Guide'.

You have to complete Supplementary Declarations (SD) forms, which Sage can help you prepare. You then transfer the information from Sage onto the official SD forms.

For information about Intrastat reporting and how Sage can help, press F1 and type **Intrastat** into the Sage Help function.

You need to submit a European Community (EC) Sales list if you're VAT registered and supply products to customers in the European Union. The information on the lists is used by the UK and other member states to ensure that the appropriate amount of VAT has been calculated.

Some of the information shown on the sales list is taken from information contained within Company Preferences in Sage, but you must enter the appropriate quarter-end and click Calculate. Sage then extracts all the relevant data and shows it on the EC Sales list. You can see the country code, the customer's VAT registration number, the total value of supplies, an indicator field and a submitted field.

The indicator field shows a zero if the supply is from business to business, but it shows the number two if the transaction is a *triangulation,* meaning that three parties are involved – for example, products ordered from a French company are sold by a UK company to a Spanish company. To save time and costs, the French company sends the goods directly to the Spanish company. The number two indicates that the goods never entered the UK.

You can use the drilldown arrows on the Values boxes to see what transactions make up the values on the EC Sales list. When you're happy with the list, click Save and Sage adds your EC Sales list to the VAT Ledger list, showing a status of pending.

The icon called Rev Charge on the VAT ledger refers to the Reverse Charge Sales list, which some businesses may have to submit to HMRC. Inland Revenue have issued a brief (24/07) for those businesses who trade in mobile phones and computer chips. For more information, please refer to the HMRC website www.hmrc.gov.uk, which explains in detail about the reverse-charge legislation.

In January 2010, the rules relating to the EC Sales List VAT 101 changed. Sage has accommodated these changes by implementing some new VAT codes. The principal changes are as follows:

- EC Sales list submissions includes sale of services.
- The submission is a combined return for both goods and services.
- Where the value of goods exceeds £70K per quarter, the submission is made monthly.
- Sage has created new VAT codes as follows:
  - T22: Sales of services to EC customers
  - T23: Zero rated supplies of services from suppliers in the EC
  - T24: Standard rated supplies of services from EC suppliers

Part V
Using Reports

'And <u>all</u> the wizards waved their magic wands and <u>all</u> the accounting problems were solved and everyone lived happily ever after.'

In this part . . .

Sage offers many reports that you can use to help manage your business. In this part, I show you how to check your Chart of Accounts layout to ensure that your Profit and Loss account and Balance Sheet are accurate. I look at the audit trail and review the different transaction types.

These chapters cover some of the standard reports you can create in Sage, but I also look at ways of exporting data from Sage and creating your own reports within Microsoft Excel.

For those of you who like using technology, Chapter 19 offers an introduction to e-banking and a review of the Accountant Link, so you can see how it can save your business time and money. This chapter also shows you how the Document Manager can help you organise your paperwork.

Chapter 18

Running Monthly Reports

....

In This Chapter

▶ Using the Sage standard reports

▶ Using the Chart of Accounts to check report layouts

▶ Running a Trial Balance

▶ Creating a Profit and Loss account

▶ Printing your Balance Sheet

▶ Viewing the audit trail

▶ Writing reports

....

*T*his chapter concentrates on the reports that you can produce at the end of the monthly accounting procedure. I assume that you've run the month-end procedure and processed all the necessary journals, as I tell you how to do in Chapter 16. Now you need to provide some meaningful information to the managers of the business. The reports must be easy to understand and use headings that are meaningful to the business.

Running reports is an opportunity to see how well your business is progressing: if the business is meeting targets set earlier; if you're bringing in as much revenue as you'd projected and how actual costs compare to the budgeted or forecasted expenditures.

Making the Most of the Standard Reports

Whenever possible, use the standard reports provided by Sage, as they're simple to run and provide most of the information that you need.

Each ledger contains its own reports. For example, you go to Customer and then Reports to see the Aged Debtors report or Customer Activity, or you go to Bank and then Reports to see reports such as a copy of the unpresented cheques. The Financials module houses the Profit and Loss report and Balance Sheet – the key financial reports that tell you how the business is doing. You find these by clicking Company and then Financials (on the Links list), and then selecting the appropriate icon on the Financials screen. You can find more information about these reports and how to run them later in this Chapter.

Whenever you preview a report, you're given three choices of what to do with the data:

- ✔ **Print:** When you're happy with the layout on the preview screen, you can print a hard copy of the report.
- ✔ **Email:** Depending on how your email system is configured, you can send the report as an attachment or link to your email software and send the report directly.
- ✔ **Export:** You can choose to export the data into Microsoft Excel and then reformat it or adjust it using the Excel spreadsheet tools.

Usually at a month-end or year-end, the accountant prepares a set of management reports to present to the owners and managers of the business. I explain these reports in upcoming sections.

Sage introduced new column-based financial reports that enable you to drill down from a summary report to a much more detailed report. Sage also has some new Profit and Loss reports and a new Balance Sheet report. You can access all these reports from Company⇨Financials⇨Reports⇨Management Analysis Reports. See Chapter 20 for more detail on these reports.

Checking the Chart of Accounts First

You must check the Chart of Accounts (COA) for errors before you run financial reports as errors in the COA can affect the accuracy of the reports. (Refer to Chapter 2 for more information on the COA.) If you try to run a balance sheet without checking, you're likely to get a message saying that errors exist in the Chart of Accounts and that the reports may be inaccurate as a result. And no one likes having a machine tell them they're wrong!

To check the COA for errors, click COA from the Company module, highlight the COA you want to check, click edit and then click the Check box. If there are no errors, Sage advises you of this. If there are errors, Sage allows you to print or preview the errors.

Figuring Out the Financial Reports

The reports that give you a view of the business-end of your business are the Trial Balance, Profit and Loss and Balance Sheet reports. You generally run each report at the end of the accounting period, whether that's every month, every quarter or annually. I cover each report in the following sections.

Trying for an initial Trial Balance

This report doesn't show up in a pretty layout – it's basically a list of numbers in nominal code order, and numbers are rarely lovely to look at – but the Trial Balance forms the basis of your Profit and Loss and Balance Sheet reports, so it's very important.

In this report, you see a list of all debit or credit balances in nominal code order for the period you specify – you have to specify a month, and Sage presents the balance at that time. The report only shows nominal codes that have a balance, so any codes with a zero balance don't make the list. As the example in Figure 18-1 shows, the debits and credits are in separate columns with totals at the bottom of each. Because of the double-entry bookkeeping principles (mandating a debit for every credit), the two columns balance.

Date: 12/11/2008		*Jingles*		**Page:** 1
Time: 16:01:24		Period Trial Balance		
To Period:	Month 5, August 2008			
N/C	**Name**		**Debit**	**Credit**
0020	Plant and Machinery		5,000.00	
1001	Stock		400.00	
1100	Debtors Control Account		17.75	
1200	Bank Current Account		938.95	
2100	Creditors Control Account			1,323.65
2200	Sales Tax Control Account			42.85
2201	Purchase Tax Control Account		247.20	
3020	Capital Introduced			6,500.00
3100	Reserves			100.00
4000	Sales of Greetings Cards			219.90
4010	Sales of Balloons			25.00
4902	Commissions Received			55.00
5000	Purchase of cards		126.50	
5015	Purchase of Party Gifts		286.00	
5150	Party Organising Costs		1,000.00	
7004	Wages - Regular		250.00	
		Totals:	8,266.40	8,266.40

Figure 18-1: Jingles' Trial Balance for the period ended in August.

Jingles is still quite a new company and doesn't have many transactions yet, nor does it use many nominal codes. As business increases, the number of codes – and hence the Trial Balance – increases in length.

In a Trial Balance, you can see at a glance the extent of your assets and liabilities and use it as an investigative tool. For example, if something seems out of whack, you can run more detailed reports to see where the numbers came from. For example, the Jingles' accountant is interested in finding out why

£5,000 is posted to Plant and Machinery and runs a Nominal Activity report to investigate further. (See Chapter 20 to find out how to run a Nominal Activity report.)

To run a Trial Balance, follow these steps:

1. **From Company, click Financials from the Links list.**

   The Financials window opens.

   Alternatively, from the main toolbar, click Modules and then Financials.

2. **Click the Trial icon.**

   The Print Output box opens.

3. **Select Preview and then click Run.**

   The Criteria box opens.

4. **Use the dropdown arrow to select the period you want to view.**

   In the example in Figure 18-1, I used August 2008.

5. **Click OK.**

   The Trial Balance report appears.

6. **Click Print, Email or Export to send the report to the destination of your choice.**

7. **Click Close to exit the report and return to the Financials window.**

Accounting for profit and loss

Owners and directors of businesses really like the Profit and Loss report (or at least they should do) because it shows them if they're making any money! The Profit and Loss report shows the total revenue (sales) that your company has made in the specified period and then deducts both direct costs and overheads for that same period to arrive at a profit or loss for the period.

The layout of the Profit and Loss report is a standard format, but you can use the Chart of Accounts function to rename headings and group together your nominal codes so that the Profit and Loss report appears with terminology suited to your business. (Refer to Chapter 2 to see how to edit your Chart of Accounts.)

To run your Profit and Loss report, follow these steps:

1. **From Company, click Financials and then P and L.**

2. **Select the Print Output that you want and then click Run.**

You have a choice to print, preview, send to a file or email. Previewing first is wise, so that you can see if you're happy with the report criteria you chose.

The Criteria box opens.

3. **Select the period for which you want to run the report by filling in the From and To dates.**

4. **Select the Chart of Accounts layout you want, using the dropdown to select a Chart of Accounts layout other than the default. Then click OK.**

   Refer to Chapter 2 for information on adding new COA layouts.

   The Profit and Loss report appears. It's split into two columns, one showing the current period and the other showing the year-to-date (YTD).

   Be aware that if you select a full year as your From and To dates, you end up with both columns showing the same figures. If you choose a single month (for example, June) in the criteria, the Period column then differentiates the current period (June) from the year-to-date figures. Of course, the numbers for the first month of the year and the YTD numbers are the same!

5. **Choose to Print, Email or Export the report.**

   Perhaps your bank manager would appreciate timely receipt of monthly accounts via email!

In Figure 18-2, the From and To dates are the same (both August 2008, the fifth month of the business year) so the Profit and Loss report shows just the month of August. The year-to-date (YTD) figures aren't very different, which tells you that the majority of Jingles' business was done in the month of August – probably a fair representation with a new business.

Sage introduced some new Profit and Loss and Balance Sheet reports, which you can find in the new Management Analysis Reports folder contained within the Financial reports. These new reports enable you to drill down from the face of the reports to investigate figures further. They also provide useful variance reports that managers of the business may find interesting. To find out how to run these reports, look at Chapter 20.

Weighing the Balance Sheet

A lot of people don't really understand what a Balance Sheet tells them, but it's a really useful tool for establishing the financial position of a company because it provides a snapshot of the business at a point in time. The Balance Sheet shows the assets and liabilities and the sources of funds that helped finance the business. From a Balance Sheet, you can see how much money is owed to the business and how much the business owes.

Date: 25/09/2008   Jingles   Page: 1
Time: 22:22:53   Profit and Loss

From: Month 5, August 2008
To: Month 5, August 2008

Chart of Accounts: Default Layout of Accounts

                                    Period   Year to Date
Sales
Shop Sales   0.00   304.60
Party Fees   3,042.44   3,142.44
Other Sales   5,000.00   5,055.00
                                             8,042.44   8,502.04
Purchases
Purchases   776.63   1,189.13
Purchase Charges   1,000.46   1,000.46
                                             1,777.09   2,189.59
Direct Expenses
                                             0.00   0.00
                Gross Profit/(Loss):   6,265.35   6,312.45
Overheads
Gross Wages   130.00   380.00
Bank Charges and Interest   (71.04)   (71.04)
                                             58.96   308.96
                Net Profit/(Loss):   6,206.39   6,003.49

Figure 18-2:
A Profit and
Loss report
for Jingles.

The Balance Sheet forms part of the management accounts of the business
and is traditionally issued at the month-end, quarter-end and year-end. Some
people prefer to issue just one set of accounts at the year-end, but others
prefer a more regular source of information and require monthly accounts.

Follow these steps to run a Balance Sheet:

1. **From Company, click Financials from the Links list.**

   Alternatively, click Modules and then Financials from the main toolbar.

2. **Click Balance to open the Print Output box.**

3. **Select Preview and then click Run.**

   The Criteria box opens up.

4. **Use the dropdown arrow to select the period From and To that you
   want to view.**

   If you have more than one Chart of Accounts layout, select the one you
   want to preview. Refer to Chapter 2 for details on setting up additional
   Charts of Accounts.

   The Jingles example in Figure 18-3 uses Month 5 August to Month 5
   August 2008 for a snapshot of August's numbers.

5. **Click OK to open up the Balance Sheet.**

   As in the Profit and Loss report, the Balance Sheet shows a Period
   column and a Year-to-Date column.

Date: 24/10/2008 Jingles Page: 1
Time: 09:43:24 Balance Sheet

From: Month 5, August 2008
To: Month 5, August 2008
Chart of Account: Default Layout of Accounts

	Period		Year to Date	
Fixed Assets				
Plant and Machinery	0.00		5,000.00	
		0.00		5,000.00
Current Assets				
Stock	0.00		400.00	
Debtors	3,567.44		3,772.84	
Bank Account	4,941.04		5,879.99	
		8,508.48		10,052.83
Current Liabilities				
Creditors : Short Term	2,079.18		2,227.83	
VAT Liability	222.91		221.51	
		2,302.09		2,449.34
Current Assets less Current Liabilities:		6,206.39		7,603.49
Total Assets less Current Liabilities:		6,206.39		12,603.49
Long Term Liabilities				
		0.00		0.00
Total Assets less Total Liabilities:		6,206.39		12,603.49
Capital & Reserves				
Share Capital	0.00		6,500.00	
Reserves	0.00		100.00	
P&L Account	6,206.39		6,003.49	
		6,206.39		12,603.49

Figure 18-3: Balance Sheet for Jingles as at 31 August 2008.

Make sure that you understand the component parts of the Balance Sheet. For example, can you agree your debtors figure in the Balance Sheet to an Aged Debtors report? Do you understand what transactions are included in the accruals and prepayments? You can check all figures by looking at your Chart of Accounts and determining which nominal codes represent each section of the Balance Sheet. You can then print a Nominal Activity report to see what transactions are included (check out Chapter 20 for how to do this).

Keeping an Eye on Your Budget Report

Providing you set your monthly budget figures within each nominal record, you can run reports comparing actual figures versus budget figures to calculate a variance. The *actual figures* are the cumulative values posted to each individual nominal record for the period you select. The *budget figures* are the values that you recorded when you set budgets for the forthcoming year; you can attribute each nominal account a budget. The *variance* is calculated by subtracting the budgeted figure from the actual. If the actual figure is smaller than the budget, the variance figure has brackets around it.

The Budget report is in the same format as a Profit and Loss report (refer to Figure 18-1), with additional columns for Actual, Ratio, Budget and Variance for both the current period and the year-to-date.

To run the Budget report, follow these steps:

1. **From the Financials window, click the Variance icon.**

   The Print Output box opens.

2. **Specify whether you want to Print, Preview, Email or Send to a file.**
3. **Click Run.**

   The Criteria box opens.

4. **Select the period for which you want to run the report and then click OK.**

Figure 18-4 shows Jingles' Budget report from April through August.

Date: 28/09/2008
Time: 21:15:35

Jingles
Budget Report

Page: 1

From: Month 1, April 2008
To: Month 5, August 2008

Chart of Accounts: Default Layout of Accounts

	Period				Year to Date			
	Actual	**Ratio(%)**	**Budget**	**Variance**	**Actual**	**Ratio(%)**	**Budget**	**Variance**
Sales								
Shop Sales	304.60	3.58	2,000.00	(1,695.40)	304.60	3.58	2,000.00	(1,695.40)
Party Fees	3,142.44	36.96	3,000.00	142.44	3,142.44	36.96	3,000.00	142.44
Other Sales	5,055.00	59.46	0.00	5,055.00	5,055.00	59.46	0.00	5,055.00
	8,502.04	100.00	5,000.00	3,502.04	8,502.04	100.00	5,000.00	3,502.04
Purchases								
Purchases	1,189.13	13.99	1,800.00	(610.87)	1,189.13	13.99	1,800.00	(610.87)
Purchase Charges	1,000.46	11.77	1,000.00	0.46	1,000.46	11.77	1,000.00	0.46
	2,189.59	25.75	2,800.00	(610.41)	2,189.59	25.75	2,800.00	(610.41)
Direct Expenses								
	0.00	0.00	0.00	0.00	0.00	0.00	0.00	0.00
Gross Profit/(Loss):	6,312.45	74.25	2,200.00	4,112.45	6,312.45	74.25	2,200.00	4,112.45
Overheads								
Gross Wages	380.00	4.47	750.00	(370.00)	380.00	4.47	750.00	(370.00)
Bank Charges and Interest	(71.04)	(0.84)	0.00	(71.04)	(71.04)	(0.84)	0.00	(71.04)
	308.96	3.63	750.00	(441.04)	308.96	3.63	750.00	(441.04)
Net Profit/(Loss):	6,003.49	70.61	1,450.00	4,553.49	6,003.49	70.61	1,450.00	4,553.49

Figure 18-4: Checking to see if Jingles is on budget.

You may consider putting the Budget report in your management accounts pack because it gives a clear indication of how well the business is doing compared to budget.

Looking Back with the Prior Year Report

Similar to the Budget report, the Prior Year report compares your figures to the prior year's numbers rather than to the current budget. Some companies use prior-year data to establish if they're doing better than last year.

To run this report, click the Prior Year icon within Financials. Follow Steps 2 through 4 as for the Budget report in the preceding section to generate the report.

The report shows actual and prior-year numbers and also calculates the variance between the two. The report also includes a Ratio column, which is calculated by taking the actual figure for each row and calculating it as a percentage of total sales.

Viewing the Audit Trail

The _audit trail_ is a list of all the transactions that have ever occurred in Sage, including those subsequently deleted. So when you make a complete mess of something, rest assured that you can never escape it. It's there for all to see – even your accountant and the auditor, who may use it at year-end!

Sage lists the transactions in the audit trail chronologically and each has a unique transaction number. This number is used alongside a search tool to find a particular transaction, which is useful if you need to correct a specific transaction.

You can clear the audit trail periodically to remove the details of the transactions, but the balances are kept and carried forward so that the accounts remain accurate. You can find an explanation of this routine in Chapter 16. However, Sage has the capacity to hold 2 billion transactions in the audit trail, so you don't actually ever have to clear it down if you don't want to.

You get on the audit trail through the Financial module. You can click the Audit icon to explore further. The Audit reports are available in brief, summary, detailed and deleted transactions. The first three reports show the transactions in varying levels of detail; the last shows exactly what it says – transactions you deleted from the system. The report lists a line per transaction, so if you have thousands of transactions, the whole report can be extremely long!

To run the audit trail, follow these steps:

1. **From Company, click Financials and then the Audit icon.**

   The Audit Trail Report window opens.

2. **Enter your choice of audit report – brief, summary, detailed or deleted transactions. Then choose the method of output and click Run.**

   The Criteria box opens.

3. **Choose the criteria required for this report.**

   Sage recommends that you run this report on a monthly basis, so enter the current month dates.

4. **Click OK to generate the report.**

   If you choose to preview the report, providing you're happy with the way it looks, you can print, export or email it from this screen.

5. **Click Close to exit the report and return to the Financials screen.**

You usually print off the audit trail at the end of each period, and it provides a hard copy of all business transactions. Often, it's printed at the year-end to provide a copy for the auditors, but it's up to you how regularly you decide to print it. Obviously the longer the period, the longer the report.

Figure 18-5 shows an extract from a brief Audit Trail report for Jingles.

| Date: | 26/09/2008 | | | | Jingles | | | Page: | 1 |
| Time: | 10:25:01 | | | | Audit Trail (Brief) | | | | |

Date From:		01/01/1980				Customer From:		
Date To:		31/12/2019				Customer To:		ZZZZZZZZ
Transaction From:		1				Supplier From:		
Transaction To:		99,999,999				Supplier To:		ZZZZZZZZ

Exclude Deleted Tran: No

No	Items	Type	A/C	Date	Ref	Details	Net	Tax	Gross
1	1	JD	1200	31/03/2008	O/Bal	Opening Balance	1,200.00	0.00	1,200.00
2	1	JC	9998	31/03/2008	O/Bal	Opening Balance	1,200.00	0.00	1,200.00
3	1	JD	0020	01/04/2008	O/Bal	Opening Balance	5,000.00	0.00	5,000.00
4	1	JC	9998	01/04/2008	O/Bal	Opening Balance	5,000.00	0.00	5,000.00
5	1	JC	3020	31/03/2008	O/Bal	Opening Balance	6,500.00	0.00	6,500.00
6	1	JD	9998	31/03/2008	O/Bal	Opening Balance	6,500.00	0.00	6,500.00
7	1	JD	1100	31/03/2008	O/Bal	Opening Balance	100.00	0.00	100.00
8	1	JC	9998	31/03/2008	O/Bal	Opening Balance	100.00	0.00	100.00
9	1	JD	1001	31/03/2008	O/Bal	Opening Balance	400.00	0.00	400.00
10	1	JC	9998	31/03/2008	O/Bal	Opening Balance	400.00	0.00	400.00
11	1	JC	1100	31/03/2008	Reversal	reverse op bal	100.00	0.00	100.00
12	1	JD	9998	31/03/2008	Reversal	reverse op bal	100.00	0.00	100.00
13	1	JC	3100	31/03/2008	O/Bal	Opening Balance	100.00	0.00	100.00
14	1	JD	9998	31/03/2008	O/Bal	Opening Balance	100.00	0.00	100.00
15	1	BP	1200	31/03/2008	UP	Deleted BP	400.00	0.00	400.00
16	1	SI	VILLAGE	01/04/2008	0001	200 Variety pack of	200.00	35.00	235.00
17	1	SI	VILLAGE	15/04/2008	0002	100 packs of	50.00	8.75	58.75
18	1	SC	VILLAGE	15/04/2008	0002C	Credit Note for Inv	25.00	4.38	29.38
19	1	SR	VILLAGE	12/04/2008	BACS	Sales Receipt	235.00	0.00	235.00
20	1	SA	VILLAGE	01/06/2008	Overpaid	Payment on Account	35.00	0.00	35.00
21	1	SI	VILLAGE	11/06/2008	1	Card - Happy Birthday	19.90	3.48	23.38
22	2	PI	PAPER	01/05/2008	0001	Inv 5467 Supply of	286.00	50.05	336.05
24	3	PI	DERBY	13/05/2008	0002	Inv 4536A 10 Packs	117.00	20.48	137.48
27	1	PC	DERBY	20/05/2008	002C	CN 4536C to credit	28.00	4.90	32.90

Figure 18-5:
An extract from the Audit Trail report – the brief version.

Forgetting the Periods and Going Transactional

Instead of generating reports based on information from a specific period, you can have Sage produce Profit and Loss, Balance Sheet or Trial Balance reports based on transactions instead of time periods. These transactional reports look very similar to period-based reports, but are calculated in a different way. For example, you have to run period-based reports for a complete month, but with a transactional report you can be more precise in selecting your data.

Transactional reports are very handy if you want to look at a specific area or time period in your business. For example, if you ran a promotion over a six-week period and want to view the effects on sales of that promotion, you can run a transactional Profit and Loss report for that specific six-week period.

You can create transactional-based reports for any date range, taking figures from the audit trail, which I talk about in the preceding 'Viewing the Audit Trail' section.

In order to prepare transactional reports, you need to group the transactions obtained from the audit trail into brought-forward figures, current-period figures and year-to-date figures to help structure the reports. These groupings are outlined below in more detail.

Going by date

You can run transactional reports by selecting a specific date range. The dates you use allow Sage to correctly categorise the transactions into three categories:

- **Brought Forward figures:** Year-to-date figures, which include the current year's activity but also include the balance brought forward from the previous year.

- **Current Period figures:** These numbers come from the From and To dates you select in the Criteria box for the period you want to report on. (See the upcoming 'Running the reports' section.)

- **Year-to-Date figures:** This category encompasses the period from the start of the financial year to the end of the period you select. For example, if you select 1 June 09 to 15 July 09, the year-to-date figures show from 1 January to 15 July 09 (assuming a December year-end). The year-to-date figures are standard comparative data that Sage uses to compare with the current-period figures.

You need to complete the Criteria box in the report with the specific dates you want to report on. For example, if you choose from 1 June to 15 July, that range is your Current Period. The report is then generated using those precise dates.

Being number-friendly

You can also run transactional reports by selecting a transaction number range rather than the date range. To use the transaction numbers, make sure that you know what the first transaction number is for the current year. Knowing this number helps Sage determine if the transaction is prior year or not, which is necessary for Balance Sheet information. You also need to specify the range of transactions numbers for the specific period you want to report on.

Running the reports

You can run transactional Profit and Loss, Balance Sheet and Trial Balance reports. To run any of these reports, follow these steps:

1. **From Company, click Financials (from the Links List) and then the Report icon.**

   The report browser will open.

2. **Highlight either the Profit and Loss, Balance Sheet or Trial Balance (from the left side of the report browser screen).**

   This gives you several report options on the right hand side of the screen.

3. **Highlight the transactional report option.**

   Notice that the icons at the top of the report browser screen have now become coloured – they were grey previously.

4. **Select, preview, print, file or email.**

   Click the icon only once – this loads up the Criteria Value screen. If you double click the report on the right side of the screen, it will automatically open the Criteria Value box, which allows you to preview the report.

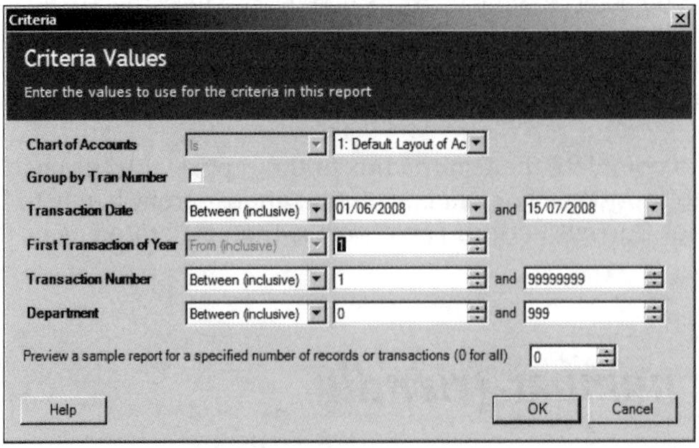

Figure 18-6: Selecting the criteria for a six-week period.

5. **When you're happy with the numbers you entered, click OK.**

   Your report is generated.

This method of reporting allows you to track your business progress for any accounting period, even a day or a week! It gives you much more flexibility over the information that you produce and certainly aids decision-making.

If you've run the Clear Audit Trail option up to a given period, you're not able to run transactional reports for that period.

Designing Reports to Suit Yourself

Sometimes you need to personalise one of the many standard reports Sage offers. You can change the existing layouts to suit yourself by using Report Designer.

Designing reports is a huge topic, and Sage used to have a separate reference book just to deal with report writing. Due to the nature of *For Dummies* books, I don't delve too deeply into this subject, I just scratch the surface by showing you how to take an existing report and tweak it slightly.

The easiest place to start is by finding a report that almost matches your needs, but not quite. You can then take this report, save it under a different file name and then reconfigure it with information that suits your business needs.

To reconfigure a report, follow these steps:

1. **Find the report you want to amend and make a note of the file name.**

   To do this, click the report icon in the relevant module. This opens up the Report Browser. For example, in the Projects module, you could select the Project Details Reports and then the Project Activity report. Make a note of the filename next to the report you have chosen. For example, the filename for the Project Activity Report is PJACT.report

2. **Open up Report Designer by clicking Tools from the main toolbar, and then clicking Report Designer.**

   Use the file explorer on the left side of the screen to locate the report, using the filename you found in Step 1.

   For example, double-click Reports, Project and then Project Details Reports.

3. **Double-click the actual file.**

   The file opens in Report Designer format, which looks pretty messy, as shown in Figure 18-7!

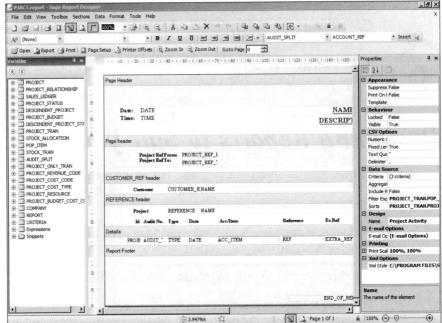

Figure 18-7:
The Project
Activity
Report
viewed
through
Report
Designer.

4. **Save the report with your new file name, before you start to make changes to it, by clicking File⇨Save As and typing in a new filename.**

   The Save As screen opens. On the left are folders containing saved reports. Sage saves the report you're tweaking in the My Project Reports folder and names it 'copy of XX'.

   I rename my file KELLYPJACT.report, as Figure 18-8 shows.

5. **Click Save.**

   You're now returned to the Report Designer screen.

6. **Make amendments to the report by using the Toolbox on the main toolbar or pressing F1 for Report Designer Help.**

   Some of the changes you can make include:

   - **Insert text:** Click **Toolbox⇨Text Box**. Use the mouse to drag and insert a text box in the appropriate part of the screen.

   - **Insert new variables:** Click **View⇨Variables**. A list opens up on the left side of the screen for new variables. You can drag and drop suitable variables into the main body of the report.

     Variables are the different possibilities for categorising something. For example, I added the variable Project Status into the report.

   Figure 18-9 shows the altered report with new variable Project Status circled.

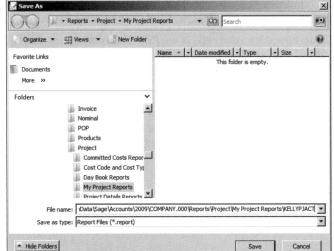

Figure 18-8:
Saving
the report
with a new
filename
in Report
Designer.

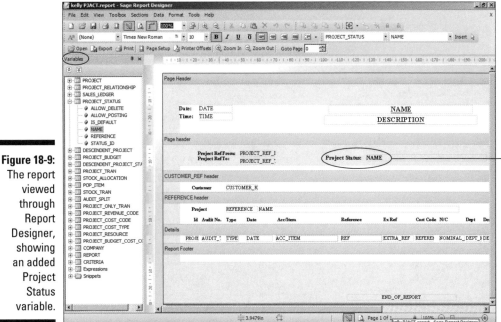

Figure 18-9:
The report
viewed
through
Report
Designer,
showing
an added
Project
Status
variable.

Variable added

Just play around with the report format until you find something that
you can work with.

7. **Click File from the main toolbar and then click Exit when you're happy with the report design. Click Yes to save the report.**

   You can now enter the report section of the module you've just amended a report for and click My Reports to see a copy of your own report with the amendments showing.

You have to be patient and prepared to spend time playing around with the format of your reports. But if you persist, you can come up with some useful and personalised reports. For the lazy ones amongst us (myself included), Sage still has plenty of standard reports to use!

Chapter 19

Tackling the Complicated Stuff

. . . .

In This Chapter

▶ Sending data out

▶ Bringing data in

▶ Using the Accountant Link

▶ Banking electronically

▶ Managing paperwork with Document Manager

. . . .

*W*hen you're confident that you've got to grips with the day-to-day mechanics of the Sage system, you can tackle some of the more advanced options that Sage offers.

The extras I explain in this chapter include the ability to extract data from Sage, make changes within a spreadsheet to that data and then import those changes back into Sage. You can also discover how to relay information to your accountant with minimum disruption to your data and your day-to-day workings with it.

I also look at the impact of using e-Banking to speed up the processing of banking transactions and how the Document Manager can help you organise your paperwork – electronic and hard copy.

Becoming competent with any of the techniques discussed in this chapter will make you justifiably proud of yourself, so get to it!

Exporting Data

You can send data from Sage to Microsoft Excel, Word or Outlook, and the next sections tell you how.

Sending spreadsheet stuff

The list of information you can send to Excel is too long to list, so to find out if you can extract what you want to extract, press the F1 key and type **exporting data** into the Help field to get a list of the reports you can extract from each module.

The idea of sending information from Sage to Excel is that you can mess about with the data in a spreadsheet to your heart's content without affecting the data held within Sage. You may want to edit the data and design specific reports and what-if scenarios to suit the purposes of your business.

To do this, from the window you want to export, click File from the main toolbar, then Office Integration, then Contents to Microsoft Excel.

Transferring Outlook contacts

You can send customer and supplier contact information from Sage 50 Accounts to Microsoft Outlook. This option is an excellent time-saving device, as it means that you don't have to type the information in twice.

The option creates a contact record within Microsoft Outlook for customers and suppliers who have a name entered on their customer or supplier record.

If you have two accounts with the same name, Sage creates two contact records, as the two contacts may be two different people, for example, if two John Smiths are listed.

You can also make changes in Sage and then send those changes to Microsoft Outlook with the amended contact details.

To export account information to Outlook, follow these steps:

1. **From the Sage main toolbar, click File⇨Office Integration⇨Microsoft Outlook Import/Export Wizard.**

   The Welcome screen for the Import/Export wizard opens, which shows the three actions you can perform: Import Outlook Diary Events, Export Diary Events To Outlook and Export Contacts To Outlook.

2. **Select Export Contacts To Outlook.**

   You can choose the other destinations if you prefer.

3. **Follow the instructions on the wizard, clicking Next to continue on to each screen.**

When you've completed the transfer of information, a confirmation message appears, saying that the transfer has been successful. If a different message comes up, follow the advice on the screen. It may be that the folder to which you're trying to send information doesn't allow access, and Sage then suggests alternatives.

Exporting to Word

You can also send data to Microsoft Word from Sage. You can send information to a new or existing document or even as a mail-merge. For example, you can send a list of customer records to Word and mailmerge the contact details with a standard letter from Microsoft Word.

Exporting to Word can be helpful, for example, if you run a sales promotion and want to contact all your customers to make them aware of the promotion. You can produce a leaflet or a letter within Microsoft Word and send the customer contacts from Sage across to Word so that the names and addresses can be merged into your Word document. You save time as you don't have to type in the individual names and addresses for all your customers.

To do this, follow these steps:

1. **From Sage, select the items from which you want to export data and click File from the main toolbar.**

2. **Click Office Integration⇨Contents to Microsoft Word and the option that suits you.**

   You choices are:

   - **New Document:** You can create a new Word document to hold the information extracted from Sage.

   - **Open Document:** You can open an existing Word document, for example, a promotions letter. You can insert merge boxes, allowing you to personalise the promotion document with the customer details.

   - **Run Mail Merge:** You can use the selected data extracted from Sage in a mail-merge document.

Choosing an alternative export method

You can also use a different method for exporting data. I sometimes preview a standard report, such as a Nominal Activity report, and after the report has been generated, export it. To find out how to run a Nominal Activity report, see Chapter 20.

To export information from a report, use these steps:

1. **Open your chosen report as normal and preview it. From the main toolbar of the previewed report, click Export.**

   The Save As window appears.

2. **Choose a folder to save the file in and save the file, using a name you can remember.**

   The file type must be a *CSV* file – a *comma separated values* file is a special file format needed for performing these kinds of tasks.

3. **Click Save.**

   You're then returned to the actual report itself.

4. **Open up Microsoft Excel and find the file you just saved.**

   When you open this report, you find that the data has been sent to Excel, and you can play around with the data and present the information in a more user-friendly way.

5. **Save the file as an Excel workbook to save the changes.**

Importing Data

A data import wizard has been introduced to enhance the existing file import options. You can import either from a CSV file or from a Microsoft Excel spreadsheet (.XLS or XLSX file).

In order to structure your files correctly ready for importing, take a look at the File Import Templates that are installed with your Sage 50 software. You can refer to Help to find out more about the templates.

To use the new data import wizard, you must follow these steps:

1. **From the main toolbar, click on File then Import.**

   Follow the screen prompts which will open the File import wizard.

2. **Click next to work through the wizard.**

   You can access Help at any time whilst using the wizard and move forward and backwards through each screen. Take a backup of your data before proceeding with the import wizard as the procedure is not reversible.

3. **Select, from the menu of the Data type window, what type of data you wish to import.**

4. **Click next to open the Data Source window. This requires you to click whether the data to import is from a CSV file or an Excel worksheet. You then need to select the file that you wish to import (using the Browse button).**

    If the first line of your CSV file or Excel spreadsheet file contains headings, you must check the box to say that it contains headings. If your Excel spreadsheet contains multiple worksheets, you'll be asked to select the one you want to import. You can select the worksheet from the dropdown list provided.

5. **Click next to open the Field Mappings window.**

    If the field in your imported spreadsheet or CSV files contains the headings appropriate to the supplied template, a mapping template will appear (similar to Figure 19.1). You'll see that the imported field name is matched to the corresponding Sage field. In most cases no remapping is required.

    Where you have no header row in your imported file, you'll have no data shown in the left side of the Field Mappings window, but you will still have the Sage headings.

    Where an asterix is shown in the 'Required?' column, a selection must be made in the imported field column to match with an entry in the Sage field. For example, if your Account Reference is Column A of your spreadsheet, then using your dropdown list you select A to map with the corresponding Sage field.

    When you have completed your mapping, you must click Save Map.

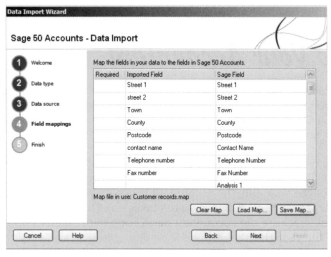

Figure 19-1: Extract of examples of CSV file structures for importing customer/supplier records.

6. **Select a filename and location and save your Data Import Map file, click save.**

   Your map will be saved in your Company .000 Import Maps folder. You can reload maps on other occasions by using the Load Map function in the Field Mappings window of the Data Import Wizard. If you make a mistake whilst mapping your fields, you can click Clear Map and start again.

7. **Click next, once your field mapping is complete, and the Finish window appears.**

   A summary of the options you have chosen in the previous windows of the import wizard appears. If you are happy with the summary, begin importing the data by clicking the finish button.

   Don't forget that prior to clicking Finish, you can always modify any of your selections by using the Back button.

8. **When the data has finished importing, the Import Results Window appears.**

   This screen is split into two parts, the top part showing the fields that have been imported and the bottom part showing the records that have not been imported. Obviously you are hoping that you have no records in the bottom half of the screen!

Check your data files after completion of the import. Use the File⇨ Maintenance⇨Check Data options.

If you leave a blank line between the headings and the actual information, it will not import correctly. Delete the line with no information and the import should then work (I know, because I made the same mistake!).

Linking to Your Accountant

How would you like to cut down your accountant's bill? Well, by using Accountant Link within Sage, you can, as long as your accountant has access to Sage 50 Client Manager. You can save untold amounts of time for both you and your accountant.

Normally, you employ an accountant to help you with quarterly VAT returns, and more likely with the year-end accounts and tax computations. At some point after the year-end, the accountant requests your data files and takes them away to work on. This task often takes months, and you're left unable to use Sage because the accountant has a copy of the dataset and hasn't finalised the year-end.

But with Sage Version 11 and onwards, this wasted time is a thing of the past: clients and their accountants can exchange data in a speedy and accurate fashion.

Essentially, you send data from the company to the accountant, and the accountant can process adjustments while you continue to work on the data. The accountant can then send the adjustments back to you to apply them to your data. The Accountant Link keeps a log of any changes made to the data in the intervening period and both users keep one another informed of those changes.

The Accountant Link is a wizard that guides both you and your accountant through the different stages of the process. To access the wizard, from the main toolbar, click Modules➪Wizards➪Accountant Link. The wizard is split into two parts: one part exports data to the accountant, records material changes and imports the accountant's adjustments; the other part allows the accountant to import the user's data, record adjustments and export the adjustments to a file and send it back to the client, ready for the company to apply those changes.

When you use the Accountant Link wizard, you're first asked if you want to export your data to your accountant or import your accountant's adjustments. I cover both options in the next sections.

Sending accounts to your accountant

If you select the wizard's Export option, you're guided through the process of exporting your file in a secure password-protected file to your accountant via email.

From the moment you export the data, Sage begins to record changes made. You can print a list of material changes and if necessary show it to your accountant before you import the records back into your system. The kinds of changes that Sage considers to be material are wide-ranging, but include transactions like deleting customer records, restoring data and creating a nominal account.

Getting back adjustments and narratives

Your accountant makes the adjustments and sends the file back to you, for you to apply the adjustments and bring the accounts up to date. The adjustments fall into two categories:

- ✓ **Adjustments:** You can apply these to the accounts automatically from the Comments and Adjustments window. Examples include journals, journal reversals, bank payments and receipts.

- ✓ **Narratives:** Instructions that your accountant sends for changes, which you need to make to your records. You must change the data manually according to your accountant's instructions.

The last section of the wizard helps you to import the adjustments your accountant made to your data.

Allow plenty of uninterrupted time to complete the import process!

You can find further details about the Accountant Link by using the Help system within Sage. Press F1 and type in **accountant link** to get more information if you need it.

Trying e-Banking

How do you fancy a seamless interface between your bank account and Sage? Well, that can be a reality with the use of e-Banking. It allows you to pay your suppliers directly from your bank account by using electronic payments. You can also check your online bank statement against the bank statement generated by your Sage program, as well as import transactions sent by your bank so that you can reconcile those bank transactions within Sage.

Before you can start using this wonderful product, contact your bank and ask for the necessary software. After you set up the banking software, you can then enable the e-Banking options within Sage.

The e-Banking features available may be limited by your bank and the account type. Some banking products allow you to download statements, which helps with the bank reconciliation, but these products may not have the electronic payments option for your suppliers.

The benefits of making electronic payments include:

- ✔ **Fast:** No need to laboriously write out cheques; you click and type your way through invoice payment.

- ✔ **Good control of cash flow:** You know exactly when that payment clears your account – no waiting for cheques to arrive and no delays while the cheques are cashed.

- ✔ **Lower cost:** Online banking transactions are less expensive than clearing cheques and cash – sometimes they're free!

- ✔ **Secure:** No need to keep cash on the premises when you can pay all your debts electronically.

Getting your statements online brings benefits too:

- ✔ **Better cash flow management:** You can easily see what funds are available at any time.

- ✔ **Efficient:** Accounts can be kept up to date by seeing up-to-date information regarding interest payments, direct debits, bank charges and so on.

✔ **Environmentally sound:** No paper statements means saving trees and sparing the planet the chemicals used to make paper, ink and stamps.

✔ **Saving time:** You don't have to wait for statements to arrive by post, you can reconcile straight away.

Configuring your e-Banking

You need to make sure that Sage can interpret the file format required by your electronic banking system. So, before you can start using e-Banking, you need to configure your electronic banking facility.

Set your bank defaults to enable e-Banking. Click Bank Defaults within the Links list from your Bank module to check this.

To configure your e-banking facility, follow these steps:

1. **From Bank, select the account that you want to configure.**

2. **Click Record and select the Bank Details tab.**

    Enter the sort code and account details. These must match the details that are to be imported from your bank. Figure 19-2 shows the Details tab.

    You must ensure that the 'Enable e-Banking' box is ticked in the bank defaults box (From the main toolbar, click Settings⇨Bank Defaults⇨ Enable e-Banking). If you do not do this, the bank type field will not show on the bank record.

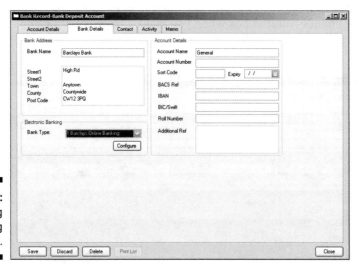

Figure 19-2:
Configuring
e-Banking
with Sage.

3. **Select the bank type that you're going to use.**

   Some examples are Barclays Online Banking and HSBC Hexagon.

4. **Click the Configure button.**

   The Sage e-Banking Configuration screen appears for your selected bank type.

5. **Enter the information requested and click OK to save the changes you've made. Click Save in the Bank Details window to close the bank record and save the changes to the record.**

You can now access the e-Banking options from the Bank Accounts window.

Opting for e-payments

As long as you have banking software that's compatible with Sage 50 Accounts and e-Banking is configured, you can use the e-Payments option and pay suppliers directly from your bank account using electronic payments (see Figure 19-3). You need to know the supplier's sort code, account number, BACS (Bankers' Automated Clearing Services) reference and account name.

Make sure that each of your supplier records is set to allow online payments. To do this, tick the Online Payments box on the Bank tab of the supplier record.

To send payments via e-Banking, you need to enter your supplier payment by using the Bank Supplier Payment option. As long as you've activated that supplier to make online payments, the reference *BACS* automatically appears in the Cheque Number box when you make a payment. When you save the payment, it automatically transfers to the e-Payments window.

Figure 19-3:
Supplier payments using e-Banking.

After you complete the supplier payment information, you can make the e-payment itself.

1. **From Bank, select the bank account from which you want to make an e-payment. Click e-Payments.**

   The Send Payments window appears, showing details of all the outstanding supplier payments that you've set up to use online banking.

   You can restrict the number of transactions that appear by selecting a date range.

2. **Select the transactions that you want to send to your bank and click Send.**

   The transfer of information from Sage to your bank account begins. A confirmation message appears, showing the number and value of payments.

3. **Click OK to continue with the payments. To keep a record of this payment, click Print.**

If any problems occur with transferring your e-payments, you're prompted to view an error log. This log explains why the transfer hasn't been successful.

Reconciling electronically

This option allows you to connect to your banking software and see an electronic copy of your bank statement that you can then use to reconcile your account in Sage.

Make sure that you have e-Banking configured and also that you set up your bank records to allow for online reconciliation.

You also need to be able to import files from your banking software. Your banking software saves this data into a file on your computer. You use this file to reconcile your electronic bank statement to Sage.

If you accidentally reconcile a transaction, you can reverse the reconciliation process by using the Amend Bank Transactions option. From the Reconciliation screen, select Tools, and then, using the dropdown menu, select Amend Bank Transactions. Select the transaction that you want to amend and click Unreconcile.

Going automatic

First of all, you need to import your banking transactions. To do this, follow these steps:

1. **From Bank, select the bank account you want to reconcile and click e-Reconcile.**

   The Amend Bank Statement window appears.

2. **Enter the statement-end date and end balance and then click OK.**

   The Reconciliation From screen appears.

3. **Open the File menu and choose Import Bank Transactions.**

   The Open window for your selected bank appears. The left side of the window shows the files on your computer and the right side shows the bank statement files.

4. **Open the folder where your bank data is saved in the panel on the left.**

   The bank files for the selected bank account are now visible on the right panel.

5. **Select the bank file you want to import from the right panel and click Open.**

   The Reconciliation From window appears, showing your imported transactions. The imported transactions from your bank appear in the top part of the screen and the Sage account transactions in the bottom part of the screen.

6. **Select a method to match transactions.**

   Choose one of the three automatic matching buttons:

   - **Full Match:** Use this button to match items with the same reference and amount.

   - **Match Amount:** Click this to match transactions with the same amounts.

   - **Match Reference:** Use this option to match transactions that share the same reference as shown on the bank statement, such as 'British Gas DD'.

   If no transactions can be matched, a message appears and you can't reconcile your bank transactions with the automatic function. You need to click OK to go back to the Reconciliation screen.

   If Sage finds more than one matching transaction, the Duplicate Transaction window appears. You must select the transaction you want to match by using the Confirm button. If you don't want to confirm the matching transactions but want to carry on with the automatic matching process, click Next. To close the window and not match any transactions, click Cancel.

Matching transactions then appear, highlighted in green. The Matched With column shows the number of transactions that have been matched.

7. **Click Confirm to verify the matched transactions and have them removed from the list.**

   You can view your confirmed transactions by clicking View and then Confirmed.

8. **When you're happy with your confirmed transactions, click Reconcile.**

   Sage marks the matched transactions as reconciled and they no longer appear on the Bank list or the Sage list.

Reconciling manually

Sage recommends that you use both the automatic and manual reconciling options. Use the automatic option first, to match the majority of the items and then finish off the reconciliation with the manual reconciling option.

To do an e-reconciliation manually, follow these steps:

1. **From Bank, click e-Reconcile.**

   The Amend Bank Statements window appears.

2. **Enter the statement-end date and end balance details and then click OK.**

   The Reconciliation screen appears.

3. **Match transactions from the bank list or the Sage list by clicking Match Manual.**

   If the Automatically Confirmed Match Manual box is checked (the default setting), then the Match Manual button confirms the transactions. If you haven't ticked this check box, the transactions are highlighted in green and you must click Confirm before you reconcile those transactions. You can view the confirmed transactions by clicking View and then Confirmed.

4. **To finish the reconciliation, click Reconcile. If you aren't happy with the reconciliation, you can exit without reconciling by clicking Discard.**

5. **Click Yes to the confirmation message that appears or No to return to the Reconciliation screen.**

   The matched and reconciled transactions no longer appear on the Sage or Bank transactions.

Working with Document Manager

Do you feel as if your desk is being weighed down by all the faxes, emails, statements and paperwork you receive on a daily basis? Sage's Document Manager, via Windows Explorer, helps you to organise all your paperwork. It allows you to match contact information and documents with customers, suppliers and bank records within Sage. You can link electronic and paper documents to their associated records on Sage.

You can use the Memo tab located on your customer, supplier and bank records to attach electronic documents, such as a Word document, or electronic copies of statements and letters produced from Sage. Or, you can make a filing system reference to note the location of an actual physical document for this record – the yellow filing cabinet in Accounts, for example.

You can also type free text into the blank section at the bottom of the Memo tab.

Adding attachments and filing system references

Adding an attachment to a record is easy. You first need to open up the Memo tab for your customer, supplier or bank record. The Attachment pane is at the top and the Memo pane is at the bottom. You can drag and drop files into the Attachment pane or use the Add Attachment button at the bottom of the screen.

When you drag a file, the file moves from its original location and ends up in the Sage file. However, you can copy and paste files to avoid this problem.

To attach a memo to a specific record, use Document Manager and follow these steps:

1. **Open the relevant record and then click the Memo tab.**

2. **Click Add Attachment. Choose the type of attachment to add and click OK.**

   The Add New Attachment box appears and asks which type of attachment you want to add. Your attachment choices are Electronic, for any electronic file and Filing System Reference, for a reference to a file location – your choices are pretty clear.

3. **Browse your computer to find the file that you want to attach if you're adding an electronic file. If you're adding a file system reference, enter the location where your paper document is held (the filing cabinet, for example). Click OK.**

   With a reference, you need to type in the name that you want to appear on the Attachment pane for this filing system reference. Make it a name that is meaningful to you, such as Invoice File Location.

4. **If you are selecting a file, double-click the filename and it appears in the Attachment pane of your record.**

   Voilà! The attachment now shows in that supplier record.

Deleting an attachment

If you subsequently find that the attachment you added to your record is no longer required, you can delete it. Simply click the Memo tab of the relevant record and highlight the attachment that you want to delete. Now click Delete Attachment and a confirmation message appears. Click Yes to continue. The attachment disappears.

Chapter 20

Running Key Reports

Sage produces so many reports that it can make your head spin just thinking about them. In this chapter, I pick out the reports I find most useful on a day-to-day basis – my personal top-ten list. I show you how to run each report, and use examples to demonstrate how to use them. You can see lots of lovely pictures – think of it as a bit like the pictures you see in recipe books – and see what Sage *should* look like!

Sage contains lots of other useful reports, you just need to have a good root through and pick the ones that suit you.

Checking Activity through the Nominal Codes

The Nominal Activity report identifies transactions posted to specific nominal codes. It includes transaction types such as purchase invoices, sales invoices, bank payments/receipts and journals, to name but a few. I use this report on a daily basis, sometimes just viewing the activity on screen but sometimes printing the information for further analysis.

This report is useful if you see a figure in the accounts that you want further information on, or if you simply want to know how much has been spent on an item for a specific time-period. For example, you notice a huge figure described as telephone expenses in a month-end report. It looks too high to be just a telephone bill, so you want to investigate further.

First of all, you check your Chart of Accounts to see what range of nominal codes are included in telephone expenses and print a Nominal Activity report for each of the codes. These reports show where the expenditures lie and if any mistakes have been made whilst entering the information.

Figure 20-1 shows a Nominal Activity report for the telephone expenses nominal code, using the demonstration data within Sage. Nothing untoward shows; it looks as if the invoice didn't come in straightaway, and therefore an accrual was made for £50 each month until the invoice was received. The accrual has then been reversed, leaving just the value of the invoice, in this case £178.72, as a balance on the account. No duplicate entries of invoices show, which you need to look for if expenses appear higher than you expect.

Figure 20-1:
An example
of a Nominal
Activity
report,
showing
telephone
expenses.

Date:	14/08/2008			Stationery & Computer Mart UK				Page:	1	
Time:	15:01:55			Nominal Activity						

Date From:	01/01/1980	N/C From:	7502
Date To:	14/08/2008	N/C To:	7502

Transaction From:	1
Transaction To:	99,999,999

N/C	7502	Name:	Telephone				Account Balance:		178.72 DR

No	Type	Date	Account	Ref	Details	Dept	T/C	Value	Debit	Credit	V	B
60	JD	30/01/2006	7502	ACCRUE	Telephone Accrual	0	T9	50.00	50.00		-	-
304	JD	28/02/2007	7502	ACCRUE	Telephone Accrual	0	T9	50.00	50.00		-	-
536	JD	28/03/2007	7502	ACCRUE	Telephone Accrual	0	T9	50.00	50.00		-	-
851	JD	30/04/2007	7502	ACCRUE	Telephone Accrual	0	T9	50.00	50.00		-	-
853	JC	30/04/2007	7502	ACCRUE	Telephone Accrual	0	T9	200.00		200.00	-	-
864	BP	28/04/2007	1200	Tel/4	Telephone to April	1	T1	178.72	178.72		N	N
					Totals:				378.72	200.00		
					History Balance:				178.72			

End of Report

To investigate your own nominal codes, follow these steps:

1. **From Company, click the Reports icon to bring up the Reports Browser window.**

2. **Click on Nominal Activity Reports to show the variety of report options shown on the right hand side of the Report Browser screen. Highlight the activity report required and then click the Preview icon.**

   This brings up the Criteria Values box as shown in Figure 20-2.

3. **Select the nominal code for which you want to generate a report and the date range you want to look at.**

   If you can't remember the code, use the dropdown arrow to identify the nominal codes. You can run the report by using a range of transaction numbers if you know them.

   If you don't put a code in the boxes, Sage uses the default codes 0010–9999. All nominal activities for all nominal codes print. If you have lots of nominal codes, you're going to run out of paper before the report finishes!

Figure 20-2:
Select the
parameters
for your
report from
the Criteria
Values box.

> **Criteria Values**
> Enter the values to use for the criteria in this report.
>
> | | | | | | |
> |---|---|---|---|---|---|
> | **Nominal Code** | Between (inclusive) | 7502 | and | 7502 | |
> | **Transaction Date** | Between (inclusive) | 01/01/1980 | and | 14/08/2008 | |
> | **Transaction Number** | Between (inclusive) | 1 | and | 99999999 | |
> | **Inc B/Fwd Tran** | | | | | |
>
> Preview a sample report for a specified number of records or transactions (0 for all) 0
>
> Help   OK   Cancel

4. **Click OK.**

   The report preview appears on screen, unless you've requested to print
   directly.

5. **Choose whether to print, email or export the report, or just view it on
   screen.**

   If you request print preview, you can scan the report on screen to make
   sure that it's presented the information as expected. If you want to print
   the report, click the Print icon at the top of the Preview screen. This
   takes you into a Print Options box, where you can click OK to continue
   printing or Cancel to return to the report.

   In Chapter 19 you can find out how to export data from Sage into Excel.

6. **Close the report by clicking the black cross in the right corner or
   clicking Close at the top of the Preview screen.**

7. **Click Close to exit the Nominal Reports screen and return to the
   Nominal Ledger window.**

Looking into Supplier Activity

How many times do you receive supplier statements that don't agree with
the figure that you think you owe them? You need to be able to perform a
quick reconciliation to make sure that they're not charging you for things you
haven't had.

You can print a supplier's Activity screen to show you the transactions
entered onto the supplier's account within a specific period and compare
that to the statement from your supplier. You can then see instantly if you
have any invoices missing.

You can also use a Supplier Activity report if you're keen to see how much you spend with a specific supplier. You can see the volume of transactions for a given period of time.

To run a Supplier Activity report, follow these steps:

1. **From Suppliers, click Reports from the Links list or the Reports icon.**

   This opens up the Report Browser.

2. **Click the Supplier Activity Reports and then highlight the report of your choice.**

   I recommend looking at the Supplier Activity (Detailed) report. Once you have highlighted the report, click the Preview Icon. This opens the Criteria Values window as shown in Figure 20-3. Double clicking on the report you wish to view also opens up the Criteria Value box.

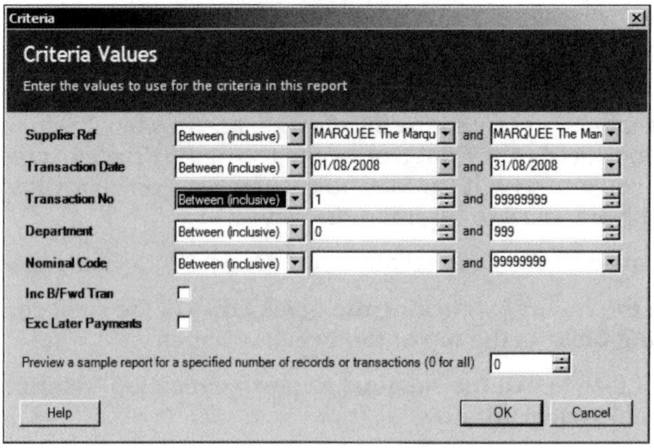

Figure 20-3:
Choose
the criteria
for your
Supplier
Activity
report.

3. **From the dropdown arrow in the Supplier Reference field, select the supplier you want to view and the transaction dates that you require.**

   In Figure 20-3, I chose the Marquee Company as my supplier and requested dates of 01.08.08 to 31.08.08.

4. **Click OK, and the report is displayed in preview format.**

   Figure 20-4 shows the Supplier Activity (Detailed) report for the Marquee Company.

   After you preview the report, you can choose to print, export or email from the toolbar on the report.

5. **Print the report if you want to and then click Close to exit the report.**

6. **Click Close again to close the Reports screen and return to the Supplier window.**

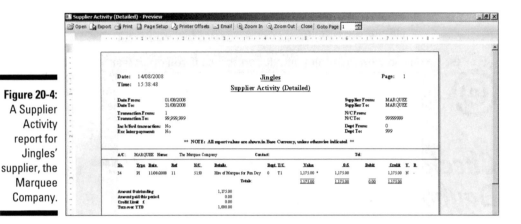

Figure 20-4:
A Supplier
Activity
report for
Jingles'
supplier, the
Marquee
Company.

Tracking Customer Activity

You may be keen to look into the activity of one of your customers for a variety of reasons. Business may have tailed off a little with a customer and you want to see how much it's decreased. You may want to see what types of goods someone has been ordering from you to get an idea of what other products you can suggest. Viewing the Customer Activity report shows you the transactions with a customer for a specified period of time. You can view all transactions, including invoices, credit notes, payments and payments on account.

Usually, you want a hard copy of a report, and you get one by following these steps:

1. **From Customers, click Reports from the Links List or click the Reports icon.**

   The Report Browser opens.

2. **Click on Customer Activity Reports and choose a report option by highlighting it and then clicking the Preview icon.**

   I recommend the Customer Activity (Detailed) Report. The Criteria Value box opens. You can also double click on the report you wish to view to open up the Criteria Value box.

3. **Select the customer you want to look at and enter the range of transaction dates you're interested in.**

4. **Click OK to run the report. Then choose whether to print, email or export the report.**

5. **To close the report, click Close or click the black cross at the right side of the screen.**

You can view customer activity on screen if you don't want to print it by selecting the customer and then clicking the Activity icon. The top half of the split screen that appears shows all transactions and the bottom part shows a breakdown of the item highlighted in the top section of the screen.

Checking Numbers with Supplier Daybook Reports

You can find daybook reports in the customer, supplier and nominal ledgers. I use the supplier daybook reports regularly to check the invoice number on the last invoice I posted. I always like to double-check to ensure that the last filed invoice is in fact the last invoice that was posted on the system. Starting off a numbering sequence for your new batch of supplier invoices only to find that you've duplicated your numbers is very annoying – correcting these kinds of mistakes is very time-consuming, and you have better things to do!

A *daybook* provides a list showing the items entered on the system in the same order that they were input. It shows transaction numbers, transaction types, account references, details of the transaction and the net, VAT and gross amount. Detailed reports often show the nominal code and the department that the transaction has been allocated to. A daybook is important because it allows your accountant to prove that the original source documents, such as sales and purchase invoices, cheque stubs, paying-in slips and electronic payments, have been entered onto the computer.

You can choose from a number of different daybooks. Using Sage, you can print daybooks for all invoices, paid invoices, credit notes and discounts.

For the purposes of finding the last invoice number, you want to choose the Supplier Invoices (Detailed) option from Daybooks. This report clearly shows the invoice reference, so if you scroll down to the bottom of the report, you can see the last invoice reference, which is the last invoice posted.

Just make sure the invoicing sequence runs in order, and you have definitely got the last posted invoice number.

To run a Supplier Daybook report, follow these steps:

1. **From Suppliers, click Reports from the Links List or click the Reports icon.**

   The Report Browser will open.

2. **Click on Daybook Reports and choose a report option by highlighting it and clicking the Preview icon.**

   I recommend the Supplier Invoices (Detailed) Report. The Criteria Value box opens. You can also double click on the report you wish to view to open up the Criteria Value box.

3. **Click OK to run the report.**

   Don't specify any dates if you want the report to list all invoices.

If you're looking for the last invoice number, you scroll to the bottom of the report and check the Invoice Reference column. After you get the number off the report, check to make sure that this agrees to the last invoice filed. If it does, you can start the next batch of invoices with the subsequent number.

Finding the Customers Who Owe You

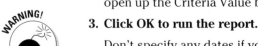

You've heard the saying, 'cash is king', well, never is it truer than in business. A business can make huge losses, but until it runs out of cash, it can still struggle on. If your business is running short of cash because customers aren't paying you promptly, you can produce an Aged Debtors Analysis report to tell you who owes you money, how much and for how long. You can see instantly which customers need a polite kick up the proverbial to help get some cash across to your bank account.

An Aged Debtors Analysis report builds up a payment profile of your customers so that you can see who pays you within 30 days and who takes more than 90 days. You can use this as a tool to determine who you prefer to continue working with. Selling to customers who don't pay you is pointless.

If you have credit controllers working in your company, make sure that they create an up-to-date report each month so that they can collect the debt as efficiently as possible.

Make sure that your bank is reconciled on a regular basis so that the reports are meaningful. You need to be sure that all the cash received has been correctly allocated to the customer accounts so that you have the most up-to-date information available.

The most sensible time to run off an Aged Debtors Analysis report is at the beginning of the month following the month you're trying to chase. For example, you can run the report for the period ended 30 June in the first week of July, when you know that all the sales invoices for June have been posted onto the system and you've had a chance to reconcile the bank up to the end of June. Obviously, you have to wait until you see the bank statements, which sometimes take up to a week to arrive following the month-end. Nowadays, however, with the advent of Internet banking, you can run off your bank statements online and don't have to wait until the end of the month before processing bank entries all in one go.

To run off an Aged Debtors Analysis report, follow these steps:

1. **From Customers, click Reports on the Link List, or click the Reports icon.**

   The Report Browser will open.

   If you can't see the Reports icon, you may have to click the little chevron next to the Letter icon; you may have too many icons to view on the screen at one time.

2. **Click on Aged Debtors Reports and highlight the report of your choice.**

   You're greeted with a raft of options – don't panic! You can run an Aged Debtors Analysis (Detailed) Report (located about one third of the way down the screen), which shows all the individual invoices/credit notes outstanding, or you can run a much shorter Aged Debtors Analysis (Summary) Report (located approximately two thirds of the way down the screen), which shows only the total debt outstanding from each customer. Both reports show the outstanding balance for each customer, and they also both age the debt, so that you can see the current-month debt and those debts that are 30, 60 and 90 days old, and older than 90 days. Once you have highlighted the report of your choice, click the Preview icon and this will open the Criteria Values box.

   You can double click on the report you wish to view to open up the Criteria Value box.

3. **Select the customers and dates for which you want to run an Aged Debtor Analysis report.**

   You normally select everyone, so leave the Customer Reference box as is. However, it's important that you select the correct dates. You need to pick up all transactions outstanding, from day one to the end of the period for which you've decided to run a report, so the end date of the report is the most important one. Choose the end of a period – a month, a quarter and so on.

   If you're trying to run a debtors report to tie in with your accounts at a period end, you need to run the report to the period end, but then select Exclude Later Payments. You only need to do this if you've processed any bank entries after the accounting period that you're trying to reconcile to. For example, if you've produced accounts to 30 June but you've continued to process sales receipts into July, then if you ran the Aged Debtors Analysis to 30 June without checking this box, the current amount outstanding is updated by the July sales receipts and the overall balance of debts outstanding don't agree with the Balance Sheet as at 30 June. By checking the Exclude Later Payments, you can run the report to exclude the July receipts and the report then balances as at 30 June.

4. **Click OK to run the report.**

   Figure 20-5 shows a detailed report.

   You can print or email the report, or export it to Excel.

5. **Click Close to exit the report.**

   This brings you back to the Reports window, where you can click Close again to return to the Customers screen.

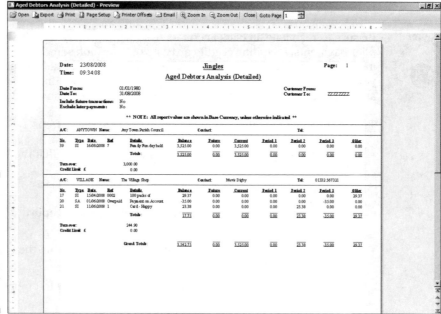

Figure 20-5:
Reviewing the detailed Aged Debtors Analysis report for Jingles.

Paying Attention to Your Creditors

If you are one of those people who's frightened to death to look at your credit card bill, you probably won't like looking at the Aged Creditors report either! It shows a list of all monies owed to your suppliers.

The report is presented in a similar format to the Aged Debtors Analysis, which I cover in the preceding section, and shows how much you owe, to whom, for how long. You can use this report to decide which suppliers you're going to pay at the end of the month. (Type **suggested payments** into the Help facility, and Sage shows you how to run a Suggested Payments report.)

The Aged Creditors report is only useful if you've updated your bank account with all relevant supplier payments, whether Bankers' Automated Clearing Services (BACS) or cheque. Make sure that you reconcile your bank account before you prepare the Aged Creditors report.

Be sure to reconcile all bank accounts from which you're likely to make supplier payments, including credit cards! If you overlook some credit card payments to suppliers, your Aged Creditors Analysis report isn't accurate, and you can potentially end up paying a supplier twice by writing out a cheque and not realising that the debt was already paid by company credit card.

To run the Aged Creditors Analysis report, follow these steps:

1. **From Suppliers, click Reports on the Link List, or click the Reports icon.**

   The Report Browser opens.

2. **Click on Aged Creditors Report and highlight the report of your choice.**

   I usually select Aged Creditors Analysis (detailed) from the raft of options. The Criteria Values box opens.

   You can double click on the report you wish to view to open up the Criteria Value box.

3. **Select the supplier that you want to run an Aged Creditors report for.**

   I usually select all suppliers. If you leave the Supplier Reference fields alone, Sage automatically selects all suppliers. You must use the drop-down arrows if you want to select a specific supplier.

   Ensure that the Date From and To fields are correct. Make sure that you tick the Exclude Later Payment box to tell Sage to ignore information beyond the *To* date.

4. **Click OK to run the report. Choose to print or email the report, or export it to the destination of your choice.**

   Figure 20-6 shows a detailed Aged Creditors Analysis report for Jingles.

5. **To exit the report, click Close.**

   You return to the Reports window. To exit the Reports window, click Close again to return to the Suppliers window.

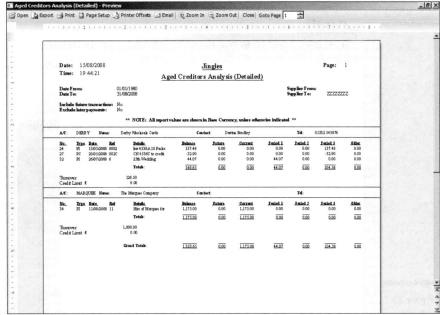

Handling Unreconciled Bank Transactions

After you reconcile your bank account, you probably have a few transactions that you can't reconcile. They may be unreconciled payments or unreconciled receipts.

You quite often have entries posted in Sage that haven't yet cleared the bank account (refer to Chapter 15 for more about reconciling). For example, you post cheques on Sage before they clear the bank account; these are known as *unpresented cheques*. The same applies for receipts; these have the rather weird name of *outstanding lodgements*.

To print an Unpresented Cheques report, follow these steps:

1. From Bank, click Reports from the Links list, or the Reports icon.

If you can't see the Reports icon, click the little chevron at the end of the row of icons to show the list of icons that aren't currently visible.

The Browser Report window opens.

2. **Click Unreconciled Transaction Reports at the bottom of the list of reports.**

   You may need to scroll down the list of reports to see this.

3. **Highlight unreconciled payments, shown in Figure 20-7, and then click the Preview icon.**

   The Criteria Values box opens.

   Double clicking on the report you wish to view will open up the Criteria Value box.

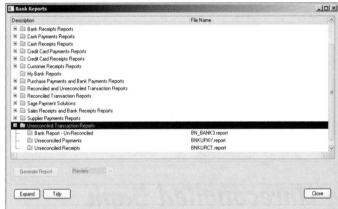

Figure 20-7:
The list of bank reports is long and varied.

4. **Enter the transaction dates that you require.**

   This is usually to the end of the month that you've just reconciled.

5. **Click OK to open the report.**

   You can print, email or export this report to your required destination.

6. **Click Close to exit the report.**

   This returns you to the Bank Reports window. Click Close again to return to the Bank window.

Figure 20-8 shows an Unreconciled Payments report from 01.01.1980 to 31.05.2008. Putting in such a broad range ensures that Sage picks up all transactions, from day one to 31 May 2008. These dates are the correct ones to select if you've just performed a bank reconciliation to 31 May 2008. Notice that the report shows just one entry: cheque number 000045, dated 31 May 2008. This appears to be an unpresented cheque; it was probably written out on the last day of the month and only sent out in the post that day, so it hasn't got as far as being paid into a bank account!

Figure 20-8:
Viewing
a list of
unpresented
cheques for
Jingles.

Date:	16/08/2008			*Jingles*		Page:	1
Time:	07:57:02			Unreconciled Payments			
Date From:	01/01/1980				Bank From:	1200	
Date To:	31/05/2008				Bank To:	1200	
Transaction From:	1						
Transaction To:	99,999,999						
Bank	1200	Bank Account Name	Bank Current Account		Currency	Pound Sterling	
No	Type	Date	Ref	Details		Amount £	
28	PP	31/05/2008	Chq 000045	Purchase Payment		336.05	
					Total £	336.05	

To run an Outstanding Lodgement report, follow these steps:

1. Follow steps 1 and 2 as for the Unpresented Cheques report.

2. Click Unreconciled Receipts.

The Criteria Values box opens.

3. Enter the transaction dates that you require.

This is usually to the end of the month that you've just reconciled.

4. Click OK to open the report.

You can print or email this report, or export it to your required destination.

5. Click Close to exit the report.

This returns you to the Bank Reports window. Click Close again to return to the Bank window.

Your accountant probably requires a copy of your unreconciled bank transactions at the year-end, so don't forget to put a copy in with your data set to send to them. Any extra work that you can do saves on accountancy costs!

Surveying Your Profit and Loss – Actual, Budget and Prior Year

I discuss the Profit and Loss account in Chapter 18, but I mention only the standard layout. Sage has some new Profit and Loss reports available in the Financial Reports section.

These new reports are structured in a column format that lets you compare your current numbers with budgets and prior-year numbers in side-by-side columns. The new reports also have a drilldown facility that gives you access to more levels of information.

To make use of the drilldown function, hover over a particular number with your mouse until the cursor changes to the shape of a hand, and then click that number to reveal more information behind it. For example, you can see what nominal codes were used to provide the number in the Profit and Loss account. To see these new reports, click Company, and then Financials from the Links list, followed by Reports (or click the Reports icon). The Financial Reports window opens. From here, you can double-click Management Analysis reports. The Profit and Loss (Actual, Budget and Prior Year) report option is within the Standard Budgeting section.

To view the Profit and Loss (Actual, Budget and Prior Year) report, follow these steps:

1. **Click on Company followed by Financial Reports in the Links List. This opens the Report Browser. Double click on Management Analysis Reports, and then select the Standard Budgeting option. Highlight Profit and Loss (Actual, Budget & Prior Year).**

   The Criteria Values box opens.

2. **Select the period that you want to run the report for and click OK.**

   The report, as shown in Figure 20-9, opens for you to preview.

Date: 25/09/2008
Time: 21:34:27

Jingles
Profit and Loss (Actual, Budget & Prior Year)

Page: 1

From: Month 1, April 2008
To: Month 12, March 2009

Chart of Accounts: Default Layout of Accounts

	Period			Year to Date		
	Actual	Budget	Prior Year	Actual	Budget	Prior Year
Sales						
Shop Sales	304.60	0.00	0.00	304.60	0.00	0.00
Party Fees	3,157.44	0.00	0.00	3,157.44	0.00	0.00
Other Sales	5,055.00	0.00	0.00	5,055.00	0.00	0.00
	8,517.04	0.00	0.00	8,517.04	0.00	0.00
Purchases						
Purchases	1,189.13	0.00	0.00	1,189.13	0.00	0.00
Purchase Charges	1,000.46	0.00	0.00	1,000.46	0.00	0.00
	2,189.59	0.00	0.00	2,189.59	0.00	0.00
Direct Expenses						
	0.00	0.00	0.00	0.00	0.00	0.00
Gross Profit/(Loss):	**6,327.45**	**0.00**	**0.00**	**6,327.45**	**0.00**	**0.00**
Overheads						
Gross Wages	380.00	0.00	0.00	380.00	0.00	0.00
Bank Charges and Interest	(65.04)	0.00	0.00	(65.04)	0.00	0.00
	314.96	0.00	0.00	314.96	0.00	0.00
Net Profit/(Loss):	**6,012.49**	**0.00**	**0.00**	**6,012.49**	**0.00**	**0.00**

Figure 20-9: Viewing the Profit and Loss (Actual, Budget and Prior Year) report.

From the information in the report in Figure 20-9, you may be tempted to investigate further the Other Sales figure of £5,055 as it looks on the high side. Using the drilldown function (clicking the number when the cursor turns into a hand) produces the detail shown in Figure 20-10.

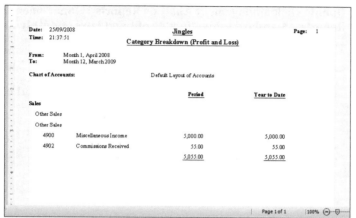

Figure 20-10:
Looking at
the category
breakdown
of Other
Sales.

Having investigated further, you can see that the £5,055 is made up of £5,000 miscellaneous income and £55 commissions received. If you don't remember the source of the £5,000 (I happen to remember it came from a grant), you can run a Nominal Activity report for code 4900 to see what's posted there.

The Profit and Loss (Actual, Budget and Variance) and the Profit and Loss (Actual, Prior Year and Variance) reports are variations on the same theme. You can find both of these reports in the Management Analysis Reports section within Financial Reports.

Doing a Monthly Breakdown of Profit and Loss

The monthly breakdown option is another of the new report layouts and is an incredibly useful report. It shows a month-by-month breakdown of the Profit and Loss account. You can drill down on any number (except for the totals) to see the breakdown of each number and what nominal code the figures are posted to. Seeing trends developing across the months in both income and expenditure is useful.

To run the report, follow these steps:

1. **From Company, click Financial Reports from the Links list. Or, click the Reports from the Financials window.**

   The Report Browser window opens.

2. **Double-click Management Analysis Reports⇨Management Analysis Reports – Standard Budgeting⇨Profit and Loss (Monthly Breakdown).**

   The Criteria Values box opens.

3. **Select the period from and to and click OK.**

   The report now opens and you can choose to print, export or email it.

Figure 20-11 shows a monthly breakdown report for Jingles.

Figure 20-11: An extract of Profit and Loss (Monthly Breakdown) for Jingles.

Date: 28/09/2008				Jingles								Pag
Time: 16:17:02				Profit and Loss (Monthly Breakdown)								
From: Month 1, April 2008												
To: Month 12, March 2009												
Chart of Accounts:				Default Layout of Accounts								
	Apr	**May**	**Jun**	**Jul**	**Aug**	**Sep**	**Oct**	**Nov**	**Dec**	**Jan**	**Feb**	**Mar**
Sales												
Shop Sales	225.00	0.00	39.80	39.80	0.00	0.00	0.00	0.00	0.00	0.00	0.00	0.00
Party Fees	0.00	0.00	100.00	0.00	3,042.44	15.00	0.00	0.00	0.00	0.00	0.00	0.00
Other Sales	0.00	0.00	55.00	0.00	5,000.00	0.00	0.00	0.00	0.00	0.00	0.00	0.00
	225.00	**0.00**	**194.80**	**39.80**	**8,042.44**	**15.00**	**0.00**	**0.00**	**0.00**	**0.00**	**0.00**	**0.00**
Purchases												
Purchases	0.00	375.00	0.00	37.50	776.63	0.00	0.00	0.00	0.00	0.00	0.00	0.00
Purchase Charges	0.00	0.00	0.00	0.00	1,000.46	0.00	0.00	0.00	0.00	0.00	0.00	0.00
	0.00	**375.00**	**0.00**	**37.50**	**1,777.09**	**0.00**	**0.00**	**0.00**	**0.00**	**0.00**	**0.00**	**0.00**
Direct Expenses												
	0.00	**0.00**	**0.00**	**0.00**	**0.00**	**0.00**	**0.00**	**0.00**	**0.00**	**0.00**	**0.00**	**0.00**
Gross Profit/(Loss)	**225.00**	**(375.00)**	**194.80**	**2.30**	**6,265.35**	**15.00**	**0.00**	**0.00**	**0.00**	**0.00**	**0.00**	**0.00**
Overheads												
Gross Wages	0.00	0.00	0.00	250.00	130.00	0.00	0.00	0.00	0.00	0.00	0.00	0.00
Bank Charges and Interest	0.00	0.00	0.00	0.00	(71.04)	6.00	0.00	0.00	0.00	0.00	0.00	0.00
	0.00	**0.00**	**0.00**	**250.00**	**58.96**	**6.00**	**0.00**	**0.00**	**0.00**	**0.00**	**0.00**	**0.00**

Ranking Your Top Customers

The Top Customers report can be a real eye-opener and is a very useful management tool. You may think you know who your top customers are, but this report may reveal some very interesting results.

The report has a simple layout and shows you the customer account and name, contact details, when you last invoiced them, their credit limit and what the turnover was year-to-date (YTD) or month-to-date (MTD), depending on which you choose.

This is the interesting bit: the customers are arranged in order of turnover, so you can see which customer is invoiced with the highest value, revealing where the bulk of your sales turnover is coming from.

You may find that your turnover is being generated by the top five customers, or you may find that you have twenty customers who spend slightly less individually with you. You may consider this to be more beneficial as it spreads the risk across a wider customer base. If one customer disappears, you aren't going to feel the effect quite so dramatically.

To run the Top Customer report, follow these steps:

1. **From Customers, click Reports from the Links List, or click the Reports icon from the Customers screen.**

   The Reports Browser opens.

2. **Click on Top Customer Reports and then highlight Top Customer List – Year. Click on the Preview icon.**

   The report opens and you can print, email or export it.

You may find it quite useful to export this report and play around with the numbers in a spreadsheet. You can put the information into graphical format to send to managers.

If you run the Top Customer List – Month, you need to ensure that you complete regular month-ends and tick the Clear Turnover Figures in the Month-End window, otherwise the information is the same as the YTD report. Refer to Chapter 16 for more information on running your month-ends.

Figure 20-12 shows a Top Customer report for Jingles.

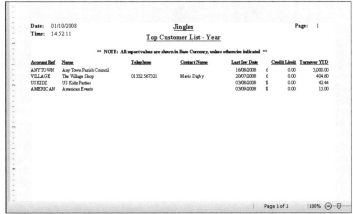

Figure 20-12:
The Top Customer report can provide surprising results.

Part VI
The Part of Tens

'Now we've got all this money, we're going to need a sensible accounting system.'

In this part . . .

This last part includes a detailed look at how function keys can help you speed up data processing and a demonstration of the wonderful ways wizards work their magic to help you with both the basic setting up of records and also some of the trickier aspects of bookkeeping.

Chapter 21

Ten (Okay, Eleven) Funky Functions

. . . .

In This Chapter

▶ Getting help

▶ Finding out about shortcuts

▶ Opening programs

. . . .

*1*f you want to wow your friends (or your boss) with a few neat tricks, then look no further than this chapter! Here, you find out how to use some of the function keys that give you some great shortcuts – for example, the copy key (F6), which speeds up processing no end and F7, which can get you out of a tight spot if you need to insert an extra line somewhere (particularly useful if you've missed a line of information from the middle of a journal). Read on to find out more.

Browsing for Help with F1

Pressing F1 launches the help system. The system is intelligent enough to know which part of the system you're working in and displays the Help screens most suited to your needs. In doing so, it saves you having to scroll through the Help index list to find the appropriate section. For example, if you're in the Batch Entry screen for suppliers, pressing the F1 key brings up a Help screen related to entering purchase invoices.

Calculating Stuff with F2

Having instant access to a calculator is pretty handy, particularly if you're in the middle of a journal and you need to add something up. Simply press your F2 function key, and a little calculator appears on the screen. You can quickly do your sums and then carry on processing information using Sage, without having to dive through your office drawers trying to find the calculator.

Accessing an Edit Item Line for Invoicing with F3

Pressing F3 displays the Edit Item line when you're entering invoices. You can add additional information and comments to your invoice, whether a product or service invoice.

Note: you need to enter some information first before the Edit box will open.

Finding Multiple Functions at F4

Pressing this button does different things depending on which screen or field you're in:

- In a field that has a dropdown arrow, press F4 to display the full list.
- In a Date field, press F4 to show the calendar, instead of clicking the Calendar icon.
- In a numeric field, press F4 to make a mini-calculator appear, instead of clicking the Calculator icon. (F2 opens a calculator in any screen, F4 opens one only if you're in a screen devoted to numbers.)

Calculating Currency or Checking Spelling with F5

The F5 key has dual purposes:

- It shows the Currency calculator when the cursor is in a numeric box. (***Note:*** you need to ensure that your currencies and exchange rates are set up for this to function.)
- It brings up the spell checker when the cursor is in a text box.

Copying with F6

F6 is one of the best inventions ever! It copies entries from the field above, which is particularly useful when you're entering batch invoices (for both customers and suppliers). For example, if a batch of invoices all have the same date, you can enter the date once, and, as you enter each subsequent invoice, press F6 when you get to the Date field. Sage copies the date from the field directly above your line of entry and enters the same date into the invoice on the line of the batch that you're working on. You can do this for any of the fields. So, if you're entering a mass of invoices from the same customer or supplier, you can use F6 to copy the details from one invoice to the next. This function has an amazing impact on the speed of data entry, and it's an absolute godsend when you set up a new system, as you often have a lot of data entry to do.

Inserting a Line with F7

The ability to add a line may seem pretty mundane and boring, but it's very useful when you're entering batches of invoices or journals. You can be halfway through entering a journal and realise that you've missed out a line. Instead of putting it at the bottom of the journal, you can press F7 to insert a line where you want it.

Deleting a Line with F8

F8 is one of my favourite function keys. Many a time, I've got to the bottom of a very long and laborious journal and been a bit carried away. Before realising it, I've started to enter an extra line of journal that shouldn't be there.

After you enter a nominal code, Sage expects you to continue to post that line of the journal and waits for you to enter a value. When you realise your mistake and try to save the journal with a zero amount on the last line, Sage doesn't allow you to post. It gives you a warning message, saying `No transaction values entered`.

But click the line you want to delete, press F8 and it miraculously disappears, allowing you to save the journal with no further problems.

Many a student has told me that they've got to that point and, not realising what to do, have ended up discarding the original journal and retyping it all!

The F8 key can be used in other parts of the system too, for example, when you want to delete a line from an invoice or order.

Calculating Net Amounts with F9

When entering an invoice, Sage asks you for the net amount of the invoice, followed by the tax code. After you enter the tax code, Sage calculates the VAT. If you don't know the net amount and only have the gross amount of the invoice, you can type the gross amount in the Net field and press F9. Sage then calculates what the net amount is.

Launching Windows with F11

F11 launches the Windows control panel. Having access to the control panel is useful, for example, if you accidentally send a report to the printer. To cancel the job, press F11. The control panel opens and you select the Printer icon. Double-click the printer where the job is waiting to print and delete the report from the queue. Click the black cross in the right corner to exit the control panel. Alternatively, you can configure this button to launch another program. Use the Help menu for instructions on how to do this.

Opening Report Designer with F12

F12 launches Report Designer, or you can configure this button to launch another program from your PC.

Report Designer is an additional feature of Sage that allows you to create your own reports or modify existing ones. If you can't find a standard report that produces the information in the way that you want, it enables you to design a report with exactly the detail needed. (I explain how to use the Report Designer in Chapter 18.)

Chapter 22

Ten (Or More) Wizards to Conjure

In This Chapter

▶ Looking at how wizards can help you perform tricky transactions

▶ Scanning the more helpful wizards and how they work

Sage helpfully provides a number of *wizards*. No, I don't mean little characters with pointy hats and wands. By wizards, I mean step-by-step instructions on how to carry out specific procedures. Sometimes they can be a bit long and laborious to use, but at other times they provide some much needed expertise. For example, they can help you to complete complicated journal entries – even the most dedicated bookkeepers can do with a bit of help sometimes!

Here, I provide a brief summary of the most helpful wizards that Sage offers.

Creating a New Customer Account

Using the navigation bar on the left side of your screen, click Customers and then New Customer in the Task pane. The New Customer wizard starts, taking you step-by-step through the twelve-window process of setting up your customers. As the wizard can take a long time, I use the quicker method of clicking Customer and then Record, but you may prefer the wizard's guidance, so make sure that you grab a cuppa first!

To have a look at the type of questions that you're asked as you work through the wizard, press the F1 function key. The Sage Help facility describes in detail the type of information you need to enter in each of the twelve windows.

Setting up a New Supplier

Using the navigation bar, click Suppliers and then New Supplier in the Task pane. The New Supplier wizard walks you through the process of setting up your supplier records, just as the New Customer wizard takes you through setting up your customer records – wizards are handy, but not too imaginative. The eleven windows you complete help you set up supplier names, addresses, contact details, credit details, bank details and settlement discounts, if applicable.

If you want to preview the types of information required to complete the wizard, have a look at Sage Help. Press the F1 function key and scroll up and down the screen to see for yourself.

You don't have to complete every field in the wizard to set up a supplier, but you do need to click through all eleven windows to get to the end and save what information you've entered, so stick with it! You can always add information to your supplier record at a later date if you feel that you've missed anything out – simply open the supplier record, make your changes and click Save – it's that easy!

Initiating a New Nominal Account

Use the Nominal Record wizard to create new nominal accounts to use in your Chart of Accounts. You only need to work through five screens – what a relief! From the navigation bar, click Company and then the New icon, which starts the wizard for you.

The wizard asks you to enter the name of your new nominal account and confirm what type of account it is – sales, purchase, direct expenses, overheads, assets, liabilities and so on.

The next screen asks you to enter your nominal category from within the Chart of Accounts – for example, product sales. It also asks you to type in your nominal code.

Save yourself some annoyance and decide on your nominal code before you start the wizard. At this point in the wizard, you don't have the option of searching your nominal code list to check if your chosen code is suitable.

The wizard asks if you want to post an opening balance. Click the appropriate answer, and then click Next to continue. That's it! You've reached the final screen, and you've successfully entered the details for your new nominal account. When you click Finish, the new record is created and any opening balances are posted to it.

Don't forget to check your Chart of Accounts for any errors after you enter new nominal accounts. You can find details on how to do this in Chapter 2.

Creating a New Bank Account

The Sage New Bank Account wizard enables you to open new bank accounts, but unfortunately it's another long process, at twelve windows. The first four windows ask the usual bank details, such as bank name, sort code, account number and so on. The last few windows concern your opening balances and entering details about them.

From the navigation bar, click Bank, and then click the New icon.

Launching a New Product

Use the New Product wizard to create a new product record. You're asked to enter descriptions of the product, selling price and cost price information, as well as nominal codes and supplier details. It also has a section on opening balances that allows you to enter those through the wizard.

To access the wizard, from the navigation bar, click Products and then click the New icon. Alternatively, you can click New Product from the Task pane on the navigation bar, instead of clicking the New icon.

Starting Up a New Project

You can use the New Project wizard to create a new project record. Chapter 13 talks in more depth about creating projects to keep track of a job's progress.

You're asked to enter details such as the project name and unique reference, which can be just a shortened name or number to identify the project. Enter information such as the project start date and end date and choose a status from the five pre-defined ones Sage that provides. If you can link the project to a customer, enter those details. The next couple of windows are optional and contain questions such as the site address and site contact details. The last-but-one window requires you to enter the price you quoted for the project.

To access the Project wizard, click the New icon from the Projects module, or click New Project from the Task pane on the Projects navigation bar.

Helping Out at Month End: Opening/Closing Stock

Click Modules from the main toolbar, and then click Wizards. Choose Opening Closing Stock Wizard to access this wizard, which forms part of the month-end routine and is a welcome method of recording your closing stock. The wizard records the amount of closing stock you have at the end of a period and then transfers it to the start of the next period. The theory is that by recording your opening and closing stock figures, the cost of sales figures can be accurately calculated by the wizard for your Profit and Loss report. (Cost of Sales = Opening Stock + Purchases - Closing Stock.) If you don't post opening and closing stock figures, the cost of sales only reflects the purchase cost and doesn't reflect stock that you have left to sell.

Work through all four screens, entering the required information and clicking Next to proceed to the end of the wizard.

The wizard asks you to confirm the closing stock nominal accounts in both your Balance Sheet and the Profit and Loss report. At the Entering Your Closing Stock Values screen, Sage requests you to enter the values of the closing stock and that of the previous closing stock value. Sage then calculates the double-entry bookkeeping and posts those entries when you click the Finish button.

Fuelling Up: Scale Charges

If your firm has lots of company car users, the Scale Charges wizard can really come in handy. The wizard allows you to calculate the fuel-scale charges levied against free fuel provided to employees using company cars for personal use. The charges are dependent on the carbon-dioxide emissions and engine-size of each car.

You're required to enter the fuel-scale charge details, and then Sage creates the journals necessary to post to the nominal ledger.

Before you proceed with the wizard, you need to have calculated the scale charge for each company vehicle. You can find this information on the scale-charge table provided by HM Revenue and Customs Public Notice 700/64; go to www.hmrc.gov.uk.

Helping with Your Bookkeeping: VAT Transfer

Known as the VAT Liability Transfer wizard, this wizard sounds very complicated, and it can be if you don't understand double-entry bookkeeping. (Have a look at *Bookkeeping For Dummies,* by Paul Barrow and Lita Epstein for more help on double-entry.) This wizard helps you create the VAT transfer journals necessary to clear down your VAT Liability account. Still as clear as mud? Read on.

Essentially, the double-entry system reverses the balances in both the Sales Tax control account and the Purchase Tax control account at the end of the quarter and places an equal and opposite entry in the VAT Liability account. In theory, the balance subsequently created in the VAT Liability account is equal to the amount owed at that quarter-end. Therefore, when the VAT has been paid across or reclaimed from the VAT office for the quarter and that payment or refund is coded to the VAT Liability account, the balance on the VAT Liability account should be zero – assuming that you've done all the bookkeeping correctly. Phew! The wizard makes going through this process a breeze.

You can't use this wizard until you've fully reconciled and printed your VAT return.

Saving Time: Global Changes

The Global Changes wizard helps you make global changes to information in customer, supplier or product accounts without having to change each account individually. For example, you can raise the selling price of all your products by 10 per cent, as the sample business in Figure 22-1 did, just like that! (I don't recommend such an abrupt and significant change, however, lest you lose more than 10 per cent of your customers!)

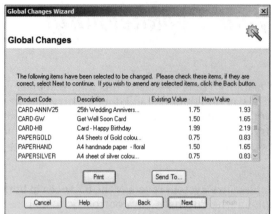

Figure 22-1:
The results
of applying a
10 per cent
increase
in selling
prices,
using the
Global
Changes
wizard.

Work through each of the windows, selecting the appropriate boxes for your global change. When you're happy with the details and can see the results shown on screen, click Finish. Sage then activates the changes. How's that for a brilliant and simple way to save yourself some time!

Handling Currencies: Foreign Trader Set-up

You have to complete the Foreign Trader Set-up wizard to activate the foreign currency functionality in Sage Accounts Professional.

After you activate the Foreign Trader option, you can't switch it off!

To activate the Foreign Trader, from the main toolbar, click Modules⇨Wizards⇨Foreign Trader Set-up Wizard.

The Foreign Trader Set-up wizard is short but sweet. Although it only runs for four screens, the impact of activating it is immense. The first thing the wizard asks you to do is to set up a new nominal account to handle currency fluctuations. When dealing with foreign currencies, you often encounter different exchange rates between sending invoices and receiving payment from them. These different rates result in slight under- or overpayments on accounts, and a foreign currency fluctuation account is an account to post those under- or overpayments to. If you've selected the default range of nominal codes, an exchange-rate variance code already exists, which you can use.

Sage also asks you which exchange-rate update method you want to use. You can change exchange rates on individual transactions, but it may be better to update the currency record as well. Sage recommends that you use the default offsetting, which always prompts you to save exchange-rate changes so that you can keep on top of things when you change any record.

The other exchange-rate update options include automatically saving any exchange-rate changes to the currency record and never saving any exchange-rate changes to the currency record.

When you complete the wizard, Sage recommends that you check the currency codes, symbols and currency exchange rates before you continue any further. Wise words!

Keeping Others in the Loop: Accountant Link

The Accountant Link is a very useful facility that enables you to send a copy of your data to your accountant via email or post. In the past, if you sent data to your accountant, you had to stop work and wait for the adjustments to your accounts. Nowadays, the Accountant Link allows you to send the data to your accountant, but still continue to work on the data yourself in the meantime, minimising disruption within your business.

After you export the data to your accountant, Sage begins to record material changes that you make to the data. You can print a list of these changes, and your accountant may request a copy of them before sending the data back to you. The accountant can send the data, with adjustments, back to you via a secure file, and you can then import those changes. The Accountant Link helps you apply the accountant's adjustments to your data to bring it up to date. At this point, the program stops recording material changes.

The Accountant Link wizard takes you through the exporting and importing process step by step (refer to Chapter 19 for more details).

Appendix

Glossary

- -

*A*ged Creditors report: A report showing all balances owed to *creditors*, categorised into debts owed for 30 days, 60 days and 90 days or older.

Aged Debtors report: A report showing all outstanding balances owed to a business, categorised into amounts owed for 30 days, 60 days and 90 days or older.

Asset: Item a business owns. (See *current asset; fixed asset*.)

Audit trail: A list of all the transactions that occur in Sage in chronological order. Each transaction is identified by its own transaction number.

Balance Sheet: A financial report that shows a snapshot of the financial status of a business at a point in time. It identifies the business's *assets* and *liabilities* and shows how those assets and liabilities have been funded through *retained profits* or invested *capital*.

Capital: Money invested into a business by owners or share holders.

Cash flow: The amount of cash flowing in and out of the business.

Chart of Accounts: A list of all the *nominal accounts* used to analyse *assets*, *liabilities*, *income* and *expenses*. It drives the format of the Profit and Loss account and Balance Sheet.

Cost: Items of expense in the accounts, such as wages costs. See *direct costs*.

Credit: A bookkeeping entry that increases the value of a liability or income and decreases the value of an asset or expense. It is always shown on the right side of a journal.

Creditor: Person or company to whom a business owes money.

Creditor ledger: See *supplier ledger*.

Customer ledger: A ledger that holds all the individual customer accounts and their balances. Also known as the debtor ledger.

Current asset: An *asset* with a lifespan of 12 months or less. A current asset can be to be *liquidated* reasonably quickly.

Debit: A bookkeeping entry that increases the value of an asset or expense and decreases the value of a liability or income. Debits show on the left side of a journal.

Debtor: Person or company that owes a business money.

Debtor ledger: See *customer ledger*.

Depreciation: An accounting tool used to gradually reduce the value of a *fixed asset*.

Direct cost: A cost that can be directly attributed to the manufacturing of a product.

Double-entry bookkeeping: An accounting method that records each transaction twice. Every debit entry has a corresponding credit entry. Doing the two entries helps balance the books.

Expense: A cost incurred as a result of doing revenue-generating business activities.

Fixed asset: An item owned by the business that has a useful life longer than 12 months.

Gross profit: The difference between *revenue* less *direct costs*.

Income: The amount of money received for goods and/or services provided.

Liability: An amount the business owes. (See *long-term liability*; *short-term liability*.)

Liquidate: To redeem an *asset* for cash.

Long-term liability: A *liability* the business owes for a period longer than 12 months – a mortgage, for example.

Net profit: *Revenue* less *direct costs* and *overheads*, including depreciation and taxes. Also known as the bottom line.

Nominal account: An account to which every item of income, expense, asset and liability is posted. Individual nominal accounts are grouped into ranges and can be viewed in the *Chart of Accounts*. (See *nominal ledger*.)

Nominal journal: In years gone by, this was a leather-bound journal. Nowadays, computers have replaced the traditional journal and a computerised journal entry screen is used to transfer values between nominal accounts by using *double-entry bookkeeping*.

Nominal ledger: The ledger that includes balances and activities for all the nominal accounts used to run the business. The nominal ledger contains all the transactions that the business has ever made.

Overheads: An *expense* that can't be directly matched to a product or service the business provides. Electricity and telephone costs are examples of overheads.

Outstanding lodgement: A deposit or receipt entered in the company's books that hasn't yet cleared the banking system.

Profit and Loss account: A financial statement that shows sales revenue less direct costs and overheads and arrives at the net profit or loss of the business.

Retained profit: *Profit* from a prior period reinvested in the business for future growth.

Sales revenue: The net value of a business's sales invoices.

Short-term liability: An amount owed for a period of less than 12 months.

Supplier ledger: The ledger that holds all the individual supplier accounts and their balances. Also known as the creditor ledger.

Unpresented cheque: A cheque written out and entered into the bookkeeping system that hasn't yet cleared the bank account. Unpresented cheques show as outstanding items remaining to be reconciled after a bank reconciliation is complete.

VAT: Value Added Tax. A tax due on purchases of most goods and services supplied by UK businesses and those in the Isle of Man. VAT is collected on business transactions, imports and acquisitions.

Index

• *G* •

• *H* •

• *W* •

Notes

FOR DUMMIES

Do Anything. Just Add Dummies

UK editions

BUSINESS

978-0-470-51806-9

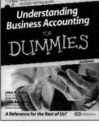

978-0-470-99245-6

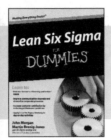

978-0-470-75626-3

FINANCE

978-0-470-99280-7

978-0-470-99811-3

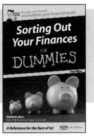

978-0-470-69515-9

PROPERTY

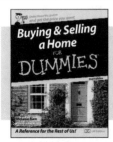

978-0-470-99448-1

978-0-470-75872-4

978-0-7645-7054-4

Backgammon For Dummies
978-0-470-77085-6

Body Language For Dummies
978-0-470-51291-3

British Sign Language
For Dummies
978-0-470-69477-0

Business NLP For Dummies
978-0-470-69757-3

Children's Health For Dummies
978-0-470-02735-6

Cognitive Behavioural Coaching
For Dummies
978-0-470-71379-2

Counselling Skills For Dummies
978-0-470-51190-9

Digital Marketing For Dummies
978-0-470-05793-3

eBay.co.uk For Dummies,
2nd Edition
978-0-470-51807-6

English Grammar For Dummies
978-0-470-05752-0

Fertility & Infertility For Dummies
978-0-470-05750-6

Genealogy Online For Dummies
978-0-7645-7061-2

Golf For Dummies
978-0-470-01811-8

Green Living For Dummies
978-0-470-06038-4

Hypnotherapy For Dummies
978-0-470-01930-6

13902_p1

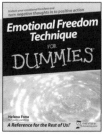
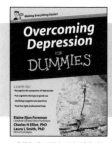

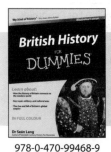
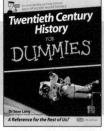
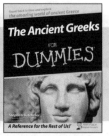

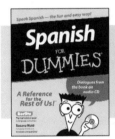

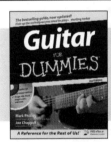

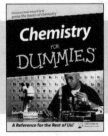

FOR DUMMIES®

Helping you expand your horizons and achieve your potential

COMPUTER BASICS

978-0-470-27759-1

978-0-470-13728-4

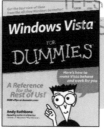

978-0-471-75421-3

DIGITAL LIFESTYLE

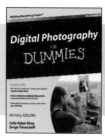

978-0-470-25074-7

978-0-470-39062-7

978-0-470-17469-2

WEB & DESIGN

978-0-470-19238-2

978-0-470-32725-8

978-0-470-34502-3

Access 2007 For Dummies
978-0-470-04612-8

Adobe Creative Suite 3 Design Premium
All-in-One Desk Reference For Dummies
978-0-470-11724-8

AutoCAD 2009 For Dummies
978-0-470-22977-4

C++ For Dummies, 5th Edition
978-0-7645-6852-7

Computers For Seniors For Dummies
978-0-470-24055-7

Excel 2007 All-In-One Desk Reference For Dummies
978-0-470-03738-6

Flash CS3 For Dummies
978-0-470-12100-9

Mac OS X Leopard For Dummies
978-0-470-05433-8

Macs For Dummies, 10th Edition
978-0-470-27817-8

Networking All-in-One Desk Reference
For Dummies, 3rd Edition
978-0-470-17915-4

Office 2007 All-in-One Desk Reference
For Dummies
978-0-471-78279-7

Search Engine Optimization For
Dummies, 2nd Edition
978-0-471-97998-2

Second Life For Dummies
978-0-470-18025-9

The Internet For Dummies, 11th Edition
978-0-470-12174-0

Visual Studio 2008 All-In-One Desk
Reference For Dummies
978-0-470-19108-8

Web Analytics For Dummies
978-0-470-09824-0

Windows XP For Dummies, 2nd Edition
978-0-7645-7326-2

Available wherever books are sold. For more information or to order direct go to www.wiley.com or call +44 (0) 1243 843291

13902_p4